HAS AN[...] A WHISTLE?

A Football Reporter in Africa

Peter Auf der Heyde

The Parrs Wood Press
<u>MANCHESTER</u>

First Published 2002

THE PARRS WOOD PRESS
St Wilfrid's Enterprise Centre
Royce Road, Manchester, M15 5BJ
www.parrswoodpress.com

© Peter Auf der Heyde 2002

The right of Peter Auf der Heyde to be recognised as the author of this work has been asserted

ISBN: 1 903158 31 1

Printed by:
MFP Design and Print
Longford Trading Estate
Thomas Street
Stretford
Manchester M32 0JT

*For my father, who played hockey but took me to
my first football game, and for my grandmother
who bought World Cup tickets for me.*

CONTENTS

ACKNOWLEDGEMENTS 6
PREFACE 7

1. Do You Know My Cousin? 9
2. Of Diapers, Policemen and Permits 16
3. Looking for the Leopards 24
4. Murderers, Thieves and Scoundrels 36
5. "I do it for the love of the game" 50
6. "For Mandela - only five" 59
7. Extra Income 72
8. The House That Peter Built 86
9. Anybody for Chicken? 100
10. Making it Big 120
11. The King of Africa 131
12. Bathed in Blood 148
13. How I Helped Bafana Qualify for France '98 . . . 160
14. Early Exit 178
15. Mr Dempsey, I Presume? 191
16. Stadiums of Death 203
17. World Cup 2002 - That's What Friends Are For . 212
18. Chairman Mao's Disapproving Look 222
19. Has Anybody Got a Whistle? 237

ACKNOWLEDGEMENTS

IN THE 20 YEARS I have been travelling through Africa, I have been ripped off by taxi drivers, made to wait endlessly by officials and bureaucrats in airports and dimly lit offices, and had teargas fired at me by dim-witted policemen. I have also encountered friendship and assistance from people I had only just met and I shared stories with them, many of which have somehow found a way into this book. My thanks go to the many trench-diggers-cum-foot-soldiers, taxi drivers and waiters throughout the continent who have taken the time to share their passion for football with me.

The people of the townships in Grahamstown did much more than share a passion with me. They opened their homes and gave me hope for a non-racial South Africa.

My appreciation goes to Gordon and Grant Igesund, Hillary and Brett Evans, Nthato Khumalo, Kamlesh Gosai, Peter Wallington, Thalia Höck and Robbie Milne, all of whom made valuable suggestions and contributions throughout the period in which this book was written. I am greatly indebted to Roelien Theron and Arnold Lampert, who witnessed the birth of this book and have seen it through to maturity.

My mother and Thomas and Katrin have had to deal with me and my obsession for over thirty years. They have managed to do so honourably. Andrea, Alexander and Marc have created the home that enables me to go in pursuit of footballing stories and then look forward to returning. Not many people would have done so with so much grace.

I have received expert help from my publisher, Andy Searle of The Parrs Wood Press, and my agent, Jim Gill of Peters, Fraser & Dunlop. Both have been encouraging throughout and I thank them for that.

PREFACE

Africa no longer needs to beg

FOOTBALL IS A TRULY global sport and you will see children kicking a ball on a dusty field in the scorching heat of Bamako, just as you will see them go for goal in the leafy suburbs of New York's affluent neighbourhoods. No longer is there any one area that can claim a legitimate right to lead The Beautiful Game. And that is as true about the action on the field as it is about activities that take place in the boardroom.

This is a fact that has been recognised by nations throughout the world and it is with this in mind that African countries have been making a concerted effort to ensure that the continent hosts the World Cup - which will finally happen in 2010. This should not be seen as a favour for Africa. It is something that is happening because it is the right thing to do. The days when Africa had to beg - cap in hand - for a slice of the footballing pie are long gone!

Not only has the continent created waves on the world footballing stage - winning the FIFA World Junior Championship as well as the last two gold medals at the Olympic Games - the continent is also recognised as a serious participant in all other spheres of football.

But even if African players are known throughout the world and some of our national teams have become serious contenders for world titles, very little is known of African football outside the continent. There is an abundance of literature portraying football in most parts of the world - but very little has been written about African football from an African perspective.

This book goes some way towards addressing this problem. It gives an insight into how The Beautiful Game is played in Africa and how important it is to the people of Africa. It looks at football at a grassroots level in the townships of South Africa, it follows the trials and tribulations of national teams at the Nations Cup and it looks at the best African teams as they compete at the world's highest footballing stage.

Like a puzzle it puts together all the pieces of football in Africa.

1

DO YOU KNOW MY COUSIN?

MY FATHER PLAYED HOCKEY. His father played hockey and so did my godfather. I, too, played hockey. Once. That was in 1980. I had just finished school and was visiting my godfather in Hong Kong. A sportsman of note, he was playing in an annual tournament organised by the Hong Kong Dutch Hockey Club. One of the teams did not have a goalkeeper and I volunteered to stand between the posts. As I can remember nothing about the actual game, I presume that I neither performed any heroics, nor did I eternally blot the 'family hockey name'.

In one of the trunks harbouring memorabilia from my youth I still have a T-shirt reminding me of my only hockey game. I also have one of those old, blurred super 8 movies I was shooting at the time instead of photographs. It shows some of the action I captured on film.

After my brief flirtation with hockey, I returned to my true love, football. To this day, I do not know why I became obsessed with football when everybody around me, stick in hand, was chasing a much smaller ball.

I was always led to believe that my obsession with the game started a year before the 1970 World Cup in Mexico. I was eight when I found the worn-out copy of a German football magazine, Kicker, in a rubbish bin at my school, the German School in Johannesburg. What I was doing - rummaging through the trash can, I have absolutely no idea. But I remember taking the magazine out of the bin and reading it from cover to cover. When I finished it, I immediately re-read it, this time starting at the last page and ending on the first.

The next childhood experience I can recall is of the World Cup itself. Being a less than adequate scholar, my parents would not have favourably considered any request to be allowed to stay up until the early hours of the morning to listen to the radio commentary of the matches being played. That did not stop me however, and, already showing a resourcefulness that was to prove useful later in life, I would sneak a small transistor radio under my blanket and then desperately try to fight off the sleep that threatened to whisk me away from the drama that was unfolding thousands of kilometres away.

I always believed that it was these early experiences which lay at the root of the obsession that followed me through childhood, puberty and in to young adulthood and still remains with me to this very day.

However, in December 1998 I was leafing through an old family photo album when I came across a letter which I had written to Father Christmas at the age of six. This was in 1967 - three years before the Mexico World Cup. In it, printed in the unsteady hand of the newly literate, I asked Santa to send me a football jersey. I mentioned no particular team, so I guess I left it up to him to decide. I can't remember if he managed to fulfill my request!

In 1974 I was lucky enough to experience my first real taste of big-time football. My parents had planned an overseas trip, which coincided with the World Cup being staged in Germany. My grandmother, who lived in Bremen, had somehow managed to secure tickets for three different games. For some the idea of a grandmother queuing up to secure football tickets might sound surprising, but with my grandmother it certainly was not. She not only understood my obsession, but also actively supported it by generously paying for an airmail subscription to Kicker.

After hearing that I was to watch three matches of the World Cup live, I could hardly think of anything else. I could picture myself in the stadium, surrounded by tens of thousands of fans who all shared my passion for the game!

Of course the World Cup was not the first match I'd watched in a stadium. I was a veteran Johannesburg football fan and I knew every corner in Balfour Park, home ground of Highlands Park, the local team which I supported.

I was also lucky enough to have had a father who - whilst not as fanatical about the game as I was - still supported me and often took me to watch matches which I could otherwise not have attended.

When I finally arrived in Germany, I was interested in little else. As the day of the first match (East Germany against Australia in Hamburg) drew nearer, I became even more obsessive. I read everything there was to read about the two teams, I predicted the score and I spoke about nothing else. On match day my grandmother, my brother and I took the train to Hamburg and followed the crowds to the Volkspark Stadion. The atmosphere was terrific. There was none of the violence that was to become a permanent fixture of international football several years later. It was like a big party and I was in the midst of it, having the time of my life. The match itself was the best game ever at the finals of the World Cup - or so I thought at the time. In retrospect, it was probably an incredibly boring affair, with the Australians wanting to restrict the damage and the East Germans content knowing that after Curran had scored an own goal for the Aussies and Streich added a second, nothing else could go wrong for them

On the train back to Bremen, I marveled at my good fortune. Here I was, a 13-year-old from South Africa, who, besides my brother, was probably the only child in my school to have seen a World Cup game live - and I still had two more to look forward to.

The second match was in Gelsenkirchen and pitted the reigning champions, Brazil, against Zaïré. In other words Rivelino, Jairzinho and Leao against Kazadi, Kakoko and Ndaye.

We again travelled by train. Sitting opposite me was a man in his forties and he asked me where I was from.

"Johannesburg in South Africa," I answered.

"Oh, then you must know Hans. He is my cousin and he lives there."

"I don't think I know Hans, what is his surname," I asked him, a bit irritated that he was preventing me from reading the magazine that I had brought along for the ride.

"Zimmer. Hans Zimmer," he said, looking at me expectantly.

"No, I can't say that I know him. Where does he live?"

"In Nairobi, Kenya."

I decided not to try to explain to him that Nairobi and Johannesburg were thousands of kilometres away, and the idea that I would know someone just because we lived on the same continent was absurd. I said nothing.

Instead, he said something: "So are you here to support Zaïré? You come from there, don't you?"

Again I decided not to give him a quick geography lesson, opting instead to take the easy way out. "Yes," I said.

That seemed to satisfy him and he finally let me continue reading.

The match was just as terrific as the first one. Brazil had very few problems and should quite comfortably have scored more than the three goals they did. Zaïré certainly did not disgrace themselves (they had done that in their previous match against Yugoslavia, when Kazadi and the man who replaced him at halftime, Tubilandu, had to pick the ball out of the back of the net nine times!)

HAS ANYBODY GOT A WHISTLE?

My final game was to be a second-round match between Brazil and Argentina, in Hannover. This was probably the best of the three matches that I watched and the 2-1 victory for Brazil was enough to keep them in the running to successfully defend their title.

But they failed! Gunned down by a rampant Dutch side, inspired by an indefatigable Johan Cruyff, who had taken football to a new level, the South Americans had to make do with the play-off for third place, which they lost to Poland.

The Dutch, in turn, came unstuck against a machine-like German team. Although they lacked a playmaker of the calibre of Cruyff, they had discipline and determination, home support, a most lethal striker in Gerd Müller and plenty of luck. It was enough to ensure a 2-1 victory and like hundreds of thousands of Germans all over the country, I took to the streets when the final whistle blew. My first World Cup, my team won - what more could a 13-year-old want?

After my World Cup adventure, I returned to South Africa, eager to share my experiences with the other children in school. As most of them had no interest in football whatsoever, my enthusiastic ball-by-ball accounts of the three matches I had watched fell on deaf ears.

My school career was hardly remarkable and I only did just enough to graduate from each successive class. By 1979 I had progressed as far as I could and, armed with a university entrance certificate, I was ready for the real world.

While steadily but continuously climbing from grade to grade, my football career was making much faster, and certainly more satisfactory, progress. At an early age, I must have been around nine or ten, I joined Viktoria FC. German in origin, the club campaigned in the second division of the 'all white' National Football League (NFL). Viktoria was very much a club going nowhere. Not good enough to ever come in contention for a promotion place, it was also thankfully not so bad that relegation was something I had sleepless nights over.

The club's most famous player was a true blue-eyed, blonde forward called Bomber Schultz. His scoring exploits were what earned him his nickname. A few years earlier, he had been a fearless striker in the first division with a club called Brothers, banging in the goals with reckless abandon. Looking as if he had walked straight off the pages of a war comic, Bomber evoked the fear of God in the defenders who had the misfortune of facing him.

But to me and the other youngsters who faithfully turned out every other Saturday to watch our heroes take on clubs like Powerlines, Corinthians or Jewish Guild, Bomber Schultz was the closest we were ever going to get to big-time football.

And it was Bomber Schultz that I tried to emulate in my own football career. I proudly wore the black and white jersey - what else could you expect from a German club? - of the under-10 Viktoria FC side.

But unlike my hero Bomber, I seldom scored and my continued presence in the team had more to do with the fact that there was little or no opposition for my place in the starting line-up.

It was then that fate intervened. One Saturday morning we were scheduled to play Parkhurst FC and, disaster of all disasters, our goalkeeper failed to pitch. Remembering that goalkeepers have to be crazy, the coach suggested I pull over the number one jersey and stand between the posts. I did, and I played a blinder! I was to be stuck in goal for more or less the next 25 years.

As I grew older, I graduated from the Viktoria under-10 side to the under-12, from there to the under-14 and then to the under-16. A change of club never entered my mind and I continued being a fanatical supporter of Bomber and his teammates in the first side, who in turn continued being as mediocre as they had always been!

By 1977, I was considered to be good enough to play for the Colts side, as the oldest of the youth teams was called. That same year also saw the collapse of the existing status quo in South African football. The NFL folded and the majority of clubs joined the 'black' National Professional Soccer League (NPSL), while a few opted for the Indian-controlled Soccer Federation. Viktoria, which was not good enough to compete in any of these leagues, threw their lot in with the newly formed Transvaal Football League (TFL).

The TFL consisted mainly of clubs which, like Viktoria, could find no home elsewhere, as well as reserve teams from some of the region's professional clubs.

At the start of the 1978 season, I was drafted into the first team and at the age of 16 made my debut in the TFL. We were not paid, although I remember that after one victory, during which I had kept a clean sheet and had done very well, we all received 10 Rand at the next training session, courtesy of a satisfied fan.

R10 in those days was quite a bit of money, more than enough for a good meal with a movie afterwards for my girlfriend and myself. As a result, I was over the moon and felt like a full professional. The money burnt a hole in my pocket and no remuneration I was to receive later in life ever gave me the same satisfaction as the first time I received money for playing football.

I played a lot of football, and not only for Viktoria. On Sundays I played Industrial League football, on Wednesdays I represented my school, and on Tuesdays or Thursdays I captained my house team in the internal school league. In most cases I would be in goal.

My aspiration to bang in the goals Bomber Schultz-like never left me and whenever I had the chance I would grab the number 9 jersey. Luckily for all the teams I was involved in, such occasions were far and few between.

One such opportunity came when, having finished school, I left South Africa and moved to Germany. I lived with my grandmother in Bremen and worked in a factory packing knives and forks. I also enrolled at school to gain a German school-leaving certificate.

More importantly for me, though, was the fact that I joined TuS Schwachhausen. It was a local club whose first team played in the Verbandsliga, which effectively was the fourth division. I decided not to tell them that I was a relatively useless striker and whatever potential I had as a footballer was to be found only if I went into goals.

For the next year I tried to score for the TuS Schwachhausen second side. I think I managed once!

Even more serious than my lack of goal scoring was the question of my future. I had long ago given up my ambition of becoming a professional player. The most obvious next choice was becoming a professional/full-time fan. That certainly had a very strong appeal but, unfortunately, I was not even distantly related to anyone who could finance this for me. It was this realisation of the realities and necessities of modern day economics that persuaded me to make an appointment with a career guidance counsellor.

On the day of the appointment I dutifully made my way towards a huge colourless building in downtown Bremen. It was a dreary, overcast day and the rain had been falling - seemingly forever. When I left the building it seemed the day was even greyer.

The counsellor, a balding bespectacled fifty-something man, patiently listened to my expectations, likes and dislikes. After I finished my short speech he took off his glasses and rubbed them on his shirt. Then he looked up at me and said: "Sorry, there is no such profession. Unless you are prepared to shift considerably, you will struggle. What I suggest you do, is to get yourself a university course book and study it and try to find something suitable."

This I did. I then proceeded to cross out everything with anything needing any of the natural sciences, which had been my worst subjects at school. I then found various other reasons to cross out virtually everything else. When I had finished with this exercise, there were two courses and professions left: social work and journalism.

Not known for making quick, or slow, decisions, I decided to study both and filled out countless application forms for German universities. Not convinced that my grades were good enough to gain entry to a German university, I also applied to Rhodes University in Grahamstown in South Africa. At the time it was the only English-speaking university offering a journalism course.

Within a short while the answers started coming in: "We regret to inform you ... you have been placed on the waiting-list and are number 473 on the list." I did not really want to hope and wait for the 472 people ahead of me on the list to fall by the wayside, so when I received a favourable response from Rhodes University I decided to bid farewell to my TuS Schwachhausen teammates, my grandmother, Germany and the bad weather, and to head back home.

2

OF DIAPERS, POLICEMEN
AND PERMITS

I ARRIVED IN MID-JANUARY 1981 and drove down to Grahamstown, where I registered at Rhodes University for social work and journalism.

Grahamstown is a quaint university town in the Eastern Cape, situated some 60 km upland from the warm Indian Ocean. At the time the town was home to some 60, 000 or 210, 000 people, depending on whether you accepted the official count of the white population only, or included 150, 000 blacks who, under apartheid, were forced to live in those large sprawling ghettoes, known as townships, on the outskirts of white cities and towns. I opted for the second choice.

The difference between 'white' Grahamstown and 'black' Grahamstown could not have been more pronounced. The townships had gravel roads with potholes the size of tyres, small tin shacks and people milling around on the streets. But as you crossed the railway bridge that divided Grahamstown into two, it was as if you were entering a different world. High fences surrounded big houses with swimming pools. The tree-lined, paved streets were empty apart from an occasional car and the odd domestic worker who would be walking home after a long day's work.

There was a third aspect to Grahamstown's social order: the university. Not quite white suburbia, yet certainly nowhere near township life, the students lived in a world of their own. Rhodes University was a liberal campus and as such it accepted black students. The percentage, though, was very low and there was little mixing going on.

White students lived a carefree life, much of the focus being on merriment, rather than serious studying. The town offered a wide choice of pubs and restaurants and there were two cinemas, both of which excluded blacks.

Needless to say, I also wanted to play football. Once again I had two choices. I could either join a team playing in the predominantly white

Grahamstown Football Association (GFA), or I could join a team in the township, where the clubs were affiliated to the Grahamstown Soccer Association (GRASA).

Even at Rhodes there were two teams. The one played in the white Eastern Province league, while the other competed under GRASA. Opting to join the university's official team meant playing on good fields, enjoying the best facilities and having warm showers after matches. GRASA teams, on the other hand, enjoyed no such luxuries. All the games were played on the only field in the township: Folley's Ground. What little grass there was, had long been eaten by the cows that grazed there during the day. There were no facilities and players changed in the open.

Choosing between the two was not at all difficult, though. During my stay overseas I came in frequent contact with exiled South Africans. There had been so many of these encounters that I had no hesitation dismissing the government's propaganda about critics of the regime for what it was: attempts by an unjust and immoral system to demonise those opposing it. I thus had no hesitation in deciding that the future of my footballing days lay with GRASA and with the people fighting for a non-racial and democratic South Africa. In March 1981 I became the goalkeeper for Phoenix FC and, at the same time, the only white player to join the ranks of GRASA.

In my very first league game for Phoenix on Folley's Ground, I got a taste of things to come. There were no nets, and goals consisted of a rickety structure that was in danger of imminent collapse. And that is exactly what happened. Unfortunately for me, I happened to be right under the crossbar as it caved in. I could have been badly injured, but I was rather lucky to have escaped with a couple of bruises and a swelling the size of a golf ball on my head. However, after the crossbar had loosely been attached to the poles, I insisted on continuing with the match, which we went on to win.

Joining a township team, even though all my teammates were themselves studying at the university, also meant that I was alienated from most of my fellow students. They could not understand why I would choose to play on a dusty field in the township.

GRASA played an overtly political role in the township, as did similar sports organisations all over the country. The white minority government had long ago banned all political organisations which posed a serious threat to its rule. It was into this void that the South African

Council on Sport (SACOS) had stepped. The SACOS policy was that it was impossible to divorce sport from its social context and that a sporting body needed to be integrally involved in all aspects of society. The organisation's slogan was 'No normal sport in an abnormal society' and it had long before become involved in overtly political issues. GRASA was affiliated to SACOS and, in the absence of any other strong community organisations, was the most influential body in the township. It politicised township residents using sport as a vehicle; it called for meetings and organised boycotts.

I found being a student quite different from attending school as the university was not as rigid as the South African school system. I developed an interest in the courses I had registered for. That also meant that I did not actually have to spend a lot of time on my studies and I concentrated on football and writing. I decided to merge the two by concentrating on sports journalism.

Seeking an outlet for the budding journalist in me, I joined the Grahamstown Voice, the mouthpiece of an anti Apartheid grassroots development agency which had been established by students a few years earlier. The Voice hit the streets of Grahamstown or, to be more precise, the streets of the township, on a bi-monthly basis.

My knowledge and love for football, a sport that was largely considered a 'black sport', made me unlike any other politically interested student. I was therefore accepted into the newsroom of the Grahamstown Voice with open arms. My rise through the sports department was rapid and within a few months I was promoted to sports editor. This, however, had little to do with the fact that the editorial collective thought I was such a good journalist. Far from it. My position as the only journalist in the sports department ensured a meteoric rise to the top of my first structured media environment.

Needless to say, all the journalists working on the paper were students and none of us was ever paid, nor did we expect payment. Most of the journalists saw their writing as a contribution to the struggle to rid South Africa of the evil of apartheid. I was no different and I spent hours writing about clubs with names such as Early Birds, Eleven Attackers and United Teenagers.

Like hundreds of other students, I honestly believed that the downfall of the white South African government was just around the corner and the work I was doing for the Voice would bring that day forward even sooner. So convinced was I of my belief, that I spent hours in debate with the editor pleading for more space for my football stories. I argued that sport in general, and football in particular, was an ideal medium through which one could change people's lives. I said it was much more real to them if, for instance, we wrote about the fact that forty football teams in the township had the use of only one gravel-strewn field, while ten teams in 'white' Grahamstown had the use of three grass football fields. The editor, one Olivia Forsyth, was not interested. She was one of those holier-than-thou student activists, who knew all the right slogans and had read all the right books, but who had little idea of what was happening on the ground.

She insisted the Voice write about economics and the downfall of capitalism in a language I am sure that not even she understood. My argument that people would much prefer to read about Linton Nqoko scoring the winning goal for Frasers United against Early Birds in the Autumn Harvest Cup fell on deaf ears and all the Lintons of Grahamstown never received the space I thought they deserved.

Years later, Forsyth left the country and went into exile, where she was unveiled as a spy. She was captured by the African National Congress (ANC) and locked up in an Angolan jail for a few months before escaping. She sought refuge in the British embassy in the capital Luanda, and after a diplomatic storm that raged for several months, was allowed to travel back to South Africa. There she became a state witness in political trials against her former friends. And unfortunately, Forsyth was not the only spy I was to encounter during my stay in Grahamstown. Another was Gordon Brookbanks, who befriended people specifically to report them to the Apartheid regime he so vigorously supported and fought for.

My contact with Forsyth and Brookbanks was not to remain the only contact I had with the security police (or SPs, as we used to call them) during my time in Grahamstown.

In pursuit of my stories, I often had to travel into the township to interview people and to gather information. At the same time, I had also become Phoenix's representative at GRASA meetings and was soon co-opted onto the GRASA executive. This meant that my forays into the township were set to increase dramatically. But entering a township was illegal, and all whites needed a permit before they could set foot in one.

The GRASA executive meetings were mostly held in a corrugated iron shack in Raglan Road, which formed a boundary between the township and 'white' Grahamstown. In winter the GRASA shack was unbearably cold, while in summer it became excruciatingly hot. Every Monday night we would meet there to discuss issues of importance. It took me a while to work out that issues such as whether or not players should be allowed to wear training shoes for matches instead of boots were as important as those dealing with training schedules and finances. This was because township residents were denied control over so many other aspects of their lives that they jealously guarded against the take-over of those which they still controlled - like football.

And because there were so many matters that needed discussing, our meetings would take several hours, during which time two security policemen would wait for me in their car, which they parked outside the shack. They knew that I knew that they were watching me. Nevertheless, they would carry out this ominous ritual every Monday. Driving away at the end of each meeting on a small scooter - my only means of transport - I knew they were following me. As I had not ventured deep enough into the township, they never stopped me, but were happy to let me know that they were keeping close tabs on my movements.

But whenever I entered the township for any other business, they reacted without mercy and, as a result I was a frequent visitor, albeit unwilling, to their offices in New Street.

One day I was travelling in the township with two friends, as well as Thomas, the young child of my girlfriend at the time, when a defence force truck stopped me. Swiftly the soldiers surrounded my car, demanding to know what I was doing. My explanation that I was in the township on football-related business was obviously not good enough, and they called someone on their radio.

"We have to tell you to wait here," the young soldier told me when he came back to my car.

So I waited. And waited and then I waited some more. It was getting very hot and Thomas was complaining. Quite a large crowd had gathered around the car and as they all recognised me as the only white player who played football in the township, they were all very friendly.

After waiting for more than an hour, a terrible smell took over in the car. Thomas had dirtied his diaper! Being a good stand-in father, I had some clean diapers with me and did a quick changing job. When I was done, I threw the dirty one into a nearby bin.

I then rejoined the others in the car and waited some more. It must have been at least one and half hours after the soldiers first went to make the call that a security police car finally arrived on the scene. In it were two SPs. I knew both of them well from previous encounters in the township. They first went to speak to the soldiers, before coming over to my car.

"Why did you change the diaper?" warrant-officer Nel said in his thick Afrikaans accent.

I was surprised. Normally they try a 'good cop' approach and exchange some meaningless pleasantries before getting down to business. This time it was different and I decided that it would be best if I just kept to the facts. "Because it was dirty," I replied.

"But where is it now?"

"I threw it into the bin over there," I said, pointing to the rubbish bin into which I had thrown the nappy.

The way Nel and his colleague jumped towards the bin meant that they must have been expecting something very exciting hidden in the nappy. Unfortunately I could not see their faces as they opened the corpus delicti and found only shit.

"We are taking you to the police station. You will follow us in your car," Nel said.

We got back into our car and followed the white Nissan through the dusty streets of Rhini, as the township was called, to the police station in 'white' Grahamstown. It was a road I had travelled often and as I parked my car outside the station I was not unduly worried. Nel and his colleague were waiting outside and escorted us into the building. "They were in the township without a permit," he explained to the policeman behind the desk. "Charge him."

The policeman asked for the particulars of my friends, but when he came to me, he just started writing. That I hated. With a surname like mine, it normally takes up to five minutes to explain to someone how to spell my name: A-u-f, then another word, d-e-r, then another word H-e-y-d-e. Auf der Heyde.

But this policeman, who had probably left school in standard six and had been working as a policeman ever since, knew how to spell my name without asking. I was worried as that implied that he had been told to expect me.

After having written down everything, we were warned not to enter the township again and told to go.

These minor incidents of harassment continued throughout my

four years of living in Grahamstown as a student and then, later, during my three years of working as a journalist in the Eastern Cape. The police arrested me, issued me with an order banning me from the township and tried all sorts of other little tricks to prevent me from entering the township. It made no difference to them whether I was going in to play football, fulfill my duties as an executive member of GRASA, or work as a journalist.

They wanted none of it and they made it perfectly clear to me that I was persona non grata on the streets of Joza, Newtown and Tantjie locations. But the continual police interest in my whereabouts ensured that I achieved a high degree of popularity among the township residents, who liked the fact that I had chosen to play football in the township and had ignored any attempts by the authorities to prevent me from doing so.

After playing successfully for Phoenix for a season, I decided to join a township-based team, New Town City. My new club also benefited from continued efforts by the police to prevent me from entering the township, as on a Saturday, thousands of residents would flock to Folley's to see this strange mlungu (as white people were called in the township) who persisted and insisted on playing for one of their teams.

On many weekends, football fans were not the only ones who came to watch me. The police too, were frequent visitors to our games and just as frequently they would fire teargas onto the field to stop the matches from continuing, thereby hoping to chase me out of the township.

Football was the most important pastime in the township and residents looked forward in anticipation to the weekend when they could watch their favourite teams in action.

At the time one of the best goalkeepers in South Africa was Peta Balac, who played for the most popular club in the country, Kaizer Chiefs. As my own popularity grew, I was given the nickname, 'Peta Balac'. Needless to say, I felt pretty good about my new epithet.

After playing for New Town City, I was asked to join Eleven Attackers and as the club was one of the strongest in the township, I jumped at the opportunity. With a new club, I was also to acquire a new nickname. After one of my better games, our fans decided that from then on, I was to be known as 'Peta No Mistakes Balac' - a name that was to stick with me for the next few years.

At the same time, my journalistic career blossomed. Albeit that my stories were very parochial, I put in just as much effort writing about our local games as I would have had I been covering the World Cup. And the satisfaction I had in seeing my stories in print was a feeling I still have difficulty in trying to explain.

At the end of 1982 I decided that I needed to broaden my journalistic horizon and during a two-month tuition break, I set off north in search of a Kenyan team called AFC Leopards. I knew very little about them, but decided that any club with a name like that was worth looking in to.

3

LOOKING FOR THE LEOPARDS

MY ROUTE WOULD TAKE ME from Johannesburg up through Zimbabwe to Zambia, then across to Tanzania and up north to Kenya. Getting to Zambia was easy enough. I started hitchhiking in Johannesburg and made it to the border between South Africa and Zimbabwe before dusk. Just as lucky the next day, I was in the Zimbabwean capital of Harare within a few hours after leaving the South African border town of Beit Bridge. After spending a night with friends in Harare, I set off early in the morning for Livingstone, on the border between Zambia and Zimbabwe.

As it was my first trip into 'real' Africa, or what I considered to be real Africa, I was naturally a bit apprehensive. But I needn't have been. Within a few hours I had not only crossed the border, but also made it to the capital Lusaka.

There I encountered my first real problems. Needing a visa for Tanzania, I had to go to the Tanzanian embassy in Lusaka. It was situated in a luxurious house in one of the better suburbs. The reception-ist directed me to an office in which the man who decided whether or not you had what it took to be allowed into Tanzania sat, looking important, behind his desk. A huge full-colour glossy portrait of the then Tanzanian President, Julius Nyerere, was hanging on the wall behind him. Without looking up from the papers he was studying, he snapped at me: "What do you want?"

"Sir, I would like to apply for a visa, sir," was my timid reply, the sub-servience in my voice not even an act.

"Have you been to South Africa?" he barked. That, of course, was the question I dreaded, but I also knew that it would be asked. At the time, South Africans could travel virtually nowhere on the continent, except to those 'countries' which it had created within its own borders in yet another futile attempt to convince the world that things were not as bad as they seemed.

As my parents were both German, I, too, qualified for a German passport, which I had always had. During my time in Bremen I had obtained something worth more than gold, a German passport giving my place of residence as Bremen and totally clean of any South African stamps. What made my passport even better was the fact that I had gone to a home affairs department in a small town and applied there.

"Surely it makes no difference whether I was born in East or West or North London. Can't we just say London?" I had asked the official. He agreed and since then, my place of birth has been recorded in my passport as London, instead of East London in South Africa.

Faced by the Tanzanian official, I was thus confident and lied. I said no, I had never been to South Africa.

Whether or not he believed me, I do not know, but he told me to pay US$20, give him two passport photos and go and wait outside.

In the reception area, under the by-now familiar smiling face of Nyerere, was a wooden bench on which I sat down. On the table in front of the bench were a few worn-out old copies of Time magazine. I took the latest. It was dated June 1982, only six months old.

After I had flicked through the magazine for at least 30 minutes, the man in the khaki suit came back and without uttering a word, handed me back my passport. I took it, murmured a very shy 'thank you' and left the building, not knowing if I had been given a visa or not.

I only dared look once I was on the street. Yes, inside my spotlessly clean passport was a 14-day visa for Tanzania, beginning the very next day. Later I was told that I had been lucky to receive a visa, as the normal procedure was to slip one or two extra ten US dollar bills between the pages. It was the first of many lessons I was to learn in the course of this trip.

As it was too late to set off for Tanzania, I returned to the hostel into which I had booked myself earlier during the day. At dawn the next morning I took a taxi to the edge of town and waited for a lift. I did not have to wait long and within a few hours I was in Kapiri Mposhi, a tiny village with only a few thousand inhabitants and one hotel, the Kapiri Mposhi Inn. It was the kind of village that would probably have not existed had it not been at a crossroads. The highway that runs north from Lusaka splits into two, just outside Kapiri Mposhi. The one road continues north to the Copper Belt and, ultimately, the Congo, while the other runs east, to Tanzania. That was the one I needed to take and as I had hitched a ride in a truck going up to the Copper Belt, the driver dropped me off at the junction.

I took my backpack, leaned it against a tree and waited. And waited.

And waited. It was not that there was no traffic; it was just that all the cars passing through Kapiri Mposhi were taking the road north. After I had been waiting for some two hours, two soldiers manning a roadblock a few hundred metres up the road to the east came to speak to me. After asking me where I came from and where I was heading, the topic naturally turned to football and, as a result, an immediate friendship was formed. They supported a Zambian team called Power Dynamos and I was astonished to learn how much they knew about international football. After talking to them for only a few minutes, I had picked up that they were incredibly passionate about not only their club, but also the national team. That was something which I noticed about many Zambians and it helped me understand the outpouring of national grief that was to befall the country a few years later, in 1993, after virtually the entire national squad had been killed in a plane crash on the way to Guinea, where they were scheduled to play a World Cup qualifier.

We spoke about Dynamos and I told them a bit about football in my country - something they were very eager to hear about. After a while they returned to the roadblock and I continued waiting, by myself, under the tree.

After about four hours, I started getting nervous. The border was still a good two hours away and I had to reach it before 6pm. It was then that I noticed an old white Mercedes Benz slowly driving towards the junction. Eagerly I watched as it drew closer and closer and when I saw it turn onto 'my' road, I became excited. I jumped up and held out my arm. The Mercedes came towards me, slowed down and stopped.

"We're only going about 40 kilometers down the road to our farm. We can't give you a lift," the driver said as he leaned out of the window.

"Thanks for stopping," was my reply as I sat down again. Feeling a bit more encouraged, I watched as the car drove off before being flagged down at the roadblock. After a minute or two, I heard the soldiers calling me. Looking up, I saw them waving me towards them. Unsure what was going on, I hurried towards the roadblock. One of the Power Dynamos fans said that the car was going to the Tanzanian capital of Dar es Salaam and was going to give me a lift.

Of course I wondered why the driver had earlier told me a very different story. But faced with a choice of getting into their car or risk having to spend a further four hours in the sweltering African sun waiting for another lift, I opted for the old Mercedes. I fetched my backpack and ran towards the car, which was still standing, with an open trunk, at the roadblock.

"Hi, put your stuff in the back and let's go," said a man, whom I recognised as the driver, as I reached the vehicle.

I did as I was told and got into the car. The same guy was driving. He must have been in his mid-forties, with short brown hair and a thin face. Sitting next to him was a much younger man, with a very boyish appearance and reddish hair. He had a grin on his face.

"Sorry about the little lie," the driver said. "We did not want to stop at the roadblock and thought if we picked you up, the soldiers would certainly stop us."

"Not a problem, I understand," I lied. In fact, I understood nothing. I was just happy to have left my tree, the heat and the dust and to be moving forward. What more could a man want?

The driver introduced himself as Ray Corbett. His companion was Timothy Dobson. He said they were both from Zimbabwe and were on their way to Dar es Salaam. Again I lied and said that I was also heading for the Tanzanian capital. They told me they were businessmen from Zimbabwe and had to attend to their affairs in Tanzania. They were careful not to divulge the nature of their business. They then told me about life in Zimbabwe and within three hours we were at the border town of Nakonde.

Crossing into Tanzania was less time-consuming than getting a visa to visit. Within half an hour we were heading towards Dar es Salaam. As it was getting dark, Ray suggested we spend the night in the next town, which he said was only 50 kilometres away.

When we got to Mbeya, it was another dead-end place. A few houses, one or two shops, a bar and, surprisingly, Alley's Guest House, into which we booked ourselves. I had already obtained some Tanzanian Shillings on the black market in Zambia and when Timothy asked me to advance the money for the accommodation, I did so without hesitation.

Over supper they explained that they were going to Dar es Salaam for only a short while and that Nairobi was their final destination. I told them about the Leopards and that I, too, wanted to make it to Kenya. They offered to take me all the way. Timothy, who did most of the talking, explained that they had not brought a lot of money, as they had a number of accounts in Kenya. He then pulled out a handkerchief from his trouser pocket and opened it. In it were a number of transparent stones. He lowered his voice and told me they were diamonds, which they wanted to sell in Kenya. He asked me whether I was willing to pay for hotel accommodation and expenses in Tanzania. In return, they would pay me £1,500 once we had reached Kenya. "I know our expenses will not be that much, but that is what we want to pay," he said.

I agreed and I spent the next two weeks travelling through Tanzania in the old Mercedes. It was an unforgettable experience. If we were on the road during mid-morning or mid-afternoon, we would stop at the side of the road. One of us would fetch a gas cooker from the trunk and we would make ourselves a cup of tea. But this was not the boy-scout kind of tea drinking, with plastic cups and powdered milk. No, we did it in style. Fine china, fresh milk and good tea. In fact, our tea drinking became a ritual, which took up a good hour every time we stopped.

And we chatted. Timothy never seemed to stop talking. And not only to Ray or myself. He would talk to anyone who happened to pass by. Within a few minutes of meeting someone, Timothy had them listening, spellbound. He spoke about everything and although I noticed that he often adapted his stories, I never asked him about them.

Neither he nor Ray shared my interest in football and neither had heard of the Leopards. Whenever I wanted to talk about football, I would have to engage the waiters or receptionists at our hotels to find out the latest footballing news.

And they, at least, were always very eager to talk. I learnt a lot about Tanzanian football. I found out about the Sunderland supporters in Dar es Salaam, who had called their club Dar Sunderland, how it was renamed Sports Club Simba, and that the club was so successful that a second club called Small Simba (how original!) was formed on Zanzibar. They spoke about other teams called Young Africans and Maji Maji. Whenever football was discussed, an instant rapport was established.

I soon found out why. Tanzanians had very little else to do or talk about as the economy of the country was virtually ruined. When Nyerere came to power in 1962 he tried to copy the Chinese example of forced ruralisation. Tanzanian officials shipped much of the urban population off to the rural areas and forced them to live in villages. This Ujoma policy, as it was called, all but devastated the country. What little economy there was had collapsed as a result. Nyerere, who seemed to care more about the rest of Africa than his own country, spent endless time and enormous resources on a war with Uganda, which ultimately drove the Ugandan dictator Idi Amin into his Saudi Arabian exile. Unfortunately, the war had cost a fortune and Tanzania was virtually bankrupt.

This economic chaos had resulted in a thriving black market. The official exchange rate for the US dollar was around four Tanzanian Shillings. On the black market it was easy to get between 60 and 80 Shillings per dollar.

I made frequent use of the black market to pay for our hotel bills. In some places, people were so desperate for foreign exchange that they were willing to give me Tanzanian Shilling without actually receiving any foreign currency in return. Instead, they requested that I deposit the money into their European bank accounts once I had left Tanzania.

By now, we had worked out the perfect arrangement for our travels. Ray did the driving, I paid and Timothy was in charge. He decided how far we would drive, where we would stay and what we would do. He obviously enjoyed the good things in life and chose the best hotels and restaurants. I could only afford to pay for these bills by exchanging money illegally on the black market. This arrangement suited me, as I could look forward to receiving £1,500, once we reached Kenya.

Our trip took us through Dadoma and the Mikumi Game Reserve, where we stayed in the Mikumi Wildlife Lodge. The lodge was like an oasis of luxury amidst a sea of squalor. It had been built in the late 1970s at a time when Tanzania was expecting a tourist boom. By the look of things, they were expecting rich tourists. Inside the hotel, it was a very different story and the shortages that we came across throughout our travels in Tanzania had also manifested in hotels such as the Mikumi Wildlife Lodge. There was, for instance, no light bulb in the lamp by the bedside and in the bathroom was a tiny piece of soap, which we had to share among the three of us.

We also decided to visit Dar es Salaam, before heading up north to the border with Kenya, which at the time was still closed. The reason for this was that Tanzania, not surprisingly, objected to Kenya unilaterally seizing the assets of the East African Community (an economic union between Kenya, Tanzania and Uganda). Kenya had taken over the railways, the ships on Lake Victoria, the airlines and the post and telecommunications. We had heard that special permission to cross the border could be obtained at the border town of Arusha. We ventured to try our luck and drove our Mercedes up north.

When we arrived in Arusha, we moved into the Mount Neru Hotel, which probably was the best hotel in the country at the time. It was filled with European tourists wearing khaki pants and shirts and those traditional safari hats that looked a bit like the helmets worn by English bobbies. These, though, were white. The tourists looked like the English explorer Stanley who had gone to Africa in search of another explorer, Livingstone, and I imagined them to stick out their hand at any moment to say: "Doctor Livingstone, I presume".

Encouraged by all the safari activity, I, too, decided to go on a small three-day excursion to the Lake Manyara and Ngorongora game reserves. I left my backpack with Ray and Timothy and joined a small group.

On my return to the Mount Neru, Ray and Timothy had checked out, leaving behind a note, telling me to meet them at the Intercontinental Hotel in Nairobi. I hitched a lift with a group of Danish United Nations workers and they dropped me at the Intercontinental Hotel in Nairobi. There I found another note informing me that they had gone to stay in the Palm Hotel in a small town called Nakuru, some 200 kilometres west of Nairobi. As it was already getting late, I booked into a hotel and decided to head out the next morning.

After a good night's sleep, I wanted to leave early in the morning as I had no idea how long it would take me to get to Nakuru. I went down to the reception to pay my bill. It was only then that I discovered that my travellers' cheques were missing. Ray and Timothy must have taken them when I left my backpack with them! As I only had enough money left to pay for the accommodation, I was in serious trouble and had no idea what I should do now. In desperation, I made a collect phone call to my parents in Johannesburg and they gave me the telephone number of Pimo and Ulli Mueller, whom they had met through friends in Johannesburg and who lived in Nairobi. I called them and explained my predicament.

They immediately fetched me and took me to their house and said I could stay as long as I wanted. I told them I had some unfinished business and set out for Nakuru the next morning.

I got a lift with an Australian journalist stationed in Uganda. He told me he was the only Western journalist still in the country, but realised that his stay was probably limited. He told me that he had been deported from Uganda a few months earlier after writing some pieces criticising the government. He had spent a short while in Kenya before returning to Uganda. He was now officially doing other work for a development agency, although he was still filing pieces for various newspapers around the world.

He dropped me in the centre of Nakuru. It is a small town with a few hotels to house the visitors who come to see the thousands of flamingoes that have made their home on the shore of Lake Nakuru. Their names reminded me of Tanzania's colonial past. There was the Midland Hotel, the Sundowner Lodge, the Waterbuck Hotel and the Stem Hotel, but there was no Palm Hotel and nobody in the town had heard of Ray Corbett or Timothy Dobson. After spending a few hours asking around, I returned to Nairobi without having been able to confront the two.

Needless to say, I had lost some of my initial interest in finding the Leopards and was faced with a far greater problem: What was I going to do in a foreign country without any money? The latter problem was solved through my parents' friends, who lent me money to tide me over till my travellers' cheques were replaced. Having solved my financial problems, I decided to go to the coastal town of Mombasa to relax for a few days before continuing my search for the Leopards.

Pimo Mueller was one of the Lufthansa big-wigs in Kenya and he gave me the address of a friend of his who lived in Mombasa and who promptly invited me to stay for a few days. I took a taxi to his house and could not believe my eyes when the taxi driver stopped at the address I gave him. The house looked more breathtaking than any picture postcard I had ever seen! Surrounded by palm trees, the cottage had its own private beach with white sand. It was everything I expected paradise to be!

I spent the next few days just relaxing in the sun, swimming in the sea and generally having a good time. The people I stayed with were very well connected and there was a constant stream of visitors through the house.

One of them was a German film director called Christian Doermer, who was making a movie about a hero from the First World War called Graf Lettow-Vorbeck. Doermer had been a child star in Germany many years ago. When I met him at the beginning of 1983, his film was already years in the making. He saw it as something of his life's work.

When he found out that I was from South Africa, he became very interested in me, as South African war hero General Jan Smuts had fought against Lettow-Vorbeck in East Africa during the First World War. Doermer wanted to know everything about South Africa. He even gave me his telephone number in Nairobi and asked me to contact him when I returned to the capital.

After living in luxury for a week I left Mombasa and went back to Nairobi, determined to write the feature about AFC Leopards. Once again, I stayed with Pimo and Ulli. On my second day back in the city I phoned Doermer, who said he wanted to see me urgently and had something to discuss with me.

When we met he told me that his cameraman had just returned to Germany and he wanted to offer me the job. He said he also wanted me to play the role of General Smuts as I was probably the only person in Kenya who could do justice to the accent. Of course, I felt more flattered by his job offer than by his remarks about my accent.

After much deliberation I decided that my search for the Leopards would become part-time, while my full-time job, at least for the time being, would be cameraman for Doermer Productions, working on the movie about Lettow-Vorbeck.

The Muellers had kindly offered me a place to stay for as long as I needed it. For the next few weeks, I got up early in the morning and took a taxi to Doermer's flat. These taxis were nothing like the taxis I had encountered in Europe and even South Africa. They were mainly vans or trucks and were called matutus. There were no official stops and passengers had to flag them down to catch a ride. Drivers would stop anywhere on the side of the road to take on passengers, irrespective of how dangerous a stop would be or how full the vehicle was already.

It was an entirely different matter if somebody wanted to get off. To alight they would somehow have to attract the attention of the driver, who was normally too busy weaving in and out of the traffic and listening to the music blaring from the radio to take much notice of his passengers.

Once I had arrived at Doermer's flat, I would wait for the instructions for the day. We had no work-schedule and the director seemed directionless when it came to making the film. He did give me a book called Battle of the Bundus, which looked at the First World War in East Africa. From it, I got a lot of ideas for locations where we could shoot and I was able to give Doermer some guidelines about how many actors we would need.

All the actors were members of the local German community, who gave their time for whatever reasons, none of which was financial in nature as Doermer paid no one.

Kenya is one of the most beautiful countries in Africa and it is easy to see why the British, French and Germans fought over the area. As early as 1924, Jomo Kenyatta had led an uprising against the British in the territory. He failed, but tried again 30 years later. This time he met with more success and the Mau-Mau rebellion, as it became known, created the base for independence, which came in 1963.

And even though the rebellion was a particularly bloody affair, with some 15,000 Kenyans being killed and a further 80,000 sent to prison camps during the eight-year state of emergency, independence was not followed by a rigorous cleansing of everything that reminded residents of their colonial past. This ensured that Doermer was able to film scenes in locations that still resembled the Kenya of the 1920s.

I thoroughly enjoyed my work. Although it had very little or nothing to do with football, I thrived not only on the practical camera-work I was involved in, but also on the research I conducted to establish locations and background scenes. I came to love Kenya, its people and the countryside. I am sure that my research merely scratched the surface. I thought of Kenya as 'a film in waiting' and was sure that sooner or later somebody would use the country to make a Hollywood film. Years later, Out of Africa and White Mischief proved me correct.

Luckily for me, Lettow-Vorbeck had not been against the idea of using local footsoldiers to build trenches and to act as cannon fodder against the British. This enabled me, in between shoots, to chat football to the locals Doermer had hired as extras.

Kenya was by no means a great footballing nation and none of the modern-day footsoldiers cum trench-diggers believed that Kenya would ever emerge as a major force in African football. But that did not stop them from being absolute football fanatics and, I was amazed to discover, football experts. They told me that British settlers introduced football to the country at the beginning of the 20th century. The first clubs were formed in the 1960s. These clubs recruited players along tribal lines. AFC Leopards, who were formed as Abaluhya, represented the majority of football fans from the Luhya tribe, while their great rivals, Gor Mahia, whose founder members included a hero from the liberation struggle, Tom Mboya, represented Luos from what was then South Nyanza district. The tribal element in football added to the excitement, tension and rivalry in the local scene. A player crossing to a rival team would be risking death.

In fact, six years later, Kenya qualified for the finals of the African Nations Cup. It had taken 16 years to achieve this and naturally the country wanted the team to do well. On paper Kenya seemed to have a formidable team that could compete with the best of Africa. They embarked on a tour of Brazil as part of their preparations. It was there that the team came apart.

There was great animosity between members of Gor Mahia and AFC Leopards, resulting in a fight in which striker George Onyango 'Fundi' was supposedly stabbed and had to be hospitalised for two weeks. Not surprisingly, the team was eliminated in the first round.

I found out that AFC Leopards were, in fact, the team of the moment. Boasting a galaxy of stars including national team players, Josephat Murila, Mahmoud Abass, Francis Kadenge, Wilberforce Mulamba and Joe Masiga, they had won the East and Central African Club Cup in 1979 and 1982. They repeated that triumph in 1983 and 1984. I was also informed that they had, in fact, won the league championship in 1981 and 1982.

The trenchdiggers amazed me in that not only did they know about their own teams, but they also had knowledge about football that went far beyond the borders of Kenya. Their knowledge seemed to know no boundaries. They knew just as much about the German Bundesliga and the English first division as they did about their own teams. Bayern Munich and Liverpool were just as much a topic of our trench-building conversation as the exploits of local clubs Gor Mahia and the elusive AFC Leopards.

But club football was not the only topic we discussed. When they found out that I was a South African of German origin, I spent much of my time rebutting jokes about the Algerian victory at the World Cup in Spain a few months earlier. Even my protestations that Germany had, after all, finished runner-up in the competition made no difference. They were dismissed with comments about the 'friendly' match between Germany and Austria, which prevented the North Africans from taking their rightful place in the next round. To this day, it is generally accepted that the two European nations, who both knew that a single goal victory for Germany would allow both countries to proceed to the next round, had contrived to get the result they wanted. Any other result or score would have meant that Algeria would top, or at least finish second, in the group, allowing them to go through. Germany had scored an early goal and both sides had then stopped playing. Instead, they had stood around for the remainder of the game, knowing that they would both be going through to the next round.

LOOKING FOR THE LEOPARDS

The Kenyans had their own World Cup story to tell and they told me how Kenya had erupted in celebration after the Harambee Stars, as the national team is called, had beaten Tanzania 3-1 in the first leg of the World Cup qualifiers and how jubilation turned to sorrow when the return leg two weeks later ended in a 5-0 defeat.

Kenya's participation in the qualifying rounds for the 1982 edition of the African Cup of Nations in Libya had also not progressed beyond the first round. They had lost their qualifying matches against Egypt at home and away and had been knocked out. They would have to wait a further six years, or three competitions, for another chance to perform on Africa's highest footballing stage.

But if their Nations Cup and World Cup campaigns were unsuccessful, Kenya did, at least, excel in the East and Central Africa Challenge Cup (CECAFA Cup). Between 1981 and 1983, Kenya won three successive CECAFA cup titles.

The trench-diggers cum foot soldiers were particularly pleased about that, especially as it meant that they had finished above their main rivals, Tanzania.

And so I spent many an afternoon engaged in conversation about football. And although I made no progress with my intended article about the Leopards, I had no complaints about the work I was doing.

After four weeks and countless discussions about football, I was faced with a difficult choice. If I wanted to continue my studies at Rhodes University and my work for the Grahamstown Voice I would have to return to South Africa. Doermer made me an offer to stay and complete the film, but I was somewhat worried that he was intending to spend the next ten years completing his project, so with a heavy heart I said goodbye to the trench-diggers and foot soldiers and booked a flight to South Africa, from where I have continued both my political work, as well as my journalistic endeavours since then.

Although I had failed in my quest to write an article about AFC Leopards, I now have among my video collection a film in which I appear in the credits. I also lost £1,500 and fell prey to two brilliant con artists. My contact with Ray Corbett and Timothy Dobson was not to be the only contact I was to have with criminals in pursuit of a good football story.

4

MURDERERS, THIEVES
AND SCOUNDRELS

THE HISTORY OF SOUTH AFRICAN sport and, in fact, all aspects of South African society, is characterised by fragmentation. Not only did government policy prescribe that all races had to have their own organisations, but within these organisations there were various splinter groups that had broken away from the mother body. The reasons for such breakaways were either political or personal. The major political differences between organisations were over the question of collaboration with the white South African government or with white sporting bodies.

Football, for instance, was in 1978 controlled by some five different organisations. The Football Association of South Africa (FASA) was the 'white' body. It became a member of the world controlling body, FIFA, in the 1950s but was suspended in 1962. It briefly saw the suspension lifted before being suspended again in 1964, and finally expelled from the world body in 1976.

The 'black' South African National Football Association (SANFA) was the biggest of the five organisations and worked closely with FASA. Also working with FASA were the 'coloured' South African Football Association (SAFA) and the 'Indian' South African Soccer Association (SASA). By 1978 the most politicised body organising football was the South African Soccer Federation (the Federation), which believed in non-racial sport and was affiliated to the overtly political South African Council on Sport (SACOS).

Three of these organisations (FASA, the Federation and SANFA) organised professional leagues. In 1985 a further split occurred when a large number of professional clubs, that were unhappy with the way in which the despotic SANFA president was running the affairs of the association, broke away from SANFA and its professional wing, the National Professional Soccer League (NPSL), and formed their own association and professional league.

Each club now had to decide whether to join the fledgling National Soccer League (NSL), as the new professional league was called, or whether they wanted to stay with the NPSL.

Bitter feuding ensued and some clubs split into two, with one group of players, administrators and supporters remaining loyal to the NPSL, while the other changed sides and went to the NSL.

One of the oldest clubs in South Africa is Moroka Swallows. Once a powerhouse in South African football, the Birds, as the club is called, has a fine tradition being in the forefront of South African football. Like other well-established clubs such as Orlando Pirates and AmaZulu, Moroka Swallows is more than just a football club. Over the years these clubs have become institutions in their own right - the club and its teams are at the very centre of the lives of thousands of South Africans.

It is thus not surprising that any decisions taken by such clubs are not to be taken lightly. When Swallows decided to cut its ties with the NPSL and seek affiliation to the new league, there was bound to be dis-satisfaction, not only among the administrators and the fans but also among the players themselves. Three stalwarts of the club, Aaron 'Roadblock' Makhatini, Joel 'Ace' Mnini and Aubrey 'The Great' Magobela, decided to stay with the NPSL.

They formed their own club, thereby following the example of Jomo 'Troublemaker' Sono and Kaizer 'Chincha Guluva' Motaung. Both had been popular players who had formed their own clubs. Both had played in the North American Soccer League and decided to incorpo-rate the names of their American clubs into their new clubs. Motaung, who played for Atlanta Chiefs in the USA, formed Kaizer Chiefs in 1971, while Sono, who is much younger and played for New York Cosmos, formed Jomo Cosmos in 1983.

Makhatini, Mnini and Magobela were open about the fact that they viewed their club as a rival to Moroka Swallows and they called it the Mighty Birds. That decision infuriated many Swallows supporters and ultimately turned out to be fatal.

Just as the original Swallows side was based in the largest township in South Africa, Soweto, the Mighty Birds chose Soweto as their home, training on one of the many dusty fields that are found all over the townships. They affiliated to the NPSL, who accepted them gladly.

The players they attracted were by no means bad. Makhatini, although still very young, was already considered as one of the best central defenders in the country. In his first year in the professional ranks, he had been instrumental in leading Swallows to cup glory. He was also selected for a South African XI that played a friendly against an invitation side. His footballing future looked very bright indeed.

Makhatini lived in a modest brick house in Soweto. He shared the three-roomed home with his parents, his two brothers and two sisters. His life revolved around football and he spent much of his time on the training field.

Wednesday, 26 June 1985 was no different. Makhatini went to training in the afternoon. His new club, the Mighty Birds, was about to start playing in the NPSL and Makhatini was one of the most experienced players in the side. He knew that much of the responsibility of leading the younger players lay on his shoulders. And he also knew that his decision to form the club had not found favour with all Swallows supporters.

What he did not - and could not - know was that three men lay in ambush next to his house as he returned from training. Makhatini got out of the car and walked towards the front door. Makhatini stood no chance. The men confronted him before he had a chance to enter the house and without uttering a word they started shooting with a pistol. Hit four times, he slumped to the ground. He was dead by the time help arrived.

Mnini lived in a different part of Soweto, not far away from where Makhatini's home was. The killers rushed to Mnini's house. They entered the yard and walked up to the door, intending to do the same to Mnini as they had done to Makhatini. But Mnini heard them approach on the pebble stones that lay in the yard. He fetched his own pistol and was waiting for them. When they realised that he could not be gunned down as easily as Makhatini, they fled.

I was, at the time, working for a photographic agency called Afrapix and was covering the rift in South African football for a number of newspapers. It was not an easy task, as most newsworthy events occurred without prior warning, making it very difficult to photograph them. At least the first game of the new NSL, between Orlando Pirates and Jomo Cosmos, fixtured for Ellis Park Stadium two days after Makhatini's killing, would be easy, or so I thought.

I arrived at the stadium with a colleague well before the kick-off and went onto the field to take photographs. Some 20 minutes before the start, the Cosmos players entered the field and began warming up. A short while later the players and the management team of Orlando Pirates arrived on the field. The players started to get ready for the game, while the administrators sat down on the players' bench.

I was busy taking photographs of the players when I saw a minibus pull up next to the field. Its doors opened and out poured a group of players who also entered the pitch. They were wearing the black and white jerseys of Orlando Pirates. I knew that at the time there existed three factions of Pirates, each claiming to be the authentic one. The one faction had decided to stay with the NPSL, but the other two groupings had thrown in their lot with the NSL and both had arrived at Ellis Park, eager to play.

In charge of the latecomers was a man called China Hlongwane and it was he who led his side onto the field. Of a jovial disposition, Hlongwane was one of the fattest men I had ever seen. Pirates was his passion and his pride, and he looked like a man with a purpose as he told his players to warm up, which they did.

When the administrators of the first Pirates team saw that Hlongwane was encouraging his players to get ready for the game, they entered the field and advanced towards him. I followed them and started taking pictures. Like a pack of lions about to pounce on their prey, they circled around Hlongwane. I saw one of them reach into his pocket and pull out a large knife. Others followed.

They had Hlongwane trapped in the middle of the circle. Suddenly one of them stepped forward and thrust his knife deep into Hlongwane's massive stomach. The assailant then retreated back into the circle. Hlongwane tried to move out, but they would not let him. Then another stepped forward and stabbed the helpless man. And then another and another. Hlongwane must have been stabbed at least 10 times before he finally managed to get away from his attackers.

This all happened so fast that nobody tried to intervene. Not the 30,000 spectators who were already in the stadium and were witnessing the attack, nor Hlongwane's players who had run towards their minibus as soon as the knives were drawn. I kept on taking pictures of the attack, unable through fear and disbelief to do anything else. Even the NSL security and the police, both of whom were present in large numbers, failed to come to Hlongwane's rescue.

Once the attackers had driven Hlongwane and his players off the field, they put their knives back into their pockets and returned to the players' bench. Problem solved!

They watched the rest of the game from the sidelines while Hlongwane was taken to hospital. Even though it later emerged that he had 17 stab wounds, doctors managed to save his life, saying that the only reason he survived the attack was because he carried so much fat. Years later he was to survive an attack during which four bullets from an automatic assault rifle were pumped into his body. He then retired from football, but died of a heart attack shortly afterwards.

The club that nearly cost Hlongwane his life, Orlando Pirates, is considered 'the people's club' in South Africa. Formed in 1912 by a group of youngsters who wanted to escape life on the streets, the club has a rich but troubled history. Disputes over ownership and fan interference in all aspects of the club, including team selection, have been as much part and parcel of Orlando Pirates as has been the club's success on the field.

The 20 years between 1970 and 1990 were especially violent and quite a few prominent committee members met unexpected deaths under mysterious circumstances. Washington Basula was murdered at home in a killing which has been linked to friction within the club. Jimmy Sojane was another committee member killed. Police, who had come to his house to arrest him, gunned down Mzwandile Malgas. All three were prominent Pirates members at the time of their death.

But it is not only Pirates members who were victims of football violence in South Africa.

In 1994 I was researching a story about the unification of South African football. After the release of Nelson Mandela from prison and the unbanning of the African National Congress (ANC), which had been at the forefront of the struggle to rid South Africa of apartheid, FIFA informed South African footballing officials that one of the conditions for the country's readmission into the world body was that a single unitary body controlled the sport.

This led to the merger of the South African Soccer Federation and the South African Soccer Association. They called the new body the South African Football Association (SAFA). President of the Federation at the time of the merger was a Durban insurance salesman called Rama Reddy. After unification he became the president of the Southern Natal Football Association (SNFA), one of the regional bodies.

I had met Rama a few times while I was still president of the Grahamstown Soccer Association and knew that he would quite willingly speak to me about the steps that led to the unification and ultimately to SAFA becoming a fully-fledged member of FIFA in 1992.

I had resumed contact with Reddy earlier in the year at a function of a football club and had briefly spoken to him about the article I was busy preparing. He agreed to co-operate and give me the 'inside story'. Due to work commitments I could not continue with the story at the time and put it aside, hoping to carry on a few months down the road.

In December 1994, however, Reddy was dead. His relatives had found his car parked on the side of the road. His lifeless body was slumped over the steering wheel and initial reports indicated that the football administrator had died of a heart attack. When Reddy's family heard that, they protested loudly. He was a healthy man who had led an active life, they said.

Pressured by the family, police looked into the matter a bit more closely and other information came to the surface. The night of his death, Reddy had attended a club prize-giving in a town some 40 kilometres outside Durban. It was also known that he was busy investigating financial irregularities within the SNFA. The organisation's auditors had told him that they were not happy with some of the expenses and that the executive should investigate these.

As a result Reddy had refused to sign the financial report and had fought with a member of the SNFA executive. It was widely believed that this member was involved in the irregularities and Reddy wanted to inform his executive of his findings at a meeting two days after the prize-giving.

When he failed to return home after the function, his family conducted a search. One of those who looked for Reddy was the very same executive member with whom Reddy had fought. Reddy's nephew, Poobalan Naidoo, who was involved in the search, later made a statement to the police that on the executive members instructions, they took a route which led them to Reddy's car. He said he had been 'sceptical' to take this route because his uncle would have been unlikely to drive there.

The heart attack theory was also discarded and it became evident that Reddy had died by strangulation. But even though they had managed to piece parts of the puzzle together, police remained baffled as to the identity of his attackers.

Their first real breakthrough came a few months into the case when an informant approached the police and told them that a certain

Moneymalen Sigamoney could help them in their enquiries. Sigamoney made a statement in which he implicated the executive member in the murder.

In the statement he told the police that he had gone to a party on the night of the murder and had met the executive member there. He knew him from an angling club, of which both of them were members. They left the party together to visit another friend, but stopped on the way to have a drink. They saw Reddy's car coming towards them and the executive member stopped it. He then got into the car with Reddy and Sigamoney followed them. They went to a secluded beach, where Reddy and the executive member spoke to each other.

In the statement Sigamoney said that the executive member suddenly placed his hand over Reddy's mouth and nose and pressed hard. He held Reddy down for about ten minutes, before letting go. He then drove the car to another place, where Sigamoney helped him move Reddy's body behind the steering wheel.

After making the statement, Sigamoney agreed to become state witness in exchange for indemnity from prosecution. The police agreed and the executive member was arrested. When the case was heard, however, Sigamoney refused to testify and the case had to be withdrawn for lack of evidence. The executive member is no longer involved in football administration, but remains in the angling club with Sigamoney.

Much later an inquest court ruled that, on the evidence before it, it could not make a finding whether any living person was responsible for Reddy's death.

Reddy was killed for less than a few thousand pounds that had been misappropriated. Others, with much more money involved, were luckier. They kept their lives and some of them even kept the money!

Money matters are very important in South African football and to the outside observer it must seem that money is the only thing that drives local football administrators. An administrator who seemed to fit this bill was Solomon 'Sticks' Morewa.

Morewa was born in a small town called Potchefstroom some 100 kilometres outside Johannesburg. His parents were by no means wealthy, and Morewa's youth no different from that of hundreds of thousands of other black children growing up under apartheid. Life was a constant struggle for the youngster. He moved to Johannesburg and enrolled at the Orlando High School in Soweto. There he became involved in political activities for which he was soon arrested. Sentenced to two years' imprisonment, he was sent to Robben Island, where Nelson Mandela was also imprisoned. On his release he worked for a number of companies, including a fertilizer plant belonging to Louis Luyt, who was later to become the most powerful man in South African rugby.

Morewa worked as a personnel clerk for Luyt and started organising football matches for the workers. Through that he became involved in the Western Transvaal Football Association, which organised football outside Johannesburg. After a while he became an administrator in Johannesburg and became active in the Transvaal Football Association. His talents as administrator did not go unnoticed and the president of SANFA, George Thabe, took him into the association's executive in the late 1970s.

From there his rise in the football hierarchy was as rapid as the rise in his popularity and when the big split, which resulted in Makhatini's death, occurred in 1985, Morewa was deemed to be the man to take over the affairs of the newly established SASA. He was made general-secretary, a position he held for several years. He kept his position once SAFA was formed after the merger with the Federation. In 1994, he was made SAFA's first-ever executive president.

But it was really from 1992 that Morewa's stature within South African society improved greatly, as did his earnings. In that year, South Africa were readmitted into FIFA and could play regular international matches, thereby greatly improving SAFA's income. However, Morewa's salary increased at a far more rapid rate than SAFA's income did. In January 1993 he was earning about £2,200 a month. This more than doubled to just under £5,000 by June 1996. If one compares this salary with that of a professional player in South Africa, who on average earns much less than £400 a month, it is apparent that Morewa was grossly overpaid.

His excessive salary, however, was not the only criticism levelled against him. He was also accused of neglecting his official duties and of concentrating too much on promoting his own interests instead of those of the association. He seemed to have a general apathy towards the less lucrative limbs of the footballing industry, such as women's football. He similarly lacked enthusiasm in answering correspondence and being accountable.

The first time I had experienced such lack of enthusiasm was in 1992, shortly after I had published the first of my South African

43

Football Yearbooks. I wrote to Morewa and offered to produce, at no cost to SAFA, a comprehensive brochure cum programme for the first international series to be played against Cameroon. I even offered to give SAFA as many free copies as they required. I put all of this in a bound proposal, which I submitted to Morewa. A decade later, I am still awaiting a reply!

When I attended the first game against Cameroon in Durban, the journalists were given a programme, which was only a few pages long, devoid of any real substance and poorly produced. I later found out that SAFA had awarded the contract to publish the programme to a printing company whose owner was a good friend of the manager of the stadium in which the SAFA offices are housed. And what infuriated me even further was that they had paid the company to do so. Instead of receiving a more comprehensive brochure from me for free, they had paid someone to publish an inferior one! I have my suspicions why Morewa awarded the contract as he did, but to print them would be libelous.

A few years later I was approached by Morewa who asked me to interview him for a monthly magazine I was writing for at the time. I agreed on condition that the administrator would allow me absolute freedom to ask any questions I liked. Morewa said he was willing to answer any question I put to him. He suggested a date and time and told me to come to his office. On the date in question, I flew all the way from Cape Town to the SAFA headquarters in Johannesburg and arrived punctually at 11am, for the interview. Morewa's secretary, a very friendly young woman called Pinkie, told me that Morewa was not in and that she had no idea when he would come to the office. She looked in Morewa's appointment book and confirmed that my interview was scheduled for that morning. As we could not reach him on his cell phone, I sat down and waited. After an hour Pinkie came to me and asked if I wanted any tea or coffee. I declined.

An hour later she again asked me and, realising that I could be in for a long wait, I accepted. For the next hour I sat in Morewa's reception room, drinking tea and reading old magazines. Even though I had long given up any hope of making my scheduled flight back to Cape Town later that afternoon, I decided at 3pm that I had waited long enough. I left my cell phone number with Pinkie and asked her to contact me as soon as Morewa appeared. I explained to her that I had a deadline I was working to and needed to do the interview the same day, or the next at the latest. She agreed to pass on the message. I spent the next day waiting in Johannesburg without hearing from Morewa or his office. The interview never took place, but I published the questions I would have put to Morewa had he been there.

I was not the only journalist who was stood up in such a fashion by Morewa. I met numerous international journalists who had come to the country to write about sport in general, or football in particular. Whenever one of them told me that he or she had an appointment with Morewa I just smiled and suggested they not use the interview as the central point of their story. One such journalist was Simon Kuper, who was doing research for his book, Football Against The Enemy. I spent quite a bit of time with Kuper and his book is one of the best football books I have ever read. But even he failed in his attempts to get an interview with Morewa.

In other words, Morewa was a highly controversial figure and many questioned not only his motives, but also his suitability to head the nation's most popular sport. But apart from allegations, innuendos and rumours that were circulating, there was little or nothing that one could pin on Morewa or other members of the executive, though most people involved in local football were worried that the sport was being held back by the goings-on at the SAFA executive.

Such was the position at the beginning of 1996, when I was appointed the editorial director of the monthly Soccer News. South Africa had just won the African Cup of Nations and everybody connected with the sport was riding the crest of a wave of victories. The last thing anybody wanted to do was rock the boat unnecessarily, but when my editor came to me and said he had received confidential documents implicating Morewa in fraud and corruption he had little difficulty in convincing me that we should look very seriously at them.

The document was a contract between a South African bank called Absa and Awesome Sports International (ASI). Everybody involved in football in South Africa knew ASI. It is a company based in Ireland. ASI had somehow managed to become the marketing agents for South African football and nobody quite knew how.

The contract certainly made very interesting reading. In it, the bank agreed to pay just less than £5 million into an overseas account in exchange for advertising rights for an international tournament, which was to be called United Bank Soccer Festival.

This festival was intended to forge sporting links between Europe and South Africa and the perception was that it would further the development of football in South Africa. The tournament saw two British teams coming to South Africa and competing against top local sides.

Similar to most other African currencies, the South African Rand is very weak. This has resulted in strict foreign exchange regulations controlling the flow of money from the country. It was thus very surprising that a company doing business in South Africa was to be paid overseas. The amount to be paid also seemed to be excessive and we decided to do some further investigation into the matter.

The contract stipulated that the amount payable for a tournament held in 1994 had been slightly more than £1.5 million. One of the teams that competed that year was Liverpool and I contacted their chief executive officer, Peter Robinson, who informed me that Liverpool had received a 'moderate' fee, around £250,000, which covered all their expenses. Further investigation revealed that Aston Villa received more or less the same. One of the South African participants in the 1994 tournament, Moroka Swallows, was paid £10,000. This left ASI £1 million. Even taking into consideration other expenses such as publicity and organisation, it became apparent that ASI had been grossly overpaid.

We approached both the bank and ASI for a comment and when neither managed to give us satisfactory answers, we decided to forward our information to our lawyers and asked them if we could publish. They said yes, and we did.

Even before we went to print Absa contacted ASI and asked them for a breakdown of how the £4.7 million was spent. They were told they could not have it, as it was a confidential matter. And that, even though it was Absa's money in the first place! It was then that I was certain we had a strong story.

When we came out, the story was at first ignored by virtually the entire mainstream press. Luckily for us, my editor also had a TV and a radio spot, which he used to keep the story going.

After hearing about our story, the South African Minister of Sport, Steve Tshwete, asked for a copy of all the relevant documents, which we duly sent him. He read them carefully and then decided to set up a judicial commission of inquiry to investigate the financial affairs and administration of SAFA and the NSL. He appointed a Supreme Court judge to head the inquiry.

When Tshwete announced the Pickard Commission, he was

approached by the executive president of SAFA, Solomon Morewa, who, with tears in his eyes, asked him to downgrade the commission to a departmental one. Morewa hoped that it would be less thorough and less powerful.

But Tshwete, who is a highly principled man and spent many years incarcerated with Nelson Mandela on Robben Island, turned down Morewa's request and pressed on.

The commission sat for a few months and then forwarded its report to Mandela, who in turn, through Tshwete, made the findings public.

In his report, the judge outlined events that had led to the granting of the marketing rights to ASI. A few months before the final agreement between ASI and SAFA was signed, Morewa received substantial amounts of money from the company. During cross-examination, Morewa told the judge that the money was an interest-free loan from a director of ASI, Brian Mahon, which he received because he needed money at the time. He could not explain why he needed money as his bank statements showed that he had a very healthy looking account, nor why a substantial amount of the so-called loan was put into fixed deposits, to which he had no access. The judge came to the conclusion that 'the so-called loan was never in fact a loan from Mahon, but was paid to Morewa by ASI for other reasons.'

Morewa failed to report the money he received from ASI/Mahon to his executive. It was not the only bit of evidence he kept to himself. Morewa also seemed to have had some difficulty in understanding the difference between an agreement and a proposal, for when he approached his executive with an agreement between ASI and SAFA about a tournament, he told his executive that it was a proposal, although he had already signed it. A year later he again reported to his executive about the same tournament. The judge found 'his report to the executive about the tournament to be simply inaccurate and misleading'.

Once Morewa had received such a substantial amount of money from Mahon, it is probably very unlikely that he was in a position to negotiate on level ground with Mahon. Mahon was contracting for ASI with Morewa whom he could manipulate into virtually any position he wished and who, in turn, would do the necessary to promote his cause within the ranks of SAFA and among its executives. It therefore came as no surprise that the marketing agreement between ASI and SAFA allowed ASI to take over virtually all of SAFA's money-earning assets for their own benefit, leaving SAFA with a virtually static income for the duration of the contract. ASI was thus free to earn as much money as it was able to from SAFA's activities.

The judge and, I venture to say, most other South Africans were of the opinion that Mahon was able to secure such a favourable contract because of his very intimate and financially-linked relationship with Morewa, and the latter's subtle influence on the members of the executive of SAFA, to convince them that the deal was beneficial to them.

Ironically though, SAFA, apparently not appreciating the position, still voted to give Morewa a 10% bonus on sponsorship obtained. This reduced their base income even more.

Morewa's bonus for 1994 was £6,500. Through an administrative error, the cheque for this bonus was written out twice. Morewa duly signed both and put them into his account. When the error was discovered, Morewa agreed to repay the extra amount at £800 pounds per month, with no interest. When asked why he allowed such good terms for himself, he said, 'money is always welcome.'

A year later his performance bonus doubled.

Not only the so-called loan and Morewa's performance bonus were criticised by the Commission of Inquiry. During investigations, it also came to light that Morewa had been given use of a Mercedes Benz by one of the sponsors. This was yet another thing that he forgot to mention to his executive and the judge said in his report that 'the whole matter is highly unsatisfactory if not corrupt.'

The vehicle was not the only accusation of corruption levelled against Morewa. It also emerged that Morewa had, as head of an education trust set up to award bursaries to football players, given himself a grant. Judge Pickard said, 'Morewa's management of the education trust and his allowing it to be mismanaged in the way it was, in itself indicates gross mismanagement, incompetence, if not corruption. He received payments from the education trust, which were unjustified and contrary to the intentions of the rules of the fund. It was frequently abused for the benefits of persons not qualifying for assistance therefrom.'

The report then was damning of Morewa and ASI. Judge Pickard said Morewa was 'no longer a fit and proper person to be at the helm of the football industry. He has proven himself to be over concerned with promoting his own interest instead of those of the association. His general attitude of arrogance and domination has made him unsuitable for the task he is required to fulfil.'

He said that Morewa was an assertive person who gets aggressive in the face of opposition, which Morewa most appropriately demonstrated by his outbursts and attacks on press reporters. 'I perceive him as quick to tears, but also quick to go on the attack when finding himself to be the subject of criticism.'

Pickard then went on to suggest that Morewa resign, or be dismissed by the executive. But far from resigning, Morewa was defiant. He said that he had been voted into office and he would certainly not resign. He received the backing of the SAFA executive, who said they would await further information before taking action. Morewa then flew to Lisbon to collect a FIFA award on behalf of South African football. When he came back, he dropped another bombshell. He announced on South African television, that, in the interest of South African football, he was going to resign at a meeting two days later.

But far from acting in the interest of South African football, Morewa was hoping, to the bitter end, to act in his own interests and he demanded such a high severance package, including a trip to the 1998 World Cup, that the executive said no. Morewa then duly withdrew his resignation and walked out of the office. This resulted in his suspension.

A short while later Morewa's lawyers contacted SAFA and in the end both sides managed to reach a compromise. Morewa was given six months' salary and all leave due. The man who was deemed not to be a 'fit and proper' person to run football, had walked away with a package worth £35,000. For this kind of money a professional player in South Africa's top league has to play for about six years, but Morewa received it because he had mismanaged the affairs of the association to such an extent that he could no longer be its head.

Once Morewa was gone, the search for a replacement began. Judge Pickard offered a description of the person he thought should take over. 'The president and chairman of SAFA should be a man of utmost integrity with a love for the game of soccer who has no financial interests by way of salary or any perks arising from his position. He must be a person who is willing to do the job for the mere love of the game.'

When I read that, I immediately thought I had just the man for the job. He always said he did it for the love of the game and as it so happened, he had just been released from jail. Nothing should stand in the way of him taking over South African football again. Or was there?

5

"I DO IT FOR THE LOVE OF THE GAME"

ONE OF THE MOST colourful men ever involved with South African football was a small, slightly stocky Indian man called Abdul Bhamjee. Bhamjee came from a merchant family and owned a sports shop in an Indian area of Johannesburg.

His rise to become the most powerful man in South African football is best described as a rags to riches story, which he himself liked telling people. He said he had to leave school at the age of twelve to help support five siblings. He worked first as a shop assistant in the dusty town of Komatipoort. Later, he sold ladies underwear as a travelling salesman, before opening a sports shop.

He joined the South African Soccer Federation and soon made a name for himself in footballing circles in the country. His own personal rise to fame coincided with that of South African football and as the sport grew, his stature grew, until he was simply known as Mr Soccer.

When he joined the Federation, it was the weakest of the national bodies. Its professional wing had little sponsorship and even less clubs with a strong appeal in the market place. But within a short period of time he had changed all of that. If there was one thing that Bhamjee could do well, it was to sell things. It appeared as if the phrase 'selling ice to the Eskimos' had been penned for him, and him alone. He started selling the product football with such vigour that the Federation was soon able to offer its clubs lucrative sponsorships for competitions. That, of course, meant that several of the top clubs in the country came across to join the Federation.

After a while, Bhamjee's relationship with the Federation soured and he left them. The exact reasons were never made public, but behind closed doors one would often hear stories of sponsorship monies that were not passed on to the Federation. With Bhamjee's departure began the demise of the Federation. More and more sponsors pulled out and many clubs left the association and re-joined the National Professional

Soccer League (NPSL).

This was the association that Bhamjee had also joined. He served as its Public Relations Officer and did so until NPSL chairman George Thabe decided that Bhamjee was getting too powerful. He suspended him in 1985 from the organisation and was obviously trying to edge him out. But if Thabe was hoping that his suspended PRO would sit back and accept his fate, he was horribly wrong. At the time there were rumours that some £100,000 of the league's money had gone missing. Bhamjee used this to convince some 18 clubs to form a rebel breakaway league, the National Soccer League (NSL), which soon eclipsed the NPSL.

During the unity talks between the various football associations that took place in South Africa during the late 1980s, Bhamjee was a thorn in the flesh of the Federation. They were unhappy to have to accept a former official who had parted ways with them under dark clouds. But such was Bhamjee's power and influence within the NSL, which by then had become the richest football association in the country, that the organisation could, to a large degree, dictate the terms under which it was prepared to merge with the other associations. One of the terms was that Bhamjee was given a post in the new association. Although officially, he was in charge of public affairs, behind the scenes he was pulling all the strings. De facto he had become one of the most power-ful men in South African football - if not the most powerful.

The first time I met Bhamjee was at one of the NSL's weekly press conferences, a custom that he had introduced to improve the league's public profile. At these conferences the league announced the fixtures for the week; club chairmen and spokesmen said why they were going to win their matches on the weekend and why their opponents were in for a hiding next to none; and most importantly for us journalists snacks and drinks were served at the end of the conferences.

At this particular conference, Bhamjee was to conduct the draw for the first round of a cup competition, which was to be played on the weekend.

"Who in this room smokes?" he asked.

Many of the journalists, quite a few of the club officials and most of the hangers-on who came for the snacks and drinks at the end of the conference put up their hands.

"Right, now take out your cigarettes."

The people in the room were obviously used to Bhamjee's ways. Out came the Lucky Strikes, Paul Reveres, Dunhills and a few other brands. Mr Soccer left his seat at the table at the top end of the room. He walked up to the first row and looked at the cigarettes they were holding. "These are shit, this is rubbish, this is junk. Throw them away."

He did the same to the people in the other rows, telling them to throw their cigarettes into the dustbin. Suddenly his face lit up. He pointed at a journalist working for an afternoon newspaper. "Now look at this fellow. He knows what he is doing. He is the best journalist in the room, you should all look up to him and try to follow in his footsteps." He held up the fellow's cigarettes. "Look here, he smokes JPS, a man of the world."

He dipped his hand into a plastic bag that he had been carrying. He took out a handful of packets of John Player Special cigarettes and started handing them out. "From now on, this is the only cigarette that you will smoke. They care about football and we care about them. JPS is the smoke for you," he grinned.

When he had finished handing out the cigarettes, he returned to his chair and continued with the draw. Not surprisingly, it was called the JPS Cup and was sponsored by the cigarette company.

He was known throughout the country for his outrageous statements. He was frequently quoted as saying, 'No publicity is bad publicity' and 'Honesty, sincerity and integrity - these are the secrets of success'.

Bhamjee loved talking and he relished being in the limelight. He particularly enjoyed conducting draws for competitions, as these enabled him to do both. And he did them with aplomb. There was one thing about Bhamjee's cup draws though, that had always bothered me. Somehow, the most popular clubs never seemed to be drawn against each other in the early rounds.

A couple of months later, South African journalists witnessed what seemed to be a possible explanation for the Bhamjeesque way of arranging football draws.

After cup competitions football journalists were asked to nominate a Player of the Series. They did this by voting for the player of their choice. The winner would then be announced at a glittering function, at which the winning team was also rewarded for its efforts.

In 1991, Cosmos did remarkably well in the BP Top 8 competition, going all the way to the final. Even though they lost the final 3-4 to South Africa's glamour club, Kaizer Chiefs, one of the Cosmos players stood out. He was the lanky striker Philemon Masinga, known simply as 'Chippa'. He scored a hat-trick in the semi-final and repeated his feat in the final.

At the awards ceremony, Masinga was considered the odds-on favourite to win the Player of the Series award. His play had been outstanding and his goals should certainly have swayed any judge who at the eleventh hour remained undecided. Or so everybody thought. On the night, Masinga was on hand to pick up his prize.

But disappointment was in store for him. When the winner was announced it was not Masinga, but a Kaizer Chiefs striker called Fani Madida who was called forward. The matter could have ended there, except this time the judges refused to take the announcement lying down. One by one they came forward and said that they had voted for Chippa Masinga as the Player of the Series and were now surprised that he had not won.

Soon it became so apparent that Masinga had in fact been the judges' choice, that the media could no longer ignore the fact. This, of course, also meant that the league could no longer ignore the fact. Far from being embarrassed about the incident, Bhamjee did a quick shuffle and announced that the organising committee had decided, in light of the outstanding performances of both Madida and Masinga, to give two Player of the Series awards and both players won.

He point-blank refused to admit that he had 'doctored' the results. Instead, he issued a statement on behalf of the organisation in which he said that he would gladly have made the votes available to the media. Unfortunately though, the statement said, it was no longer possible to do so.

"The voting papers were destroyed after the selection was made as a dispute was never envisaged. In future competitions the ballot will be made available for public scrutiny," the statement read.

Incidents such as these did nothing to diminish Bhamjee's popularity. He was far too clever for that. He knew what to do and when to do it. He chose his friends carefully and wooed sections of the media. Many a politician, official and journalist received expensive gifts from him. To have been on his 'A list' of friends was certainly worthwhile, as it could bring you really expensive gifts, like the Rolex watch that he gave to Sam Ramsamy, who was the first president of the South African Olympic Committee after the country's readmission to the Olympic Games in 1992.

He also handed out money. Many a journalist covering football in South Africa had his meager earnings boosted by Bhamjee. He claimed it was for the 'coverage of NSL activity'.

But it was not only the rich and famous who were courted by Bhamjee. He did the same with the common people. Obviously they did not receive gifts, but Mr Soccer knew just the right language in which to address them. His catch-phrase (and in fact the catch-phrase in the country at the time) was 'The People'. This mysterious, faceless and nameless mass was what drove politicians in the country during the 1980s and 1990s. Football was the people's sport and Bhamjee was its custodian. He spoke about 'The People' and was considered, by himself and by others, as their guardian angel who did everything to see to it that 'The People's' Will prevailed. One of the first group of visitors African National Congress leader Nelson Mandela received after being released from jail was a National Soccer League delegation, led by Mr Soccer himself. Bhamjee said at the time that he had gone to Soweto to make sure that 'our father is home'.

That he did not come short in the process goes without saying. He printed most of the material for the association, did their programmes and was paid handsomely for that work. He also ran his sports shop in Fordsburg, specialising in football goods, and called it Fedfan, from the times that he was still involved in the Federation. Not only that, he also ran an extremely lucrative mail order business.

To understand why the South African mail-order business is such a lucrative one, one needs to understand a little bit about South Africa and its geography. South Africa is a huge country, more than double the size of Great Britain. The distances between cities are vast and there is a large rural population. Most South Africans at that time had no access to shopping centers, malls and the like. But there was one thing that bound them together: the love of football.

In every little hamlet there is at least one football team and, more than likely, a football league. And these teams were particularly proud of their football kit. Even though some of the people living in these out-lying areas had little or no money, they would somehow manage to scrape together enough to ensure that their football team was kitted out with a decent set of jerseys.

Enter Bhamjee. He had the jerseys; the only problem was how to get them to the masses. For that he used his own football magazine, which was little more than a mail-order catalogue.

"I DO IT FOR THE LOVE OF THE GAME"

He paid journalists to write articles about the most popular players and clubs - none of them critical of course. He would throw in a few posters and then add four or more pages advertising his own mail-order items and sell the complete package as a football magazine. At the time, there existed very little opposition to his football magazine and, by all accounts Bhamjee's magazine not only sold well, mail orders for his products came flooding in.

But if Bhamjee was doing well for himself, he was doing just as well for South African football. He was particularly innovative and enjoyed introducing new marketing ideas into the sport. One of his best was the so-called Charity Spectacular. This was a day-long football extravaganza at which South Africa's four most popular teams competed against each other. In the morning the two semi-finals were played, in the afternoon the two winners would pair off for the final. In between, there was music and other entertainment for the spectators.

Football fans certainly took to the concept like a fish to water. Bhamjee organised this Spectacular as the traditional season-opener and every year it was sold out. In the 1990s, the Charity Spectacular was often played in front of over 100,000 people, even though the official capacity of the stadium in which it was played is much less.

The money generated from the Spectacular, through gate-takings, sponsorship and broadcasting rights, was donated to various charitable organisations and over the years millions have been given away. This was not done without controversy though, as every year there are reports of a large percentage of the money not actually reaching charities.

The four clubs that participated in the Spectacular were chosen by popular vote. Football fans throughout the country were invited to vote for their favourite club by sending in a postcard or phoning in to give their nomination. How fair and accurate this system is, nobody knows; throughout the years there have been several accusations of teams participating in the tournament despite the fact that they did not get as many votes as some of the clubs that had been excluded.

Another successful innovation that Bhamjee introduced to South African football was the double-header, which enabled fans to see two matches in one afternoon. Both double-headers and the Charity Spectacular remain important features on the South African footballing calendar.

Bhamjee's greatest triumph, though, was the planning and building of the FNB Stadium. He called it the Stadium for the Nation, or the People's Stadium. His vision was for it to be South Africa's Wembley Stadium, with a seating capacity of over 100,000. It was located on the outskirts of Johannesburg, close to the biggest township in South Africa, Soweto. Bhamjee somehow convinced a major South African banking institution to bankroll the construction of the biggest football stadium in the country. The idea was that it would become the national stadium and the headquarters of football in the country.

Mr Soccer basked in glory on the day that the construction of the stadium began. He had invited the country's media and dignitaries from all walks of life. Presenting himself as one of the people, he wore a construction hat and took great pleasure in doing the first spadework in front of running microphones and on national television.

With the construction of the FNB stadium, Mr Soccer had reached his zenith. From there, he could only go down. And plummet he did, more dramatically than anybody had expected. In February 1992, Abdul Bhamjee, aka Mr Soccer, appeared in court on charges of theft. He looked forlorn and dejected and much older than his 52 years on the day he was sentenced to an effective 14 years in jail for theft.

What had happened?

It seems that Bhamjee, who liked to tell everybody that everything he did, he did for the love of the game, was not being very truthful when he made these utterances.

Bhamjee had been charged in court with 35 counts of theft. One of the charges related to the negotiation of broadcasting rights for league matches with the South African Broadcasting Corporation (SABC). On behalf of the NSL Bhamjee had negotiated a contract and agreed upon a set fee for the broadcasting rights. These had been presented to the SABC Board, which had then made the money available. At the same time, a second contract, which included a considerably lower figure, had also been drawn up. This had been presented to the NSL executive, which had agreed to the terms. Bhamjee, together with a few others, had pocketed the difference. In the three of the most serious cases alone, Bhamjee had stolen £260,000.

The SABC's then chief legal advisor, Leandor Gaum, testified at the trial that he had drawn up the original contracts, but that his signature had been forged on the contracts which had been presented to the league.

Bhamjee's defence was that he was entitled to 10% of all the sponsorship that he raised for football. The magistrate presiding over the case was not at all convinced. He said that 'the mere fact that the 10% commission he claims he was entitled to from all sponsorship monies he raised was agreed upon by former NSL official Cyril Kobus (who was also charged and jailed), former chairman Rodger Sishi (who was forced to resign in disgrace) and Bhamjee himself was handled in the highest secrecy and confidentiality, showed that he (Bhamjee) knew that he was committing a crime.'

He went on to say that Bhamjee had been in a position of trust and he knew that he had to consult the management committee of the league, especially when it involved a sensitive issue such as the league's finances. For someone involved in soccer administration for as long as he had been, Bhamjee must have known that he was not acting lawfully by intentionally and purposefully misappropriating funds. 'Bhamjee was a talented man who put so much energy into soccer, but is guilty of the most mammoth and series of thefts,' said magistrate MJ Strydom.

He found Bhamjee guilty on 33 of the 35 counts and sentenced him to an effective 14 years in jail. Bhamjee's lawyers appealed against the conviction and sentence. They claimed that 'the sentence of 14 years' effective imprisonment is severe and unreasonable and induces a sense of shock, especially if one keeps in mind the money's (sic) expended by the appellant in furthering the aims of the NSL, the selfless devotion, over many years, by the appellant to the cause of the NSL.'

The appeal court obviously did not agree that Bhamjee's work for the NSL was as selfless as his lawyers had wanted them to believe, and decided that the former PRO was to remain in jail, thereby bringing to an abrupt end the illustrious footballing career of the flamboyant Indian shopkeeper, Abdul Bhamjee, who was also known as Mr Soccer.

Some would argue that his sentence was not in the interest of the sport, claiming that even though Bhamjee worked money into his own pocket, he did a lot of good for football in the country, bringing money and marketing to the sport.

Bhamjee served only four years of his sentence in jail, before being released on parole. He returned to running his sports shop, but has since steered clear of any further involvement in South African football. His magazine no longer exists. When I saw him at the shop at the turn of the century, he no longer looked like the glamorous PRO that he once had been. He had aged and looked like a bitter old man.

Being in jail robbed Bhamjee of another of his greatest aspirations:

seeing South African football re-emerge from the wilderness of sporting isolation. When South Africa finally played its first international match after being readmitted to the world controlling body, FIFA, Bhamjee was sitting in a prison cell, far away from Durban where it was all happening.

6

"FOR MANDELA - ONLY FIVE"

IN 1992, SOUTH AFRICA was readmitted to the world controlling body, FIFA. To celebrate, they planned a spectacular comeback, but ran into unexpected problems as the South African Soccer Association (SASA) could not find high-profile opposition. A hastily arranged tour by Cameroon was then organised. South Africa won the first match in Durban 1-0, lost the next in Cape Town, before drawing the final game in Johannesburg.

After this series, South Africa faced Zimbabwe away in its first-ever competitive game. This was scheduled for August 1992 and I made arrangements with another football journalist, Mark Gleeson, to travel together. I was, at first, a bit reluctant as Gleeson had served in the Apartheid army and his father was a high-ranking officer in the South African military, but in the end the need to share expenses over-ruled any political objections I had to sharing a hotel room with him.

We were two of a handful of journalists who felt the occasion was important enough to warrant the two-hour flight to the Zimbabwean capital of Harare.

But before South Africa could take on Zimbabwe, there was a very important issue to take care of. Important at least to the millions of South African football fans who would be watching the match live on television. They knew that fans in African countries like to give their national teams nicknames.

The 1992 African Cup of Nations final, for instance, was between the Elephants (Côte d'Ivoire) and the Black Stars (Ghana). In this case the animals triumphed 13-12 over the galactic planets in the penalty shoot-out. Elephants are not the only four-legged creatures to be parading on the African football field. Just ask the Argentinians - as defending world champions, they were beaten 1-0 by the Indomitable Lions (Cameroon) in Italia '90. The Lions were not the first of the cat family to appear on the world footballing stage. In 1974, in Germany, the Leopards (Zaire) became the first sub-Saharan African country to qualify for the finals. On the field they were far less threatening than their animal namesakes were - they were slaughtered 9-0 by Yugoslavia. And in 1994 it was a two-legged creature - the Super Eagles (Nigeria) - which came within a few minutes of knocking out Italy. The Nigerian side was not always known as the Super Eagles though. They started off as the Green Eagles and only added the Super once their performance on the field improved.

Other animals include the Stallions (Burkina Faso) or, if a legless animal is preferred, the Mambas. The Mozambican team is named after this snake.

Other teams draw their names from statesmen - dead, as in the case of the Pharaohs (Egypt), or alive as in the KK XI (Zambia), who took their name from the then Zambian ruler Kenneth Kaunda.

Astute followers of politics will question the wisdom of this, as frequent name changes could be necessary. Take England, for instance. They would have to change their names ever so often. The Harold Wilson XI won the World Cup for England in 1966. Four years later the Germans knocked out the Edward Heath XI. But they still did better than the Harold Wilson XI, a comeback team which failed to qualify for the 1974 version in Germany. The Margaret Thatcher XI in 1986 lost to Argentina in the quarter-finals. The John Major XI in 1990 went one better by finishing fourth. The Tony Blair XI did not have much success in 1998 though.

But in Africa things are different. From 1964 to 1991, the Zambian team had no reason to undergo a name change. Assisted by the fact that only one party was allowed and Kaunda was always the only candidate in presidential elections, the Zambian football team had a high degree of stability - at least when it came to their name. Similar stability could be found in many other African countries. Had the Kenyans opted for the name Jomo Kenyatta XI instead of the Harambee Stars, they could have done so from 1964 to 1978, during which time the former political prisoner led the East African country. Having led Kenya to independence, Kenyatta remained Head of State until his death in 1978. Since then, there have not been that many reasons to change their name, as Daniel Toroitich Arap Moi took over on Kenyatta's death and has ruled since then. The Swazis were even better off. They could have competed as the King Sobhuza The Second XI for over twenty years.

There are also the Red Devils (Congo), the Desert Warriors (Algeria) and the Leone Stars (Sierra Leone). The latter team is not to be mistaken for the Lone Stars (Liberia), who presumably get their name from the fact that George Weah is the only footballer from Liberia anybody has ever heard about and as such they are really a lone star kind of team.

Given the importance of such nicknames, there was no way that a nameless South African team could take on the Warriors (Zimbabwe). The problem was solved when a journalist first used the term Bafana Bafana in an article about the team. The name he gave the team proved to be prophetic, as the Bafana Bafana (young boys) went about their first competitive match with all the naivety displayed by the young and inexperienced.

They were completely fooled by the Zimbabwean coach, Reinhard Fabisch, who managed to instill a false feeling of superiority in the young boys through the Zimbabwean press.

Believing the stories of the home side being underdogs and there being major problems in the Zimbabwean team, the South Africans thought they needed to do little more than arrive at the Independence Stadium in Harare to collect their two points. (Remember the time when life was easy and a win was two points?)

The team arrived at the stadium a good hour before the scheduled start and went into the change room. A short while later there was a knock at the door and the match commissioner entered and told them that they could now have their 15-minute warm-up time, as international rules allow. The South African coach then was Screamer Tshabalala, who had taken over the coaching position a few months earlier from Jeff Butler.

Butler had been forced to resign after it emerged that there were several inconsistencies on the curriculum vitae that he had submitted with his application. He claimed that he had coached and played for several clubs which, in fact, was not the case. It would appear that Butler had taken over parts of the CV of another Jeff Butler, who had played league football in England.

Tshabalala had been a successful player with a number of clubs before going into coaching. He had taken over at a club called Mamelodi Sundowns and had brought them much success, winning numerous championships and cups. In part his success was due to the calibre of players he had at his disposal and whenever he needed a new player he was told by the club owner Zola Mahobe to go out and buy him. Much later it was discovered that Mahobe was in fact financing the club with money his girlfriend was stealing from a South African bank.

Tshabalala had remained at Sundowns when the source of Mahobe's money was discovered. With police closing in, Mahobe fled the country. His girlfriend, Snowy Moshoeshoe, was not so lucky and she was arrested and sentenced to a lengthy jail term. Mahobe later decided that rather than live a life on the run, he would come back to South Africa and do his time. He has since been released from jail.

While all of this was happening, Tshabalala remained at Sundowns, a post he kept until being appointed assistant to Butler. After Butler's resignation, Tshabalala took over and led South Africa out of isolation.

But he had little experience in international matters and when the match commissioner informed him that he could take his players onto the field he declined, saying they were busy at the time.

And busy they were. Tshabalala had brought a small tin with him from South Africa. In it, he was burning things. He then handed out ash from the tin to the players, instructing them to sprinkle the ash into their boots. He hoped that this ritual, which is widespread in African football, would ensure a South African victory.

When the referee blew his whistle the South Africans walked out onto the field. In front of a hostile crowd of 40,000 the Bafana Bafana were completely overwhelmed, or the Zimbabweans had better ash in their boots. Whatever the case, the hosts won 4-1.

Two months later I again boarded a plane to follow Bafana Bafana. This time the Nigerian capital of Lagos was my destination. As there were no scheduled flights between Nigeria and South Africa, the football association had chartered a plane. Or so I thought. In fact, they had entrusted a travel agency called Fli Afrika to make all necessary arrangements to get us to Nigeria for the game on time.

And again the name proved to be prophetic, for through Africa we flew.

Fli Afrika had chartered a plane - as they were supposed to do - and had managed to get the team, the officials and a handful of fans and journalists onto the plane for a 9pm take-off - as they were supposed to do. They had not, even though they were supposed to, arranged for landing rights in Lagos and at about 2am the next morning the pilot had no alternative but to announce that he was landing.

Nobody quite knew where we were landing and as the pilot had not informed us we all expectantly waited for the plane to touch down. My hopes of seeing bright lights and a huge sign announcing where we had landed were soon dashed, as there were neither. And once we had disembarked we discovered that there was virtually nothing at all. The airport was locked, the building was in total darkness and there was not a single person in sight. After standing around the tarmac for about one and a half hours, we finally found someone. He had no key. One of the journalists, who spoke a spattering of French - by now we knew that we had landed in French-speaking Côte d'Ivoire - informed the man that we would like to enter the airport building. He hurried off into the darkness, presumably setting off to find a way of getting us into the building. After a further 30 minutes' wait, he reappeared accompanied by an official whom he had obviously just woken up. He muttered something in French and although I did not understand it, I picked up that it was not along the lines of 'Good morning, would you like some croissants with your coffee?' Yet he still opened the building for us.

Wearily, we entered and most of the players immediately made for the plastic chairs to try to get at least some sleep. And then we waited and waited and waited some more. Two hours later - by now it was getting light - the owner of the travel agency, Mr Cameroodien, who had presumably come along on the trip to ensure that nothing went wrong, summoned us and said we would be leaving for Lagos in an hour.

Not that I believed him, but I thought I should still get ready, which, of course, as I had very few things to pack, took me all of 30 seconds. I then proceeded to do exactly what I had done before I was told to get ready: I waited.

After another hour's wait, Mr Cameroodien, who at this stage was probably fearing for his life, something quite a few of the players and journalists were very willing to exchange for a good bed or a seat on an airborne flight, told us that he was taking us to a hotel in downtown Abidjan for a few hours before catching a scheduled flight in the afternoon to Lagos. I had high hopes that this would prove a bit more successful, as neither Fli Afrika, nor Cameroodien (who, I might hasten to add, is a very pleasant man who always tries his best) had anything to do with our further flight to Lagos.

At 1pm, we were back at the airport, sitting on the floor in front of the check-in counter, waiting for the tickets and a plane. Neither was there. By 4pm we were still sitting on the floor in front of the check-in counter and still waiting for a plane. And we were starving!

Finally, at 7pm, we left Abidjan via Togo for Lagos, where we arrived two hours later. Lagos was hot, humid and crowded and not particularly pleasant. Even though I have returned to Lagos a few times since that first visit, I have not changed my opinion about the city.

As we left the terminal building, I could see that hundreds of people had been waiting for the arrival of Bafana Bafana. Their message was clear: the Super Eagles were going to slaughter the Bafana. Some of them said that out of respect for the recently released African National Congress (ANC) leader, Nelson Mandela, the home side would restrict themselves to five goals. It was an opinion that was obviously widespread, as more and more people held up five fingers and said: 'For Mandela, only five - without him, ten.' I was happy to escape their taunting and sit in the bus that was to take us to our hotel.

We had been booked into the Sheraton Hotel. Both sides stayed in the same hotel. The ride from the airport took forever. Driving through the streets of Lagos is like driving through a massive supermarket. Hawkers offer everything, from magazines and cigarettes to toys, soft drinks and even animals. A local journalist told me that in Lagos 'you could live in your car and buy all you need while cruising through the streets'.

But then 'doing business' is a firmly entrenched tradition in Nigeria and it seems unlikely that it will ever change.

Eager to better themselves, millions of Nigerians have streamed to Lagos, turning the capital into a sprawling city of close to 10 million people.

This, however, has created a situation where the city comes to a virtual standstill at times because there are too many people. Not surprisingly, the congestion was one of the reasons why the government decided to build a new capital in Abuja.

But, unfortunately for us, Bafana were not scheduled to play in Abuja. They were going to play in Lagos and thus it came that three hours after having arrived at the airport, we were still in the bus en route to the hotel.

After South Africa's poor showing in Zimbabwe, it was clear that Bafana Bafana was going to have a very tough time indeed against the Super Eagles, who were considered the overwhelming favourites in the group. The local media made no attempt to hide the fact that they believed South Africa were in for a hiding and even the Nigerian players, whom I would bump into in a lift or on a hotel floor, had an air of superiority about them that must have caused some consternation for the vastly inexperienced South Africans.

For us journalists, it was an entirely different matter. South Africa was very much the flavour of the month and we were continuously asked for comments. 'Did we believe we stood a chance? Could we see that the Super Eagles were the best team in Africa? What was Mandela like? When was South Africa going to be free?' They wanted answers for everything and as the newspaper and broadsheet industry in Lagos was one of the most thriving in Africa, it is hardly surprising that there was a never-ending stream of journalists that prowled around the hotel, waiting for that big scoop that would separate them from the rest of the bunch. It never came!

Instead, we received an invitation to play them in a 'friendly international journalists match'. It was an offer we gladly accepted and as the South African national broadcaster was going to televise the World Cup qualifier live, they had arrived with a huge crew, which in turn meant that we would have no problem in fielding a pretty strong side.

Bafana Bafana was scheduled to have a training session in the Surelere Stadium in Lagos on Friday, a day before the match. We were going to play our friendly straight after that.

We travelled to the stadium by bus, once again taking close to an hour through the overcrowded streets. The stadium was typical of many others throughout Africa. No doubt built with the help of some Eastern Block country, many of which saw their contribution to Africa's development as building huge stadiums to be used for Independence Day celebrations, football matches and such activities. This particular stadium stood tall and large amidst a sea of shacks. The training session offered a welcome change for the people living in the shacks and they flocked to the stadium to watch the South Africans who, they believed, were going to be the next team to fall by the wayside as the Super Eagles soared unfalteringly towards USA '94.

For us that meant that we would have a few thousand people who were going to watch us play. Added to the pressure of having to impress in front of thousands, was the importance of the match. In newspapers sold all over Lagos, our Nigerian colleagues had predicted not only an easy victory for the Super Eagles, they had also announced to the locals that they were going to start the ball rolling, so to say, by convincingly thrashing the South African journalists the day before.

I had been chosen to play in goals (whenever media matches were scheduled I volunteered to go into goal as I knew that very few offered to stand between the poles and I therefore seldom had any opposition for a place in the starting line-up). I solved the problem of not having boots by asking Andre Arendse, the South African reserve goalkeeper, if I could borrow his after his training. As I had known him for a long time and had become quite friendly with him, he had no problem with my request and handed me his pair of Kappa boots. The game could begin!

We started shortly after 11am and I soon found out why the South African players had ended their training session by 10:30am and returned to the hotel. It was unbearably hot and humid and I was soon sweating like a pig, as were my teammates. But that did not prevent us from playing our hearts out and instead of being easy pushovers for the home side, we were matching the Nigerians shot for shot, tackle for tackle.

We had a good side. In the sprawling townships that were to be found on the outskirts of every South African city and town, football was by far the most popular pastime and virtually every boy living in these townships had grown up kicking a ball on the dusty streets. The journalists were no different and some of them possessed an amazing amount of skill that drew cheers even from the locals who were watching us.

I made a useful contribution. While I couldn't prevent them from scoring early in the second half, I was able to make several good saves later on. As one of our strikers had managed to beat their goalkeeper with a well-timed scorcher from outside the area in the first half, the score at the end was 1-1, a result that pleased us much more than them.

The next day I took a taxi to the stadium. On his way there, the driver had two crashes. Both times he swore at the other driver, before driving on. I arrived at the stadium four hours before the kick-off. Three local journalists invited me to wait with them at the press centre outside the stadium. After a two-hour wait, I decided to go onto the field, but I could not make it past the first gate. An hour before the start of the match I started worrying, as I was stuck with several thousand fans in front of the gate. Preventing the crowd from getting in was a huge soldier, who used a six-foot pole to keep the crowd at bay. After a while though, not even the pole could prevent the fans from getting aggravated and the soldier decided that he should protect himself by firing teargas at the crowd. Coughing, with tears streaming down my cheeks, I wondered if I was ever going to get into the stadium.

Somehow I managed and with thirty minutes to go, I finally sat on the field. The atmosphere was terrific. Music was blaring out of huge loudspeakers scattered around the stadium, the smell of meat being cooked on an open fire drifted across the field from the vendors who were selling it outside, while children ran around the stadium selling peanuts and small green and white Nigerian flags. I loved it.

And it got even better! The cheer that erupted throughout the stadium when the Nigerians entered the field to warm up was something that I had not yet heard anywhere else. Not when Zimbabwe trounced us in Harare a few months earlier and certainly not when South Africa opened their international record with a 1-0 victory over Cameroon in Durban several months earlier. No, it was a cheer that was reserved for the kind of adulation that only players of the calibre of Ricky Owubokire, who had been top goalscorer in Portugal the season before, and Victor Ikpeba, the young rising star in French football with Monaco, could command. It was something that we South Africans could not understand - at least until such time that we, too, had players that were recognised as great footballers throughout the world.

We were soon to realise just how great the Nigerian players were, as they tore into our defence. Mark Anderson in goal for South Africa faced a barrage of shots from the Nigerians and it was no surprise when they went ahead in the 34th minute through a well-taken Owubokire goal. From there, there was no coming back for the Bafana and it soon became apparent that the best they could hope for was to keep the score respectable. Goals by Samson Siasia and two from Rashidi Yekini gave the Nigerians a convincing 4-0 victory and ended a miserable day for the South Africans.

Are four goals respectable? I don't know, but when a team like Nigeria scores them, I would say that they must come pretty close to being respectable. Just over a year later, the same Nigerian side would slam three past Bulgaria at the finals of the World Cup and come within a few minutes of knocking out Italy, who instead went on to qualify for the final.

After the match, the journalists rushed back to the hotel to file their stories. As usual, rushing in Nigeria meant that one was stuck in traffic for hours somewhere on the streets of Lagos. Needless to say, back in South Africa copy editors all over the country were becoming nervous as their copy deadlines were rapidly approaching.

As I was working for a monthly, I had no such problems and could hang around the foyer, watching the South Africans slouching in. As rapidly as they had appeared, the players disappeared to their rooms. A short while later, the Nigerian players arrived. They were accompanied by a string of gold-chained young men, all dressed in the latest fashion, and a whole army of young ladies, gorgeous and dressed to kill.

While the players rushed to their rooms, the hangers-on stood around the hotel lobby, waiting for the players to have a quick shower and come down again. Once a few of the players returned to the lobby, they would leave the hotel, again accompanied by a group of their hangers-on.

Once all the journalists had filed their stories, a group of us decided to go to the nightclub on the top floor of the hotel. As we stepped out of the lift, the boom-boom of disco music hit us between the eyes. We paid our ten Nairas (2 Naira = 80 Pence) at the door and were allowed in. It was packed. I could see quite a few of the South African players on the dance floor, while others were sitting at the tables surrounded by the same kind of drop dead gorgeous females that I had seen earlier with the Nigerian players. Most of the Bafana players seemed to be in the best of spirits.

To this day, that is something which I do not understand. Whenever I played football, be it a kick around in the park or an important cup-tie, I would feel absolutely sick if I ended up on the losing side. The same could certainly not be said about South African players. Often after a defeat the players would have the party of their lives - as was happening now.

After a few drinks I decided that it was time to go. As I was leaving, a group of South African officials, accompanied by none other than the gorgeous girls brigade, came in. It was obvious that this was not their first point of call and it was just as obvious that they were not going to be there for a short while only.

After breakfast the next morning, I waited in the lobby for the bus that was going to take us to the airport for our return flight. Cameroodien told us that we would take the same scheduled flight with which we had come, back to Côte d'Ivoire, from where we would leave with the charter back to South Africa. Quite a few of the other journalists, as well as some of the officials - many of them still looking rather tired from what had obviously turned out to be quite a late night - were also waiting. As we were waiting, Gregor Wille stepped out of the lift. He was one of the few white players in the South African side and although he had never actually earned a cap, he spent a few games on the bench.

He walked straight up to one of the groups of officials and stuck out his hand at one of them. I had seen the official the night before in the nightclub with a prostitute and I doubted that he had had much sleep. Wille's face was very serious and I was somewhat surprised, as football players were not known for their good manners. The official was obviously as surprised as I was, but took hold of Wille's hand. What followed next is something that I will never forget. Wille, still holding the man's hand, said to him, 'Welcome, welcome to the Aids club'. He then let go of the official's hand and returned to the other players, who were laughing their heads off at what they had just seen.

Not so the group of officials. They looked far from amused. Some looked angry, others looked sheepish, but certainly none of them had seen the lighter side of what had just transpired. I don't think anything else ever came from the incident, although, not surprisingly, Wille never again was called up for the Bafana.

Shortly afterwards, we left for the airport. The roads in Lagos seemed permanently jammed, irrespective of what the time was and after spending another two hours in the bus, we were finally dropped off at the airport, where we were told that there was no plane. That was the good news. The bad news was that even if there had been a plane, it could not fly, as there was no fuel.

After another three-hour wait, we were finally told to check in. At the check-in counter there was chaos. In Africa there is a thriving trade system. People buy goods cheaply in one country and then take them elsewhere to sell them for a profit. The route between Lagos, Lome and Abidjan was obviously a very popular one for the informal trade sector and not only were hundreds of people trying to check in for flights, they also had huge parcels, wrapped in plastic, which they wanted to take onto the plane.

After queuing for an hour or so, our whole group, bar two, had managed to check in. Unfortunately, I was one of the two. By the time I had arrived at the check-in counter, the woman behind the desk had run out of boarding passes. "Could you not just write the seat number on the ticket?" I inquired naively.

"No, that is not possible," she barked back at me.

"How long will it take before you get some more boarding passes?" I asked.

"I don't know."

There was little else I could do but wait. So I waited. After about half an hour, I was getting a bit nervous, as the flight was about to leave and she was seemingly doing very little in the way of trying to solve the problem. I sat down in front of her desk and made as little attempt to move as she was making to find a boarding pass.

I think that must have impressed her, as she suddenly shuffled off, mumbling to herself. She returned a few minutes later holding two boarding passes. She proceeded to write our flight details as well as a seat number on them and handed them to me. I gave one to my colleague and the two of us ran towards the exit gate.

We need not have bothered, as even after I had taken my seat next to an incredibly fat woman, the cabin crew made no attempt whatsoever to prepare us for take-off. I had luckily been given an aisle seat, which is just as well as I knew that if I was to be sandwiched between two incredibly fat women, I would be finished.

Suddenly I could hear angry voices from the front of the plane. I looked up the aisle and saw a woman trying to force her way onto the plane.

The plane was full - but not the kind of full with every seat taken. No, it was full with every seat taken and just about every available space used for parcels of every shape and size. Later, a Nigerian journalist explained to me that passengers on planes in Africa do not trust the airlines with transporting their goods in the hold. They were scared that their luggage and goods would vanish somewhere between the point of departure and the point of arrival. A while later, I understood why they had that fear!

But the screaming woman was as determined to get onto the plane as the crew was to keep her off. After a short while, the three male members of the crew managed to throw her out, quickly closing the door behind her. We were finally ready for take-off.

There were no further hiccups and after a two-hour flight, we landed in Abidjan.

As we had a ten-hour wait before our charter was to leave for South Africa, I decided to take a taxi to the Houphouet Boigny stadium, where the home side was taking on Botswana in what turned out to be an incredibly one-sided World Cup qualifier. Even though we arrived only ten minutes into the game, the Ivorians, who were the reigning African champions, were already leading by two goals. The Elephants had an excellent striker in Abdoulaye Traore and he ran rings around the Botswana defence, who, at the end of the game, could count themselves lucky that they only conceded six goals.

Surprisingly, very few of the Ivorian players were under contract to clubs in Europe, although at least a handful of them undoubtedly possessed the skill to play abroad. A photographer sitting next to me explained that as the economy of the country was one of the best in Africa, the clubs had money, which in turn meant that they could pay their players well. Some of the better players, like Traore, were at the time earning close to £4,000, which for African standards is very high. In the South African side at the time, for instance, there was no player who was still based in the country who was earning more than £600.

At the end of the match, we took a taxi to the Soviet Hotel and checked in. At midnight, we went down to the lobby to board the bus to the airport. The team manager and doctor were missing and we spent thirty minutes waiting for them. We arrived at the airport at 1.30am and checked in for the flight. We were then told that the plane had not yet arrived, but that it should be coming shortly. Two hours later, we were still waiting, though at least we had moved to the departure lounge, which was more comfortable than the check-in lobby.

Finally, at 4am we left for Johannesburg, where we touched down at 1.30pm on Tuesday afternoon - eight days after leaving South Africa.

In that week, I had been to three African countries (Côte d'Ivoire, Togo and Nigeria), watched two World Cup qualifiers (Nigeria vs SA and Côte d'Ivoire vs Botswana), played one game myself, and had come to the conclusion that in future I would make my own travel arrangements. It had been quite an eventful week!

7

EXTRA INCOME

HAVING LEARNT FROM my Nigerian travels, I had decided to make my own arrangements for my next trip, which happened much sooner than I had expected.

My destination was again West Africa, but this time it was Ghana I was flying to, accompanied by a footballer whom I was helping secure a contract overseas.

The player was - depending on which passport one believed - either Richard Sibeko, a 24-year-old South African, or Richard Kwame Padmore, a 21-year-old Ghanaian. I had met him while he was playing for a club in South Africa called Ratanang. The owner of the club, after committing fraud, had decided that he would rather seek refuge in the neighbouring country of Lesotho than take his chances with the South African courts. The club had then been sold, but the deal had excluded three players, including Richard.

The young footballer had arrived in South Africa from Ghana in 1991. He was a solid, strongly built defender who had - not by accident - earned the nickname 'The Ox'. The former manager of the club had told me that Richard was keen to try his luck overseas and that he wanted nothing more than to play football in Europe.

I contacted the coach of a Durban-based club called D'Alberton Callies. Gordon Igesund had himself played in Europe for many years and had since been involved in several player transfers to clubs overseas. His moonlighting as an agent had been rather successful and one of his players, Sean Dundee, was making big waves in Germany at the time.

He said that he was keen to help Richard get overseas, but he felt it was better if the defender spent another season in South Africa playing for Callies to prepare him for European football. Richard agreed and I went down to Durban and negotiated a contract for him. I had arrived in the big world of footballing agents!

I was soon to find out that it was not a very easy world to be involved in. Richard needed boots, Richard needed accommodation, Richard needed clothes, Richard needed just about everything, and he expected me to get these for him.

We spent a few days driving around Durban looking for accommodation. The club had a few apartments in town, but Richard refused to stay in them, saying that he needed to pray in the middle of the night and that the others would disturb him. Much later, in Ghana, I was to understand what he meant by that.

After having sorted out Richard's practical arrangements, I returned to my job as journalist, while he returned to his job of preventing the opposition's strikers from scoring. He must have done that pretty well, as a few months down the line I got a call from Igesund informing me that Richard was now ready to go to Europe on trial to an Austrian club called Sturm Graz.

He went and, not surprisingly, they liked what they saw and confirmed that they were keen to sign him. So far, so good. But that is when the troubles began. We had informed Sturm Graz that they were getting a 21-year-old Ghanaian on trial, but when they looked at his passport, he was the 24-year-old South African, Richard Sibeko.

When Richard arrived in South Africa a few years earlier, the country was still suspended from the world controlling body, FIFA. All foreign players playing in the country were blacklisted and could play nowhere else. This had not prevented a whole flood of foreigners from coming to South Africa. They had been issued with false papers and had been given false names. That is how Richard Padmore became Richard Sibeko.

That, of course, was not the kind of story we could tell Sturm Graz, as they were not interested in the politics of South Africa; all they wanted was a player from Ghana. We decided that Richard and myself would fly to Ghana, apply for a new passport and organise his international clearance, which he needed if he wanted to play football in a different country.

There was one flight per week from Johannesburg via Zimbabwe's capital of Harare to Accra and I booked us on that. As Ghana had no diplomatic ties with South Africa at the time, I could not get a visa for the country before leaving. Luckily though, the stopover in Harare was about six hours, which was enough to go into town, plead with some bureaucrat for a visa and then hopefully make it back in time to the airport to fly further.

We arrived on time in Harare and Richard, who had made the trip a few times before, instructed the taxi driver to take us to one of the fancy suburbs where the Ghanaian embassy was situated.

It reminded me of my first trip to Kenya, when I had to apply for a visa to enter Tanzania. This time round it was not Nyerere's smiling face that looked down at me, it was that of Flight Lieutenant Jerry Rawlings, the young charismatic leader who had swept to power in a coup d'état a few months earlier. The khaki-clad bureaucrat behind the desk was possibly a bit friendlier than his Tanzanian counterpart, but he seemed just as uninterested in helping us achieve our goal.

It was only after Richard started speaking to him in the Ghanaian dialect, Fanti, that he looked up and took notice. And when I told him that Richard was a footballer, the ice was broken. In fact, he became quite animated and I was worried that, in the excitement of speaking to a professional player, he would forget the reason why we had come in the first place. But I did not have to worry, as less than an hour later we left the building, my visa neatly stamped in my passport.

Later that night I was sitting next to 'my' player, en route to Accra to organise a passport and an Austrian visa for him.

The airport in Accra was similar to many others I had seen throughout Africa. Pictures of the president (in this case Jerry Rawlings) hang prominently in public places, porters hustle for luggage and grim-faced officials sit behind glass booths. Posters advertising hotels and taxi drivers offering 'the cheapest and safest drives into town' were also to be found.

Contrary to many other airports in Africa though, I got my luggage reasonably quickly and soon Richard and myself were travelling by taxi through the streets of Accra to his mother's house.

I immediately took a liking to Accra. It had an African flavour, but not the overcrowding of a city like Lagos. It was clean and even the air did not seem that polluted.

Richard's mother lived in a small two bed-roomed house on the outskirts of Accra. His father had died many years earlier and his brother was a commissioned soldier, who was at the time on duty outside the country. Richard's mother shared the house with his sister Winifred, a big likeable woman, who was without work. Richard was contributing to the upkeep of the family and every month had dutifully sent home some of the meager salary he was earning playing in South Africa.

His mother was particularly happy to see him and after introducing me as 'my manager' I was also welcomed with open arms. I shared Winifred's room with Richard, while she moved in with her mother.

Our first port of call was the building housing the Department of Home Affairs in downtown Accra. It was a tall, colourless building, no doubt filled with colourless bureaucrats whose main purpose in life is to make the life of others as difficult as possible.

Whether it was filled with those sort of people I never found out, because I never actually set foot in the building. As we arrived at the gate, we were met by a stranger, who asked us what we wanted.

"I need a new passport," Richard said with his thick West African accent.

"No problem," the man said. He opened a scrapbook, pulled out a blank piece of paper and gave it to Richard. "Just write your name on it, your age, your occupation, place of birth, give me two colour photographs and come back in three days."

Needless to say, I was more than nervous, but after further discussions had taken place between Richard and the man, he said that I should give him US$200 and that we should come back in three days to get the passport. Hoping that Richard knew what he was doing, I gave him the money.

Three days later we returned to the building and lo and behold, the man appeared and gave Richard a brand new Ghanaian passport.

Having successfully achieved the first goal of our journey, we now set about trying to achieve the second one, a task that was to prove much more difficult than the first.

To be allowed back into Austria, Richard needed a visa and we went to the Austrian embassy in search of such a document. The embassy in Accra was obviously a very small one. All consular duties, like issuing visas, were conducted from a residence in one of the better parts of Accra. The houses were big, the walls around them huge and each and every house had a little wooden hut, not much bigger than a kennel, but much higher, standing next to the gate. These little huts were meant to provide shelter to the security guards who sat outside the property day in and day out.

The Austrian embassy also had its guard standing outside. Compared to the Austrian ambassador, a fiftyish woman with gray hair, they actually did a lot of work, just sitting there. The embassy was open no more than four hours a day and as there was no massive Austrian community living in Accra, nor was there an influx of Ghanaians wanting to visit Austria, the ambassador was certainly not overworked.

It was therefore all the more surprising that she seemed totally uninterested in our visit.

"Yes, what can I do for you?" she asked after letting us wait the obligatory five minutes while she did absolutely nothing.

"We have come to apply for a visa to enter Austria," I answered.

"Fill in this form and come back with the ticket," she said.

And that is exactly what we did. We left the leafy suburb, made our way back to Richard's home and put together all the things that we thought would assist us in obtaining a visa as quickly as possible. A short while later, we were outside her office again, hoping to spend only a short while there before finalising Richard's travelling arrangements.

"You can't get a visa, he needs a letter from the people in Austria," she explained after having looked at the visa application form.

My good mood vanished with those words. I just knew that getting such a letter was always an incredibly difficult thing, especially if one was trying to organise it from a country such as Ghana where even a letter to a neighbouring city could take a few weeks.

"The club would like him there at the end of the week," I very politely told her.

"I don't care."

There was nothing we could do, so for the fourth time that day we flagged down one of the many taxis that drove around Accra. This time we were lucky, as the taxi that picked us up was no more than 15 years old, practically a new-born by Accra standards.

There was a telephone shop near Richard's house from where one could phone just about anywhere in the world. That was in theory. In practice it was a very different story. It was a case of having the patience to be able to wait for those few moments that occurred infrequently every day, during which one could actually get a line to the outside world. This shop, which was really just a small wooden shed with two telephone wires running through the roof into the room, was to become like my second home in Ghana as I spent at least two hours of every day there.

First, we tried to get hold of Johan Scharman, the agent setting up the deal for us in Austria. When we finally did, he was not very pleased. Far from it.

"That is not very good news. Sturm want him now, they want him to play this weekend, they do not want to wait," he said impatiently.

Even though Scharman was no stranger to Africa, having played in South Africa in the 1970s, he had no idea of what it was like on the rest of the continent and I think that he thought I was just being lazy.

"There is very little I can do if the consulate does not want to issue us with a visa," I tried to explain to him. "The woman has said that she wants a letter from Sturm, explaining why Richard must get a visa."

"Yes, I understand, but it is not good. It is really not good. See what you can do," he said.

The next day we returned to the consulate. The same woman met us at the door. (I later found out that, apart from the security guard at the gate, she was the only person working in the consulate.) "I still can't give you a visa," she said.

"Have you not yet received the letter?"

"No."

Richard nudged me and scratched his thumb with his index finger. I looked at him puzzled.

"Offer her some money," he whispered. "That way we will get the visa fast.'

I was very glad that she had not heard him. I am sure that if she had, my career as a football agent would have come to an abrupt end - even before it had started. "I can't do that," I replied. "I will explain why later."

I turned to the 'gnaediges Fraeulein' and tried to speak to her as sweetly in German as I could. "Please, it is very important that Richard gets the visa as soon as possible. Is there anything we can do to speed the process up?" I asked.

"Nein!" She was obviously not a woman of many words.

I told her that we would come back the next day and that I was very confident that the letter from the club would be there. In the taxi on our way back to the phone booth, I explained to Richard that an Austrian bureaucrat was not like a Ghanaian one and was probably not that easily persuaded by a couple of dollars. I said that the kind of money we would have to pay her to do us a favour was far beyond what I could afford on my journalist salary. "Once you make it big and I take most of your salary, it will be a different story," I joked.

Our attempts at phoning cheered me up quite a bit, as I managed to connect with Scharman at the fifth attempt already, only one hour after we started. "They will still not give us the visa. She has not received the letter from the club and will not do anything until that is there."

"Oh shit. Phone me back in thirty minutes, I will quickly get hold of the club and find out what is going on," he said.

I agreed, even though I wondered why he never offered to phone me.

We spent the next thirty minutes talking to Jane, who managed the phone shop for her uncle. She was very grateful for having a job. "It is not easy here. There are no jobs and education is expensive. Without this, I would not know what to do," she said. She had left school after eight years, her parents no longer being able to afford to pay for school-books.

What I found very endearing about her was that she simply accept-ed the situation and tried to make the best of it. She did not complain, but rather tried to do as well as she could under the circumstances. That was a quality I was to encounter often in Ghana and it is probably also one of the reasons why Accra had little of the poverty that was a part and parcel of so many other African capitals.

Jane climbed even higher in my estimation when she said that she was a football fan. She supported a club called Hearts of Oak. The club was based in the capital and was one of the most successful teams in the country. Twice they had played in the final of the African Champions Cup and they were well placed to win the local league again.

We spoke about some of the great players that had come out of Ghana in recent years. Players like Abedi Pele, who won the African Footballer of the Year three times running from 1991, or Tony Yeboah, who was top scorer in the German Bundesliga. I even managed to impress her when I started talking about Ibrahim Sunday - the first play-er from Ghana to have played in the German Bundesliga. He had a short and undistinguished career with Werder Bremen (which is why I knew him), before becoming a coach for a minor league team outside Bremen.

Soon it was time to phone Scharman again and this time around we made an even faster connection. "The letter has been faxed to the con-sulate in Accra", he said. "Try to get Richard on a flight tomorrow."

I said fine, but thought that he needed urgently to take a course in African studies and hopefully then he would not expect miracles all the time.

The next day we made our way to the consulate early, as I still want-ed to try and book a flight once all the paperwork was sorted out.

We entered the same office and the same woman looked at us. "Can I help you?" she asked.

I was flabbergasted. Not only had we been to the consulate four times in the last four days, she had spoken to us on each of these occasions. Under normal circumstances I would have made some stupid comment, which would have resulted in the visa not being issued for the next month or two, but as I was just as eager as Richard to have this sorted out, I meekly said, "We have come for a visa, you should have received the letter from the club by now."

"I have, but I still can't give you a visa, there is a problem."

That was all I needed. I was tired, exhausted, I wanted to go home to South Africa. But instead of being able to make arrangements to fly home, I was at the mercy of some lowly bureaucrat, who had obviously decided that her most important task in life was to make mine as unpleasant as possible. "What is the problem now?" I asked.

"The club has said nothing about medical insurance in Austria and without that, I can't issue a visa."

"But, but...you said nothing about that...and...," I decided to keep my mouth shut until I could control what came out. "If we get a letter from the club saying that they will cover the insurance, is there anything else that we need before the visa can be issued?" I asked once I had calmed down.

"Yes, he needs a valid return ticket to Ghana."

This was turning into a nightmare. But instead of saying something along those lines, I merely said that I would arrange everything and would be back once I had everything in place.

I phoned Scharman and explained the situation to him. He was not pleased and told me that I should phone him back a bit later. I was not pleased either, but I still phoned him back. He said he had spoken to the club and they would immediately send another letter. He ended the brief conversation by saying that I should buy the ticket for Richard and would be reimbursed once the club had received his clearance.

I paid Jane and went off in search of a ticket. At least that proved to be one of the smaller - although costly - problems I encountered during the trip. The flights were pretty full, but we did manage to get a confirmed seat at the end of the following week. After my experiences in Nigeria, I was not sure if that amounted to much, but Richard assured me that he would get on the plane if his visa was in order.

Armed with the ticket, we went back to the consulate the next day. It was the same story. The guard let us in, the consul (or whatever she was) hardly looked up from the desk and asked us what we wanted. She knew exactly what we wanted, but she obviously enjoyed asking the question, as it gave her the kind of power most powerless bureaucrats can only dream of.

"Please madam, we would like to get a visa. We have the airline ticket and you should have received the letter from the club by now, confirming the insurance," I said, having decided that the 'humble-pie' approach would be the best one under the circumstances.

"Yes, I have received the letter. Let me have a look at the ticket." I gave her the ticket and she looked at it skeptically. "That seems to be fine, but I can only give you a visa for four weeks," she said.

Richard interjected. "But I am going to play...."

I looked at him angrily and interrupted him. "That's very kind of you, we appreciate that. When can we come back to get the visa?" I asked.

"You can come back on Friday," she answered.

"Thank you, we will do that," I said, pushing Richard out of the door. As soon as I was sure that she could no longer hear us, I turned to him. "Richard, do you want a visa or not? If you tell her that you are going to play football there and are probably going to stay there, we can wait for a few more months, if not years. Once you are in Austria, the people there will be able to sort you out. Scharman can do something. Let him work a bit for his money."

Happy that our ordeal was nearly over, we returned to his mother's house. She had cooked a meal for us and we sat down at the table she had prepared.

The first few times we had eaten, I had asked why neither his mother nor Winifred joined us, but Richard had only laughed. "Men have to eat alone. The women prepare the meal and make everything right for us, but we have to sit down and eat by ourselves. That's the way it is." I had tried to encourage Winifred to join us at the table, but she had always said no.

So Richard and I sat down to eat. His mother had prepared fufu for us. This was a traditional meal of porridge served in a pot with a rich sauce of mostly fish. Each person would eat with his hands, dipping them deep into the pot to get to the fufu. The bones of the fish were spat onto the floor.

It had taken a short while to get used to the idea of such intimate meals, but once I had, I thoroughly enjoyed them.

After lunch, we went to the communications centre, which was the somewhat optimistic name that Jane's uncle had given his wooden shed and tried to phone Scharman to give him the good news. He was happy, but not over the moon, and I became quite irritated with him.

"Johan, that is the best we can do. If the club is not happy, they can fly over themselves and sort it out. If they want to buy a player from Ghana, they must accept that it is in Africa and that things here are not done in the same way in which they are handled in Europe. We worked bloody hard to make sure that Richard got his visa and I am pleased that we managed to get it." If the price for the phone call had not been so high - even though Jane had by now decided that she liked us and gave us special rates - I would probably have given him even more of an earful, or at least pointed out that it was a bloody Austrian bureaucrat that had caused the delay, not some third world official. Instead, I told him that I would contact him once we had the visa in our hands and give him the exact travel arrangements.

The next day we went to the craft market, as I wanted to buy some curios to take back to South Africa with me.

The market consisted of three sheds, filled with stalls. These stalls seemed to be grouped together in terms of the goods they sold. In one row there were a whole host of stalls selling brightly coloured cloth, in another they were selling woodcarvings. You could buy masks, music cassettes, small ornaments, leather goods and many other things in the other.

The vendors were particularly good at hustling. "Come, come to my stall. You don't pay for looking. Looking is free," they said as they tried to nudge you towards the entrance of their stall. Luckily for me, Richard managed to keep them at bay.

"Leave him alone, he is with me and we don't need anything." Needless to say, that did not go down very well with some of them and they glared at Richard. "Man, we are just trying to make a living, don't be so hard on us," the vendors said.

After walking up and down the rows a few times, looking at everything, I decided to buy a wooden trunk, beautifully carved out of dark oak, and a leather bag, which was being sold at the same stall.

"How much do you want for these two?" I asked the eager salesman.

"Two hundred dollars," he said.

"You must be joking," I replied and turned to leave the stall. It was a ritual I had performed many times in markets all over Africa before.

He grabbed hold of my arm, trying to prevent me from leaving.

"Wait, we just talk. That is my starting price. How much do you want to pay? That's how business is done here in Ghana."

"I can't do business with you if you start like that. I can pay twenty dollars for both." I moved towards the door again.

"What? That is not enough. What is your best price?" he said as he pushed himself in front of me, preventing me from leaving.

I tried to squeeze between him and the doorframe. "I don't really need it, so I can't pay more than fifty dollars."

"That's not a good price, I've got a family with children, one hundred and fifty. That is fair."

"Forget it, then we can't do business."

"No, no, we talk. We can come together, I am sure. One hundred, that's a very good price."

I looked at Richard. He was nodding his head. I decided to push him further. Sixty dollars. Last price."

"Please, one hundred, that is not a lot."

I took out seven crisp ten-dollar bills and held them out towards him. "Seventy dollars, if you want it, take it, otherwise you can leave it."

He seemed unsure. As I pushed past him, he grabbed my arm again. "Wait, we can talk some more."

"No we can't," I said as I started putting the money back into my wallet.

"OK, OK." He took the money. "Can't you make it just ten dollars more, please?"

"Nope."

He put the leather bag into the trunk, which he wrapped in newspaper. Richard took it and we left his stall. As we moved away, I could hear him muttering to himself. I regarded that as a good sign. I had certainly not paid too much.

Richard looked at me. He was amazed. "Where did you learn that?"

"I've been around and I enjoy the challenge."

The next morning we again left early, eager to make sure that we would get the visa. The gate to the consulate was still locked and we sat down on the side of the road. "Do you think you can make it overseas?" I asked Richard.

"I know I can make it. It is not up to me. If it is God's will, I will make it."

I envied him his conviction. "Do you think God wants you to succeed?"

"I don't know, we will see."

It was not the first time that I had come across this kind of attitude. On the one hand, I thought that it was good that people could have such strong beliefs, on the other hand though, this attitude had also helped many a despotic African ruler stay in power for much longer than was good for the local population. Religion invariably teaches people not to question authority, even if it is unjust and discriminatory.

Richard certainly was very religious and it was only in Ghana that I realised why he had not wanted to share a room in Durban with a non-believer as it would prevent him from praying at odd hours.

We continued chatting about the new life he was about to embark on in Europe and the difficulties he would be facing. After a while the security guard at the gate unlocked it and we went inside.

"Good morning, can I help you?" the consul asked.

"Yes, we have come for the visa."

"That will be fifty dollars."

Needless to say, this is not something that she had mentioned before, but luckily I had brought enough money. I gave her fifty dollars and she went to fetch the passport. Without looking at it, I took it. "Thank you," I said, hoping that she could sense the contempt in my voice.

Outside the building we opened the passport and saw the page on which she had stamped the visa. I looked at it. No more than five centimeters wide and eight long, it had caused me more aggravation than I thought was possible. We had taken ten trips to and from the embassy, the visa had cost fifty dollars and my biggest wish now was that the woman behind the desk would be transferred to Lagos.

The flight back to South Africa was on Sunday, so I had another day in Accra. On Saturday morning, Richard took me to the beach and we bathed in wonderfully warm water. It was the best therapy I could hope for to let me forget the last two weeks.

In the afternoon we did something even better. We watched the local derby between Hearts of Oak and Goldfields, which for Ghanaians is like one of the great derbies. Think Rangers and Celtic, Inter versus AC or Boca against River. It thus came as no surprise that the stadium was packed.

It was a brilliant match. The players had incredible skill and from the first whistle they went forward in search of goals. And goals we saw. Five of them, with Goldfields winning 3-2.

Richard, who seemed to know everybody in the stadium, introduced me to the Goldfields officials after the match. "This is my manager, he is from South Africa."

I was a bit nervous about how they would react to this, but Mandela's release and the possibility of a new government had obviously done wonders, as they seemed incredibly eager to speak to me. The president told me that he wanted to come to South Africa to play a friendly and asked me to help him organise it. I promised to see what I could do, once I had returned. (I did speak to a number of clubs on my return, but none of them were interested, as they had no knowledge of the club, or the country.)

On Sunday, we left for the airport early. Richard said that we should be there at least two hours before the flight. "It is not like leaving South Africa," he said.

When we arrived at the airport, I immediately saw what he meant. It really was not like South Africa. Only passengers were allowed to enter the airport building and all others were kept away by a barrier set up around the entrance. Two heavily armed soldiers stood guard at the door, frisking people going inside.

They looked at my ticket and told me to enter. I went to the Air Ghana counter and stood in the line. After waiting for half an hour I was at the head of the queue. "What do you want?" the woman at the other side of the counter asked.

She reminded me of the Austrian bureaucrat. "I want to fly to South Africa," I said, as I handed her my ticket.

"That'll be ten dollars."

Having spent two weeks in the country, I knew better than to explain to her that I had already paid for my ticket. I took out ten dollars and gave them to her. As if it was the most natural thing in the world, she handed me my boarding pass.

As I was leaving the counter, a man appeared and said that he needed to talk to me. He pointed to my trunk and said that I could not take it out of the country. "What do you mean I can't take it out of the country?"

"It belongs to Ghana, the customs people will not let you take it out. But I can help you."

I knew what he meant. I took out ten dollars, gave them to him and asked him to help me. He pulled a piece of paper out of his pocket and signed it before giving it to me. It was from the Department of Arts and

Culture and was, in effect, a permit to be allowed to take a national treasure out of the country. Why my US$70 trunk was considered a national treasure, I had no idea, but having successfully overcome the second hurdle, I proceeded to move to immigration.

I handed the man at the desk my passport. He looked up at me. "Your visa is not correct."

"How much will it cost to make it correct?"

"Twenty dollars."

I gave him twenty dollars and he stamped my passport. He gave it back to me without looking up. "Next please."

With my passport I moved to customs. Having learnt from the check-in, the department of whatever and the immigration desk, I decided to try and save some time by putting ten dollars into my passport, which I handed to the customs official. He opened the passport, saw the money and took it. He closed the passport and without looking at my hand luggage or asking any questions he motioned for me to move further.

The last stop before the departure hall was the Department of Health. I did the same as with customs and put ten dollars into my vaccination certificate. I gave it to the woman sitting behind the desk. It was obviously just the medicine she needed, as she took it and said, "I hope you enjoyed your stay."

I think I did. At least most of it. I was certainly never going to be a great fan of the Austrian Foreign Service and I had done my bit to generate income at the airport. But ultimately, the trip had been successful and as I sat in the plane flying back to South Africa, I thought of Richard. I thought how difficult it must be for him to try to establish himself not only in a new team, but also in a new country.

I was also proud, though. Proud that I had enabled him get a chance to make something out of his life. It was now up to him to take it further.

8

THE HOUSE THAT PETER BUILT

SEVEN YEARS LATER I visited Ghana again. This time to cover the African Cup of Nations, which the country was co-hosting with Nigeria. The two countries had agreed to host the tournament after the Confederation of African Football (CAF) had withdrawn Zimbabwe's hosting rights. A visit to the southern African state a few months earlier by a CAF committee had shown that preparations for the finals in 2000 were far from adequate and they desperately needed an alternative host.

I was working for Soccer News and the German Press Association (dpa), but because Soccer News had just gone from being a monthly magazine to a weekly, I decided that I did not want to spend too much time out of the office. I booked to fly to Accra for the last ten days of the competition, arriving in time to watch matches from the quarter-final stage.

South Africa played their first round matches in Ghana's second largest city, Kumasi. This sprawling city of some 500,000 people is the heart of the Ashanti Kingdom. The Ashanti are one of the most influential tribes in Ghana and its members are to be found in all high-ranking spheres of Ghanaian life. Kumasi is regarded as the football capital of the country and is home to one of Africa's most popular clubs, Asante Kotoko. Their fans soon adopted Bafana as their team, and strengthened by their support during the games, South Africa had no problem topping the group.

Although there were several upsets in the three other groups, all favourites, except Zambia, managed to go through to the knockout stage. The Zambian team, whose fans had expected the team to comfortably sail through, leaving at least Burkina Faso and Senegal behind them, failed dismally. Fearing what would happen to them on their return, they refused to take a direct flight home to Lusaka, opting instead to lie low for a while in Johannesburg.

In hindsight, that is probably something that the Ivorians wished they had done too. After drawing with Togo, losing to Cameroon, but beating Ghana, the 1992 champions managed only a third place finish in group A and were eliminated by a single goal. On their return to Abidjan, they were taken from the airport to a military camp, where they were all locked up and lectured on the themes of nationalism and patriotism. They were released only after intervention by the world controlling body FIFA, as well as several European clubs who did not want to have to miss their players because a military ruler had decided his country's national team had shamed the nation.

Those two incidents were not the only ones that made this tournament a special one. History was already made by the time the referee blew the final whistle at the end of the 90 minutes of the opening match between Ghana and Cameroon.

It was the first time since the start of the competition that none of the 28 players used during a game belonged to a club in Africa. Instead, the players were contracted to clubs like Wolfsburg, Real Madrid, West Ham United and Fenerbahce.

Cameroon's 14 'foreigners' had the better start and went ahead after 20 minutes, when French-based Joseph-Desire Job went through on the left flank. His pinpoint cross found Spanish-based Laurent Mayer, who volleyed the ball against the crossbar. It bounced back into the field of play and English-based Marc-Vivien Foe had no trouble heading past a stranded Turkish-based Richard Kingston.

The hosts came back strongly in the second half and deserved their equaliser on the hour. German-based Charles Akkunor played the ball to Portuguese-based Kwame Ayew. He made no mistake and pushed the ball past Turkish-based Boukar Alioum.

At that stage, I was still writing my stories from the comfort of my brother's living room in Johannesburg, but naturally I was eager to get to the action.

Ten days into the competition, I boarded a South African Airways flight to Accra. A friend from Cape Town, Marcelle, had just moved to Ghana to take up a position with a computer school and I had arranged to stay with her. She picked me up at the airport and took me to the house she was sharing with another South African.

The house was in a quiet cul de sac in one of the better parts of Accra. It belonged to a real-life prince, Prince Kofi, a fantastically rich businessman who had decided to open a computer school in the country. Not trusting his own countrymen, he had decided to leave the running of the school in the hands of a group of white South Africans, of which Marcelle was one.

At first I was incredibly impressed by the fact that he was a prince, but after being told that in Ghana there are hundreds of princes, my initial awe lapsed somewhat.

What was particularly nice about Prince Kofi's house though, was that it was centrally located. A short walk took me to a traffic circle, from where it was easy to catch a taxi into the centre of town. None of the taxis had meters and it was advisable to discuss terms before embarking on the journey. Elsewhere in Africa I have had situations where the driver would take me to my intended destination, only to charge an exorbitant fee. An argument would ensue and in the end at least one of the participating parties (the taxi driver or me) would end up with a long face. (Mostly it was the taxi driver who would end up with the long face.)

Marcelle also had a driver that Prince Kofi had made available to her, and Eric was quite happy to drive me around Accra when he was not busy on official computer school business.

The first thing that I needed to organise was my accreditation. Having been at numerous competitions in Africa before, I knew that this was one of the most time-consuming and irritating obstacles that had to be overcome before starting to work.

I had been told that the accreditation was available at the Accra stadium and stopped a taxi to take me there. The stadium, which had been the venue for the 1963 and 1978 African Nations Cup finals, was near the centre of town. It looked deserted, though, and apart from a few workers who were milling about, there was nobody to be seen. I asked one of them where the press centre was and he directed me there.

In the press centre, there was a little bit more happening. Two journalists were working on computers, while two others were having an argument about the strength of the Ghanaian side. I asked them if they had any idea where to get the accreditation.

"You have to go to the Department of Information, they have everything there."

"I have only just arrived in the country, could you perhaps show me where the department is?"

"No worry, I will take you."

We went out of the stadium and walked along a busy street. The Department of Information was not very far from the stadium and the journalist who had shown me the way said that I just needed to go in and ask.

I went inside the building and found a woman sitting behind a desk in the foyer. I told her I had sent in my accreditation form for the Nations Cup quite a while ago and had also sent in, as requested, a photograph and US$100. I would now like to pick up the accreditation, I said.

She said that I would have to go to an office on the first floor, as they would be able to help me there. I went to the office and knocked on the door. Somebody inside said 'yes', and I entered.

There were two people sitting at a desk. I told them that I had come to pick up my accreditation. "Everybody is on lunch now, you have to come back in an hour," was the reply.

I realised that I was not going to have any luck if I tried arguing with them, so I left. Outside the building was a small tin shack, which operated as a take-away cum restaurant. Standing in the red sand around it were a few chairs. I sat down and ordered something to drink.

An hour later I returned to the office. The same two people were sitting behind the desk. I repeated my story.

"We do not have any accreditation cards here, you have to go to the Department of Youth and Sport."

I looked at them in amazement and wondered why they did not give me that information an hour earlier. I decided it would be best if I said nothing and left.

The Department of Youth and Sport was just across the road from the Department of Information. As directed, I went to an office on the second floor, knocked and entered. It was a big office, with two desks. I could see that I was in the right place, as on one of the desks was a laminating machine, as well as a camera that is used for instant photos. There were three men sitting in the office. They were watching Cartoon Network on TV. I told them that I had come for my accreditation. They said that the person who dealt with the press was not there at the moment and I should wait outside.

I sat down on a chair in front of the office and waited. And waited, and waited. After an hour somebody came. As he was about to enter the office, he looked at me and asked me if he could help me. I told him why I had come and he said I should follow him.

As we entered the office, the three men jumped up and stood to attention. He was obviously their boss as only once he had taken a seat behind the one desk did they sit down. He asked me my name.

"Peter Auf der Heyde from Soccer News in South Africa."

"Did you send in your form with a photograph?"

"Yes, sir."

"Then you should be on this list," he said and started to scroll down a list he had. After a while he found my name. "The card should have been done already. You have to go to the Department of Information, they should have it there."

"But I have just come from there," I said.

"Yes, but the card should be there."

I crossed the road again and went back to the woman sitting behind the desk in the foyer of the building.

"I was told that my card should be here."

She got off her chair and picked up a cardboard box, which had been standing on the floor behind her. It was the size of a shoebox. She put it on the desk in front of me and asked me my name.

"Auf der Heyde, Peter," I replied.

"What?"

"The name is Peter Auf der Heyde from Soccer News in South Africa. If you wish, I will look as that might be easier."

She pushed the box towards me and I took out a bunch of cards. They belonged to journalists from Côte d'Ivoire, Cameroon, Ghana, Algeria and Gabon. There were none from South Africa.

"My card is not here," I said.

"Then you have to go back to the Department of Youth and Sport. They will issue you with one."

I was tempted to jump over the desk and throttle her, but I managed to control myself. "OK, I will go."

And off I went. Back to the same office. I knocked at the door and entered the same room where the same three men were still watching Cartoon Network. Their boss was not there.

"My card is not there. The lady said I have to get a new card here."

I had obviously impressed them with my tenacity, as one of them said that I could wait in the office. The next thirty minutes I watched Looney Tunes on Cartoon Network with them. In the middle of Tom and Jerry the boss came back.

"You are here again? Is the card not there?"

"No."

"Then we must make you a new one. Sit there for the photograph."

I sat for the photograph. Then he recorded my details on the computer. "I have to wait till we take another photo, we get two at a time, so you can come back tomorrow at about ten," he said.

"OK, I can do that," I said. "But will it definitely be ready as I have to fly to Kumasi for South Africa's game against Ghana," I lied.

"Yes, no problem," he replied.

I left his office and returned to Prince Kofi's house, having spent six hours trying to sort out my accreditation without having finalised anything.

The next morning I returned to the Ministry early. After all, I had come to Ghana to watch football and I was determined to do so. I knocked at the door and was told to come in. "The man from South Africa," one of the Cartoon Network addicts said. "Your accreditation is ready. Just have a seat and we will find it for you."

I could hardly believe my luck. The accreditation was ready and I had spent no more than a day in obtaining it! That was pretty good going for a continental competition. They handed me the laminated card and I quickly left their office, before they could change their minds.

As there were several hours before the start of the quarter-final match between Algeria and Cameroon, I decided to do some more sightseeing in Accra and flagged down a taxi.

"How much to drive me around for three hours," I asked.

"Four hundred cedis."

"No, no. You think I am a tourist and you want me to pay too much. Yesterday I paid three hundred for the whole day; I can give you two fifty. If you want it, it is good, if not, I can find somewhere else."

He agreed and I got in. I told him to drive to Bob's Place, as I had been told that I could change money there. Although the black market was not particularly good in Ghana, as the economy of the country is relatively strong, it was still worthwhile to leave out the banks in any financial transactions, as they charged huge commissions.

Bob's Place, which was like an Irish pub, was the focal point of expat life in the capital. At night it would be filled with foreigners downing Guinness and watching sport on satellite TV. They showed the Nations Cup matches on satellite, which was a much better bet than trying to decipher the blurry pictures sent out by the local station.

I changed US$200 and returned to the taxi.

"I would like to go to Next Door," I requested. Next Door was a restaurant/disco, next to one of the most popular beaches in Accra, Labadi Beach. It was truly African and at night was packed with people dancing to local musicians performing on a makeshift stage. They served local cuisine and local beer.

The drive there was fascinating. Accra is a bustling city, but fairly clean. Hundreds of businesses line the roads. We passed the 'God Help You' plumbers, which shared a building with 'Cool Media Advertising.'

I told the taxi driver that I needed a film for my camera and he took me to the 'Devine Photo and Wedding Studio', where, he assured me, I could get anything I needed. I bought a film and we drove further.

From my dealings with Richard Padmore, I had realised that Ghanaians were very religious and as we drove towards the beach, I saw quite a few churches. Many of them were in 'normal' houses and only the sign on the door that said 'Jesus Worship Centre' indicated that the building housed a church. Further on, we passed the 'Heaven Video Theatre and Church', which presumably did not conduct both businesses at the same time.

But if there were many churches, there were even more restaurants. The 'Peaceful Garden Restaurant' was next door to 'Buckingham Palace' - I never did find out what that was. Just a few shops further was the 'Love Tea Spot and Fast Food'. As I wanted to go to 'Next Door', we did not stop until we got to Labadi Beach.

Labadi Beach is one of the most beautiful beaches I have ever seen. White sand, thick vegetation and warm water. I ordered something to drink, sat down and looked at the sea. After a while I returned to the taxi and asked him to take me to the stadium.

Although there was only an hour to go before the match was due to start, the stadium looked nearly as deserted as it had the day before. Journalists, who had been in Ghana for the whole tournament, said that the stadiums were empty for most of the matches. It was only when Ghana's Black Stars played that the stadium was filled.

And those who decided to stay at home did not miss much.

Although Cameroon had to survive a late comeback from Algeria, they did what was expected of them. The Indomitable Lions, helped by some slack marking, swept into a two-goal lead inside half an hour, but then took things a bit too easy. They allowed the Desert Foxes to come back strongly after half-time. The North Africans scored with eleven minutes left and then threw everything forward in attack, but failed to find the equaliser and Cameroon booked a place in the semi-final.

As I needed to file my story for dpa immediately after the final whistle, I rushed into the press centre. All four computers were occupied.

Three of them by people who did not look like journalists, nor did they wear accreditation badges. I placed myself behind one of them and looked over his shoulders. He was on the Internet and writing to somebody using the free e-mail service provider, Hotmail.

"Excuse me, are you going to be much longer?" I asked him.

"I have only just started, so I could be a while," he said.

I looked at the other people sitting in front of the computers. They, too, were writing e-mails. I recognised them as being the same people who had earlier helped journalists find their seats.

"I need to file a story, could you please let me use one of the computers?" I asked very politely.

"I will be finished just now," he said.

"But these computers are here for the use of journalists, not for you to write an e-mail to your girlfriend."

"I said I would be finished just now."

I wanted to find a supervisor to complain, but was scared to leave the area, as I would lose my place in the queue. That, I knew, was not a good thing. Never leave a queue, if you want to get to the front.

Luckily for me, a loud-mouthed Italian appeared and he too needed to use the computers. "I want de computers, you let me work there now," he screamed at all four people using the computers.

One of the people sitting at one of the terminals turned around. "I am a journalist, I am filing a story," he said.

"OK, you can stay, but the others, you go." With that he started pushing the man I had been speaking to off his chair.

He obviously decided that this was a battle he was going to lose and he got up. The two females followed him and I jumped on one of the chairs they had been occupying. The computer was still connected. It was displaying the bluemountain.com page. They had been sending a greeting card to someone!

I managed to send my story and returned to Prince Kofi's house to watch another of the quarter-final matches on TV.

Cameroon's opponents in the last four were Tunisia, who had eliminated defending champions Egypt in the quarter-finals.

A 10-man Bafana team, who had defender Eric Tinkler sent off, had also made it through to the semi-finals, after having beaten the hosts, Ghana, 1-0. There the South Africans faced arguably the best team in the competition, Nigeria. To make matters worse, the match was scheduled for Surelere Stadium in Lagos, scene of a humiliating 4-0 defeat a few years earlier. I had travelled with the team to Lagos at the time and had sworn to myself that I would not return unless I really had to. Watching South Africa play in the semi-finals was not something that I really had to do, and I decided to stay in Accra to watch Cameroon.

The semi-final between Cameroon and Tunisia was a much better game than the quarterfinal. Even though the Indomitable Lions started the match as favourites, Tunisia dominated the first half and should have gone ahead. Woeful shooting let them down and the sides changed ends goalless.

The second half belonged to Italian-based Patrick Mboma, who scored twice and set up a third to ensure a 3-0 victory for Cameroon and a place in the final.

I was in two minds as to whom to support in the second semi-final. On the one hand, of course, there was the patriotic wish of wanting to see the Bafana make it to their third consecutive final, on the other hand there was also the realisation that I would have to travel to Nigeria for the final, if South Africa were in it.

As it happened, thirty minutes into the game, it became apparent that South Africa was coming to Accra to contest the play-off for third place. The Super Eagles opened the scoring through Tijani Babangida after only forty seconds. He added a second on the half hour and even though sixty minutes remained, it was almost impossible for South Africa to claw their way back into the match.

Even though the play-off for third place is possibly the worst game to play during a competition - it is very much like a consolation prize - the game between Tunisia and South Africa proved to be quite exciting.

Not surprisingly, only 3 000 people turned up. They saw Bafana lead 2-1, with only minutes remaining. The North Africans were then awarded a penalty. Khaled Badra stepped up to take the spot-kick. His shot was so weak though, that Andre Arendse in goal for South Africa managed to keep it out. The goalkeeper turned from hero to villain a minute from time though, when he chased a harmless cross and slipped on a bumpy part of the field, allowing one of the Tunisians to head in another goal.

In the end though, it was the South Africans who celebrated, as they managed to win the deciding penalty-shoot out.

I was already standing at the computer when the final penalty kick was taken as I did not want to have a repeat performance of what had happened during the previous match.

THE HOUSE THAT PETER BUILT

As I was filing my piece, I heard somebody call my name. "Peter, servus, wie geht es?"

I looked around, it was Richard Padmore, who I thought was in Austria. "Richard, how are you, what are you doing here, have you got a few minutes, I will quickly finish my story and then be with you, OK?"

I finished filing and turned to Richard. He looked different. Even though he had twice visited me in South Africa since signing for Sturm Graz six years ago, he had changed. He had a thick gold chain around his neck and several rings on his fingers. He looked much more grown-up. When he spoke English, I could hear that he had not lost his Ghanaian accent. He told me that he stayed behind in Ghana after the mid-season break to recuperate after an injury. I knew that he had left Sturm Graz and moved to another club in Austria called Lustenau. He said that he would drive me to Prince Kofi's place, as he wanted to spend some time with me.

"I have been looking for you since the competition started, but I knew that if Bafana played, I would find you," he said.

We walked together to his car. It was a blue Opel. Three men sat inside. Richard introduced them. "They look after things when I am not here. They are also players, but do not play for a big team." He told one of them to move to the back and beckoned me to sit in front.

"I am glad that I found you, I want to show you my house," he said.

We drove to Prince Kofi's house. When we arrived, he told his three helpers that they should wait at the car, while we went inside.

During his time in Austria, Richard had obviously become much more confident, as he soon had Marcelle and her housemate, Jacky, hanging on his every word. Things had not gone very smoothly for him this season, he said. After helping Lustenau gain promotion to the first division, he had picked up a serious knee injury and had not been able to play. Doctors in Austria had tried everything, but nothing had worked, so he decided to return to Ghana in the hope that traditional healers would be able to help him. He expected to remain in Accra for a few more weeks before returning to Austria.

"Can you come and see my house now?" he asked.

"No, Richard, I have to write a few previews of the final tomorrow, but I could come and watch the match at your place," I said.

"OK, I will fetch you tomorrow at 1pm."

During his time in Austria, he had obviously picked up some of the European customs, as quite contrary to what I expected, he was on time on Sunday.

We drove through Accra to his house, which was on the outskirts of the city. "I bought this house from the money I've been earning as a professional. When I am in Austria, the three players live there, as well as my wife's sister."

He told me that several professional players have houses in that area. "Do you see that big house? It belongs to Abedi Pele's brother, Kwame Ayew. It is a huge house," he said as we passed a mansion. "My house is near here."

His house was much smaller than Ayew's, but I am sure that it had a much nicer gate. The gate consisted of wrought-iron rods. What made it special was a huge corrugated iron football, which covered both sides of the doors. One of his helpers jumped out of the car and opened the gate, splitting the ball in half. Richard must have seen my look, as he said: "Gates are very important here. We like to show what kind of people we are."

The house consisted of three bedrooms, a kitchen and a dining room cum lounge, which was filled with photographs of himself playing for Sturm Graz and Lustenau. There were also a few pennants of clubs he had played against hanging on the wall. A huge television set stood in a cabinet in one corner.

"Watch this," he said proudly, as he turned off the light. He switched on an oval-shaped glass lamp that spread a luminous green light throughout the room as it revolved.

"Very nice," I lied.

"Let us eat something before the match starts. Gloria, bring the food please." He sat down at the table, where two places had been set.

"Is your wife not going to sit with us?" I asked.

"No, you know what it is like in Ghana."

Gloria brought us fufu with fish. "You like this, I remember," Richard said.

After lunch we sat down in the lounge and Richard turned on the television. We were just in time, as the game was about to start. He said that he favoured Nigeria. "They will win 3-1."

Nigeria, who had not lost at home for nineteen years and were unbeaten in the Nations Cup for eleven games, were not only Richard's favourites, they were mine too. I predicted a 3-0 score-line.

Both of us were wrong. Cameroon's win represented their third victory over Nigeria. The Indomitable Lions had beaten the Super Eagles in 1984, in 1988 and again in 2000. They took a 2-0 lead before allowing Nigeria to come back into the match and equalise. As there were no goals in extra-time, a penalty shoot-out had to decide the winner.

It was here that Tunisian referee Mourad Daami came to prominence. But, unfortunately for him and for the Nigerians, it was for all the wrong reasons. After one of the Nigerians had seen his shot saved, Cameroon was leading the shoot-out 3-2. Former African Player of the Year, Victor Ikpeba, then stepped up to take his shot. He drove it hard against the crossbar, from where it bounced down. Television replay showed that it had crossed the line, but Daami ruled that it had not and Nigeria had their backs against the wall. Even though Marc-Vivien Foe missed the next attempt, Rigobert Song converted the fifth kick for the Indomitable Lions and Cameroon won 4-3 on penalties.

Needless to say, it was a result that did not go down too well with the fans, and police had to use teargas to control the crowd baying for Daami's blood after the match.

After I had filed my story, Richard took me to Prince Kofi's house. We agreed to meet later that night at 'Next Door'.

When I arrived at the restaurant, he was not there yet and I sat down at a table overlooking the beach. A three-piece band was playing and the place was packed. I ordered some food, as Richard had said that he might be late. Midway through my supper, I saw three Bafana players enter the restaurant. John Tlale was the reserve goalkeeper, who had been a member of the squad at all three Nations Cup finals, but had yet to play for his country. Daniel Mudau, or Mambush, as he was widely known throughout South Africa, was the leading scorer in the domestic league, but hardly ever played for the national team. During this tournament he had come on once. With them was Alex Bapela, who was even more of a fringe player than the other two.

John saw me first and came over to my table. "Hi Peter, you waiting for some ladies here or what?" He gave me a toothless grin.

I liked him. He had been my magazine's first Footballer of the Year a few years ago and since then our paths had crossed at regular intervals. I invited them to join me at the table and they sat down.

"So what did you think of the final? I thought Cameroon deserved to win, even though the one penalty should have been a goal," I asked.

"It was a good game. Both sides are good," he replied.

"So what did you think of the Nations Cup?"

"Ah, so-so," Daniel said. "I was disappointed that I did not play more. I have no problem when the players are doing a job, but if they are not, then others should get a chance. I think I deserved a chance, but I never got one."

All three players said that they had not enjoyed the tournament very much and that things had not gone as they would have liked them to. Listening to them, it was clear that the atmosphere in the camp was far from harmonious. Daniel especially was outspoken in his criticism. "I don't know what else I have to do. I score in the league, but I don't get a chance in the national squad."

We continued speaking about the competition for a while. Richard joined us during our conversation. Daniel was particularly pleased to see him, as they had played together for a club called Ratanang in 1992. They immediately connected and for the rest of the evening they shared stories about their careers.

Before we knew it, it was well past midnight. Richard offered to drive the players to their hotel as they were flying back on Monday morning. He looked at me expectantly.

"Don't worry about me, I will find my own way back. I might go to another club for a while."

The four of them then left. I listened to a few more songs before leaving. I flagged down a taxi and told him I wanted to go to Miracle Mirage, a nightclub in the city. I had been told that it was an interesting place. Twenty minutes later, he stopped in front of the club.

As soon as I opened the car door, I was surrounded by a group of youngsters. "Extra lubricated, twenty cedis for ten. With Chaka Chaka you need them," they said.

As I had no intention of using any of the services on offer from the Chaka Chaka - as people earning their money in the oldest profession in the world are called in Ghana - I had no use for extra-lubricated condoms, not even at only two cedis per condom. "No thanks, I won't need them."

They followed me until I managed to evade them by ducking into Miracle's entrance.

Inside, I soon saw why the boys were probably running a thriving business. The club was filled with Chaka Chakas. As soon as they saw a prospective customer (and anybody male was a prospective customer), they would swarm up to him and start chatting him up.

"Hi, my name is Lucy. I am from Accra. Where are you from?"

The first few times, I made the mistake of being friendly and answering them. I later found out that that was a huge mistake, as it was virtually impossible for them to lose interest once a conversation had been started. It was only by becoming quite rude that they got the message.

Once I had managed to shake off all the unwanted attention, I found out that I was not the only South African in the club. Six or seven Bafana players were doing their thing on the dance floor. I joined them and spent a couple of hours with them. By the time we left the club, it must have been close to four in the morning. They had only four hours left in the country before flying back to South Africa.

I at least had more than half a day to recuperate from the heavy night. I headed straight for bed when I arrived back at Prince Kofi's house.

A few hours later, Richard arrived to take me to the airport. Prince Kofi's house was not far from the airport and twenty minutes later, he dropped me off. "It is still the same, only the passengers are allowed to enter the airport building, so we have to say goodbye here," he said.

Having done that, I went to check in. This time around though, there were no bribes to pay and we left Ghana on time.

Sitting in the plane, I thought of the two weeks I had spent in Ghana. I thought of Richard and the many possibilities that had opened up for him as a result of playing professionally in Europe. I thought of Mambush and the criticism he and the other players had levelled against the coaching staff. And soon I was drifting off to sleep.

9

ANYBODY FOR CHICKEN?

THE TOURNAMENT IN NIGERIA AND GHANA was not the first finals of the Nations Cup that I had covered. The first time was in 1996, when the finals were held in South Africa. The Confederation of African Football (CAF) had originally awarded the right to host the competition to Kenya, but their preparations had gone so disastrously awry, that even CAF, who should have been used to just about everything by then, had decided that it would be an absolute disaster if the East African nation was to try and stage the finals. Instead, CAF approached the South African Football Association (SAFA) and asked them if they could take over as hosts. Having failed dismally to qualify for the 1994 World Cup, as well as the finals of the African Nations Cup in the same year, SAFA had decided that it would be foolish to say no, especially as it came with automatic qualification.

I had been employed by the German Press Association (dpa) as sports correspondent for Africa and one of my first tasks was to cover the finals of the Nations Cup.

As the country had only recently been allowed back into international football, there were obviously still quite a few teething problems that needed to be overcome. Accreditation for journalists was chaotic and many a foreign correspondent did not have very nice things to say about the local organising committee. Luckily for me, I was in a very different boat. One of the advantages of covering an event in one's own country is that there are fewer problems getting all the paperwork sorted out and within a relatively short space of time, I had the laminated press card that would allow me to cover the event.

A much bigger problem awaited me though: dpa wanted stories from me, many, many stories. The editor in charge had obviously not been to Africa, as his brief to me was that I should submit two stories within ten minutes of the match having finished. Sitting somewhere in the press box at Wembley Stadium, that might not be too much of a problem, but to manage that from South Africa was an entirely different matter. But, as has been the case throughout my career as a football journalist, I improvised by using the television broadcast. Dpa were happy, as they received their stories.

Less happy must have been the organisers of the competition, as very few people bothered to watch the games. One of the reasons for this lack of interest was that even before the first ball had been kicked, the defending champions Nigeria had pulled out. The reason they gave was that they were looking for guarantees for the safety of their players, but behind the scene everybody knew that their withdrawal had been a political response to South Africa's criticism of Nigeria's decision to execute author and political activist Ken Saro-Wiwa. South African President Nelson Mandela led protests against the planned execution, but Nigeria did not budge and from that point on, relations between the two countries soured considerably.

With one of the major drawcards being absent, local football fans showed very little interest in matches that did not involve the Bafana and at times there were only a few hundred in the stadiums. That situation changed dramatically whenever South Africa played and from their first match against Cameroon, it became apparent that local fans were willing to put their weight behind South Africa's attempts to win the trophy at their first appearance in the finals.

For the players there was much at stake. Most of them still played their club football in South Africa and they earned very little. Playing for the national team not only gave them an opportunity to make a name for themselves and thereby possibly land a lucrative contract overseas, it also gave them the chance of making money.

When the players approached SAFA officials to discuss their win bonus, the association told them that they would not accept their proposal. Understandably, the players were not very happy with this and they considered a player revolt. It was not the first time that there had been conflict between the players and the association.

After South Africa's first win in a competitive match - against Congo in 1993 - a victory party in a local hotel afterwards had nearly turned violent when players insisted on getting money that had been promised to them for matches they had previously played.

This conflict of interests between officials and players seems to be an ongoing occurrence in African football (many would say in world football), and money is not the only issue at stake. There have been many cases of African players contracted to European clubs who get called up for an international match by their country, only to find that when they arrived at the airport, no ticket had been booked or paid.

For European journalists this apparent fixation of players with money matters when it comes to the national team is something they often cannot understand. They think that playing for a national team is an honour and not something that should be done only for monetary gain. What they fail to comprehend is the fact that players in Europe, who earn several tens of thousands of pounds a week, can afford not to be too concerned about the financial remuneration for playing in the national team. African players, many of whom receive less than 600 pounds a month, could not.

In this case the conflict between the players and the association was so severe that there was the danger of damaging South Africa's Nations Cup campaign. Luckily for all concerned, national team coach Clive Barker came up with a brilliant suggestion. He suggested that SAFA place a bet on Bafana winning the competition with a London bookmaker. If South Africa won, the money would be available to pay the players, if not, it did not matter. The association agreed and therefore the players had a lot to play for.

Although they lost to Egypt in the group stage, Bafana easily qualified for the quarter-finals, where Algeria were the opposition. Even though South Africa went into the match as favourites, they had a tougher task than anticipated and only a late goal five minutes from the end gave South Africa a 2-1 victory. But for the fans it did not matter. Bafana were in the semi-finals and that was all that mattered.

There they faced Ghana. Although the Black Stars have yet to qualify for the finals of the World Cup, they not only have a fine pedigree in continental competitions, they are also considered one of the strongest nations in youth football. In 1992 they became the first African country to win an Olympic football medal, when they finished third in Barcelona. They have also won the world junior championship twice.

The Ghanaians went into the match seriously weakened though, as their best player, Abedi Pele, had been kicked off the park in their quarter-final victory over Zaire. Without him, the side had lost its playmaker and, as a result, South Africa had very little trouble. The 3-0 scoreline was a fair reflection of the game.

The win not only ensured Bafana a place in the final; it also created unprecedented footballing interest throughout the country. Suddenly white people, who had previously not cared at all about football, became experts. Everybody talked about the big match against Tunisia and for once in South Africa's divided history, the country was one.

A capacity crowd of 80,000 crammed into the stadium. Even FW de Klerk, who had been the last Apartheid president, now suddenly showed his support for the new South Africa. He was in good company, as players from the national rugby and cricket teams, both of which are regarded as 'white' sports, came to the game.

Before the match, South African officials paid a visit to referee Charles Massembe's changing room. The Ugandan referee was no stranger to South African football and had on numerous occasions been in charge of matches involving South African clubs and the national team. During these, I had often noticed that he made decisions that seemed to favour South Africa. He awarded South Africa freekicks when he should have waved play on and failed to give corner-kicks for the opposition.

The first half was evenly contested and the teams changed ends without a goal having been scored. Early in the second half, South African fans had to endure a moment of panic as Massembe reached for his pocket after Bafana player Innocent Buthelezi committed a serious foul. Buthelezi, who was known as the strong man of South African football, had already been cautioned in the first half and a second booking would have meant that South Africa would have had to play out the remainder of the game with ten men. Massembe must have realised just in time that he would have to send Buthelezi off, so he waved play on. The midfielder was substituted shortly afterwards.

Another substitution proved to be even more inspirational. With the clock ticking away and the match seemingly heading towards extra-time, Barker brought on striker Mark Williams. The forward turned out to be the match-winner, as he scored twice, giving South Africa a historic victory. The country erupted with Massembe's final whistle. Never before, not even when Nelson Mandela had been released from prison, had there been as much celebration throughout the country. All-night parties were held and for the first time ever, the country was one, united in a victory that had given hope to a nation emerging from a troubled past.

Two years later, all of that had been forgotten. The euphoria created by the first non-racial democratic elections, in which all South Africans, irrespective of race, had been allowed to participate, had given way to an unflattering reality. Crime and unemployment dominated the headlines, racial harmony had not materialised and in many ways South

Africa was as much a divided country as it had been before the victory in 1996.

For politicians and SAFA alike, the 1998 finals in Burkina Faso provided a ray of hope. They were hoping for a repeat performance in West Africa to rekindle what had started after the victory against Tunisia.

However, they were certainly not going to go to Burkina Faso as favourites. Only two countries Egypt (1959) and Ghana (1965) had ever managed a successful title defence and both were achieved when only a few countries entered the competition.

In addition, the South Africans are notoriously bad travellers. Their only victory on the road in 1997 was against the Democratic Republic of Congo (DRC), which at the time was still known as Zaire, and even that was achieved in the neutral venue of Togo.

The Bafana lost away friendlies against England, France and Germany, and suffered embarrassing defeats against football minnows Congo, as well as in the Confederations Cup against Uruguay and the United Arab Emirates.

The poor Confederation Cup showing resulted in coach Barker resigning. His successor, Jomo Sono, promptly suffered an even more embarrassing away defeat in a regional competition against lowly Namibia. After the 3-2 defeat the Namibian press renamed the South African team 'Banana Banana'.

If all of that was not enough to cause concern amongst the fans, the association seemed also to have pushed the self-destruct button in preparing for Burkina Faso. Travel arrangements were left until the last minute, and a week before the competition no one was certain when the team would be travelling to the West African state.

To add to the chaotic circumstances team officials were taken by surprise a day before the team's planned departure when they were informed that the players had to have meningitis injections. This forced yet another delay in preparations, as the players were not allowed to train for two days after receiving their vaccinations. In addition, some of the players' passports were not ready, and no proper arrangements had been made for the squad's food to be flown to Burkina Faso. Many countries had decided that they would not rely on local food in the West African country, but few countries had left the transport of their own food so late.

A week before the start of the competition, Sono had not yet announced the names of the technical staff he was to take with him. He threatened to resign after he was forced to cancel a training session when too few players turned up.

I was at the time working for the monthly magazine, Soccer News, but had been approached by a television production company that had been commissioned by the title sponsors of the event, Coca-Cola, to produce a daily insert. They wanted me to do the research for the show. It was an offer I gladly accepted and one that proved to be invaluable later on.

Burkina Faso is, in many ways, an anomaly in Africa. It is one of the few countries that is in a position to export food.

Another main export is people. Half a million Burkinabe work in neighbouring countries, mainly Côte d'Ivoire. But this focus on the free market has not always been part and parcel of local society.

A decade ago, the country was still known as Upper Volta. At the time it was classified as the poorest nation in the world. Though no such classification existed, it would probably also have qualified as one of the most unstable politically.

In the 20 years following independence in 1960, a number of coups were staged. In 1983, a left-leaning army captain called Thomas Sankara came to power - also through a coup. One of the first things he did, after changing the name from Upper Volta to Burkina Faso, was to introduce a modest Renault 5 as his and his ministers' official car. A short while later he ordered a 25% across the board cut in government salaries. Needless to say, decisions such as those won him widespread popular support, but did not go down too well with fellow leaders and in 1987 a group of junior officers seized power.

Aware of the mass appeal Sankara enjoyed throughout the country, he was taken outside the capital Ouagadougou and shot.

A new military government was installed, headed by Blaise Campaore. He civilianised himself and organised presidential and general elections in 1991, putting himself forward as presidential candidate. He won a landslide victory, possibly helped by the fact that he was the only candidate. The opposition boycotted the elections, claiming it would be unfair as Campaore dismissed demands for it to be supervised by an independent national conference. Only a small percentage of the population voted in these elections. Seven years later, his support was questionable, but he remained in power.

The last government elections were held in 1996 with a multitude of parties contesting seats. Compaore's Popular Democracy-Labour Movement (ODP-MT) was the overwhelming winner, just as they were the first time around. The government allows a free press and criticism, though people on the street speak of subtle repression that keeps them in check.

It was Compaore's government that encouraged the African Football Confederation to hold the 21st African Cup of Nations in Burkina Faso. It was a decision many questioned, as they were said to lack the infrastructure to host a major media event.

I was eager to find out if this was true and was looking forward to arriving in the country. Coca-Cola, who were the title sponsors of the event, had booked me on an Air Afrique flight to Burkina Faso's capital, Ouagadougou. I was not the only journalist on the flight, as the company had sponsored several other journalists who were booked on the same flight.

We made two stops en route - the first in the Côte d'Ivoire capital, Abidjan, the second in Lome, the capital of Togo. As I had visas for neither, I was not permitted to leave the airport buildings. In Lome, we were asked to identify our baggage as we changed planes, and I presumed that the porters wanted to make sure that the right bags were sent with us.

As I had not yet been to Burkina Faso, I did not know what to expect when the plane landed. We arrived in the late afternoon and cleared customs without any difficulty.

But if I had arrived without any difficulty, the same could unfortunately not be said about an important part of me - my luggage. As I was standing at the conveyor belt and watched as more and more of my fellow passengers picked up their baggage and left, I had that sinking feeling in my stomach that only somebody who has been in a similar situation can understand. I placed great importance on my two bags. Not because the items contained therein were of great material value: it was simply because I did not want to spend time in a country like Burkina Faso without clothes or basic necessities like a toothbrush and shampoo.

While I was standing around I was watching the TV crew arguing with the porters, who had just unloaded the TV equipment from the aircraft. They were saying that it was not 'normal' luggage and they should therefore be paid extra. They wanted US$300. This, the TV people said, was excessive. As is usually the case in such situations, a compromise was reached, dollars were exchanged and life could continue.

I was not so lucky. I was still standing at the conveyor belt, watching as it became emptier and emptier. As soon as there was no more luggage on it, it stopped altogether. I was still without my bags.

In desperation, I turned towards an official-looking man standing around, doing nothing. "Excuse me sir, I think my luggage has not arrived, what do I do now?"

"No, no anglais."

So much for officialdom in Burkina Faso, I thought. Luckily an employee of Coca-Cola, who was aptly named Hope and had been seconded to chaperone the journalists, had arrived in the country a few days earlier and she told me that I was certainly not the only person to have arrived in the country luggage-less. She ushered me, as well as two other South African journalists who were also missing some of their luggage, to a tiny office in which an official was sitting. He was obviously being harassed by others who, like me, had arrived in the country while their suitcases had not. They were screaming at each other in French. After a while, the passengers left and we now faced the man. "Oui" he asked us.

"No française, I only speak English. You speak English?"

"A little, what do you want?"

"We want our suitcases, they have not arrived. But we still identified them in Lome, so we know that they left Johannesburg."

"You must fill out the paper and we see." He gave each of us a form, which we proceeded to fill out. It contained the usual questions. What did your suitcase look like (both black), what type of luggage is it (a large sports bag and a smaller one), did it have a name tag (yes - I was lying), what did it have in (I added just a bit extra in case they don't find it and I could claim), and give a contact name and telephone number. Having filled in everything, we handed the forms back and looked at him expectantly.

"We will see," he said. He obviously did not understand the psychology of making a distressed person feel better.

"But when will I get my bags?"

"We will see," he answered.

By now it had become late, and those lucky enough to have their suitcases were eager to leave. We were not, even though we realised that as ours had been the last flight in for the day, there was no chance of us getting our belongings before the next day. Hope told us not to worry, as in most cases the luggage had been found. She promised that she would come back early in the morning and wait at the airport for the missing bags. Reluctantly, we agreed to leave.

Outside, even though it was close to ten, it was hot and humid and we were happy to be able to sit in the coolness of the 16-seater bus that was waiting for us outside the airport. Hope explained to us that we were lucky as we were going to sleep in villas that had been built to accommodate delegates to an Organisation of African Unity (OAU) meeting, which had been held in Ouagadougou a few years earlier. "This place is very poor, you will see, but we are staying in luxury," Hope explained.

The villas turned out to be less luxurious than I had imagined, but certainly they were comfortable enough and clean, and most importantly they had air-conditioning. The bus dropped the journalists at their villa and then took me to another one, which I was going to share with the television crew.

I was given a room and somebody had a spare toothbrush, which he gave me. I awoke early the next morning, eager to find out what was going to happen about my luggage. Hope, who was staying somewhere else, was not at the villa yet but I was told not to worry, Coca-Cola would sort it out.

A short while later, Hope arrived with a twenty-something woman, whom she introduced as Cindi-Anne, who was in charge of things. Cindi-Anne said that we would be leaving for Bobo-Dioulasso, the town in which the South African team was playing, in the early afternoon, to give us some time to wait for the bags. She also gave me a Coke T-shirt, which I changed into. She said that I should just find my bearings and that the bus would be back in the afternoon to pick me up. She promised to send the driver to me as soon as he had the luggage.

After waiting for practically the whole day, I realised that the return of my baggage was not as imminent as Hope and Cindi-Anne had made me believe and that I might have to wait even longer.

The bus finally arrived at 6pm. The driver said he would take us to Bobo-Dioulasso, but he first had to do a few things. What it is that he was doing, I had no idea, but it consisted of something like this: he would drive to a house, somebody would come out, a few pleasantries were exchanged, the driver would get into the bus, drive to another house and the same thing would happen. In between, he also stopped at a market and bought himself some food, which he ate whilst driving from friend to friend.

It was already 8pm by the time we finally left Ouagadougou. The road to Bobo-Dioulasso was bad - very bad. There were potholes everywhere and the driver seemed to take very little notice of them. Every time we hit one, the bus would bounce into the air and we would be thrown around. The driver, whom we nicknamed Jacques Villeneuve, obviously wanted to make up for lost time, as he was speeding along at 120 kilometres an hour, even though the roads were probably better suited for a speed of 60 kilometres. Normally the trip between Ouaga (as travellers called the capital) and Bobo should take about five hours. Not so with Jacques Villeneuve. He was obviously intent on breaking the record for the distance - I was more concerned that he might break everything else, including my bones, in a head-on collision.

As we left Ouaga, I had chosen to sit up front next to Jacques, not knowing what I was letting myself in for. As I looked straight ahead of me, my eyes must have been as huge and round as saucers. In the darkness I could only make out the silhouettes of trees and huts flashing past and now and then I would see the glare of the lights of an oncoming car straight ahead. More often than not, it looked as if the car was heading directly for us, but somehow Jacques always managed to avoid a crash. To make matters worse, if they could get worse, Jacques seemed to be incredibly tired and at times his head tilted forward as if he was about to go to sleep. The only way I could prevent this from happening was if I spoke to him. That, of course, was difficult. He spoke little English, I even less French. But as my life depended on it, I did the best I could. I think I managed to keep his attention by throwing in a few French names that I could pronounce. "It is good to be in Burkina Faso it is a beautiful place; Didier Deschamps. How many people live here, Marcel Desailly? Do most of them Laurent Blanc live in houses or Olympique Marseilles or flats?"

And so it went on and on and on. After travelling for an hour and a half, I had not only gone through every city and footballer in France that I knew, I had even started to rattle down the menu of my favourite French restaurant. It was all to no avail though and I was still as petrified as I had been when we started the journey. As I was now fearful that I would die of a heart attack, even before I was killed in the inevitable bus crash, I decided that I had to do something. Jumping out of the bus was not an alternative, nor was strangling the driver. We had all tried to reason with him, but he had merely slowed down for a few minutes before putting his foot down again and reaching speeds of 120 kilometres per hour. I then thought of something else. I told Jacques I needed to pee. The bus screeched to a halt and I stumbled out. I asked the other journalists - most of whom had also taken the opportunity of jumping out of the bus for some fresh air - whether somebody wanted to swop places with me. Nobody volunteered. I then said that's fine, but I am no longer sitting in front and if they wanted to risk Jacques falling asleep at the wheel because nobody was talking to him, so be it, but I was definitely going to sit at the back.

As I got on the bus and sat down in the last row, my colleagues had picked up that I was being serious and after a lengthy discussion, one of them went to the front and sat down next to Jacques, who roared off as soon as the last person had entered the bus (but before the door was closed.) The quick pit stop had done nothing to convince him that it would be quite fine to arrive in Bobo an hour later than planned. On the contrary, he must have felt that he had to make up for the lost time, as he immediately pushed the speed even further. Deciding that I did not want to know in advance when I was going to meet my maker, I put my head down and tried to fall asleep. That was near impossible. Every time that I was about to doze off, Jacques would either hit a pothole or swerve to avoid hitting something on the road.

After a further two hours, we must have arrived in Bobo. Jacques parked in front of quite a fancy villa. It had a high wall surrounding it and a guard sitting outside. Cindi-Anne, who I later found out had flown to Bobo by plane, was already there when we arrived. She said we could choose any of the rooms that were not already occupied and we should make ourselves comfortable. I asked her about my bags.

"Sorry, we have not yet heard anything. Hope went to the airport, but they were not there. We will talk about it in the morning."

I was too tired to complain about it and decided instead to find myself a room to catch up on some much-needed sleep. I found a huge room with a king-size bed and a fan. The floor of the room - as well as the whole house - was tiled and thin wire mesh guarding against insects covered the windows. I had been told before that the mosquito was the national animal of Burkina Faso and I should come prepared. I had come prepared. I had mosquito repellent as a spray and I had mosquito repellent as a roll-on stick. Or I should have had them. But unfortunately, both were in my bag, which was somewhere between Lome and Ouagadougou.

ANYBODY FOR CHICKEN?

Mohen, who was the assistant sports editor of a newspaper in Durban, and whom I knew from having lived in the city a few years earlier, gave me some of his mosquito repellent and after covering my body from head to toe, I jumped into bed. I was out in a few minutes.

The next morning Cindi-Anne held a meeting with us. She told us that we had been sponsored by Coca-Cola to come to Burkina Faso to report on the finals. There were seven journalists, of whom five were from South Africa and the other two from Zambia and Zimbabwe. There were two photographers and a four-man television crew. I was considered a part of the television crew, although Cindi-Anne was aware that I was going to report on the finals for various print and radio media as well.

She told us that we were going to receive our meals in the villa, that Jacques Villeneuve (though she called him by his other name: The Driver) would be available to drive us around. It was her other news that gave us the greatest pleasure though: she said we were free to use the facilities that were in the villa.

After our brief meeting, I went outside to get some sort of feeling for where we were. The villa was in a small street, obviously in the wealthy part of town, as all the neighbouring properties had similar villas. Jacques, who was waiting by the car outside, said that these houses had been built for some meeting and had then been sold to rich Burkinabe. They in turn had hired them out for the duration of the Nations Cup. We were within easy walking distance of the compounds housing the teams that played in Bobo, including the South Africans, Zambians and Egyptians. They stayed in similar villas, though theirs were not as luxurious as ours.

After breakfast, most of us decided to take a trip to the Hotel L'Auberge, where the CAF officials stayed. It also served as the press centre and, as we were all eager to get our accreditation sorted out as soon as possible, we asked Jacques to take us downtown.

Luckily for us, there was quite a bit of traffic and even though he tried his best - weaving in and out - he could not manage to reach the speeds that he had maintained travelling down to Bobo.

The press centre was as chaotic as I had come to expect of large competitions in Africa. At the one end, journalists were jostling for positions closer to the table behind which officials - who were not only overworked, but were also out of their depth - were trying their best to cope with the onslaught. At the other end stood some ten tables with outdated computers. A group of journalists who had already received all the freebies there were to receive and had managed to secure their accreditation, stood in a corner chatting about football, while a few beautiful ladies stood around looking rather lost. I had come to recognise these ladies from other events. They were always similar in type: Beautiful, long painted fingernails, fancy hair-do's and high-pitched voices that could be heard throughout the entire room. Journalists had a habit of picking them up wherever they went and then taking them along to various press centres and events. This has often caused problems as in most stadiums press seating is very limited and often these hangers-on would occupy press seats while journalists had to stand.

Having not yet secured my accreditation, I decided that I would join the group of journalists jostling for positions in the hope that it was the queue for the press passes. It was, and after forty minutes or so, I had finished all the formalities and was told to come back in the afternoon when the press card would be ready.

I left the press centre and walked around a bit, looking at the city. Bobo was the second biggest city in Burkina Faso. It had hotels with such inviting names as Relax Inn and OK Inn, but even though I had spent only one night in the place, I already knew that very little about the place was relaxing. And even less was OK. Far from it.

Burkina Faso literally translated means the Land of the Incorruptible Men.

Incorruptible, perhaps, but not exactly unmaterialistic.

Everywhere one looked, there were signs of entrepreneurship. Lining the roads in Bobo-Dioulasso were hundreds of vendors and small open-air restaurants and bars.

The bustling streets were crammed with bicycles and mopeds. But the cars seemed to regard them - and red traffic lights - as minor traffic irritations for which one should slow down a bit, but certainly not stop. Mopeds, or mobylettes, as they are called, were the major form of transport.

In the afternoon, I returned to the press centre and managed to get my accreditation without too much hassle. It was only later that I found out how lucky I had been, because earlier the accreditation process had been a disaster. In temperatures that reached 40 degrees C, journalists had to wait and wait. At least they were in good company, as participating teams also had to stand in line.

First everybody had to wait due to a strike by the officials, and then they had to wait as the plastic they needed to laminate the passes had run out. Teams that arrived in the country later were more fortunate. They did not have to appear personally, they just received their player passes. However, instead of a photograph of the player, a big black square appeared.

Under the circumstances, I was quite content to take my accreditation and count my blessings. Jacques then took us back to the villa.

When I entered my room, I knew I was in trouble. Lying on my bed were two more Coca-Cola shirts. I took that to mean that my bags had not yet arrived, but as none of the Coke people were around I could not ask them. One of the photographers, who had arrived before us and had therefore not needed to go into the centre to organise his accreditation, said that Cindi-Anne had come to the house and dropped off the shirts. She had said nothing about the bags.

That evening we had our first supper as a group. The meal was brought to the villa from elsewhere, as our kitchen was only used to keep our drinks (a never-ending supply of Coca-Cola and water) and to wash the dishes. The food, consisting of rice and roasted chicken, as well as vegetables, was placed on the living room table and whoever was there at the time started eating.

After dinner, I went to speak to Cindi-Anne about my bags. She was staying in a similar villa not far from ours with some other Coca-Cola executives. She had bad news - in this case no news was bad news. She said that she had no idea what had happened to my luggage, though she did promise that she would continue trying to find out when it would finally arrive.

The next day, South Africa played its first match of the tournament against Angola. It was an uninspiring match, in which Angola were obviously quite happy to go for a draw. Bafana lacked strength upfront, and but for a shrewd move by coach Jomo Sono would have lacked a player too. South Africa's 'wunderkind', Benni McCarthy, threw a punch at his opponent after being fouled. His experienced captain, Lucas Radebe, was quick to react. He indicated to the youngster that he should fall down and act injured. McCarthy did as he was told and was carried off the field. When he wanted to get up from the stretcher, Sono came running over and told him to stay. He was carried into the change room.

Sono, whose claim to fame is having played in the New York Cosmos side with Beckenbauer and Pele in the 1970s and as a result called the club he formed in South Africa Jomo Cosmos, brought on another player. Referee Sidi-Bekaye Megassa from Mali fell for the trick and failed to red-card McCarthy. For this error, Megassa was taken off the list of referees at the finals.

After the match Jacques rushed me home - and for the first time I was pleased that he harboured aspirations of being a Formula One driver. I needed to get home fast to send my stories to dpa, as it was virtually impossible to do so from the stadium. Not only were international calls prohibitively expensive, there were also too few lines for the number of journalists wanting to use them.

In the comfort of our villa, we had two international lines and as most of the other journalists conducted post-match interviews, I had only to fight with the photographers to send my stories to Germany.

Once I had finished my work I walked across to Cindi-Anne for an update on the luggage saga. Same story - no bags. She gave me some more Coca-Cola shirts and I returned to our villa for supper, which consisted of chicken in sauce and potatoes. After dinner I decided that I no longer wanted to walk around in the heat in my jeans and I borrowed short pants from one of the other journalists in our group.

The next day, I watched the matches of the other group (Egypt vs Mozambique 2-0 and Zambia vs Morocco 1-1), waited for my luggage (I had enough Coke shirts, so Cindi-Anne did not give me any more), and had chicken for supper.

In fact, most of my days in Bobo were spent like this. We watched football, sent stories, ate chicken and I waited for my bags. All of this happened while my collection of Coca-Cola shirts was growing.

There were plenty of stories to write. South Africa were held to another draw by Côte d'Ivoire, but then slammed Namibia 4-0. In the match McCarthy, who had been left out of the team against the Ivorians, became the first South African to score four goals in one match. What was even more remarkable, was that he had done so within the space of 13 minutes. In the other group, Zambia, one of the pre-tournament favourites, were hammered 4-0 by Egypt. Following the defeat, the Zambian Minister of Sport, William Harrington, who had accompanied the squad to Burkina Faso, held urgent talks with the players and officials. After the discussions, Harrington went to Burkhard Ziese, who was in charge of the team and suspended him with immediate effect.

I had earlier spent quite a bit of time with Ziese, who was one of many German coaches working in Africa. After his suspension, he had no place to go as there were no flights out of Bobo, so he had to hang around the team quarters and watch as veteran player Kalusha Bwalya and assistant coach George Mungwa took charge for the final group game, which they won against Mozambique 3-1.

Interestingly, even though the Zambians were knocked out of the competition after their game against Mozambique, they stayed in Bobo for several days. They had earlier arrived in the country with a charter flight and were also meant to leave the same way. But when they were told that an aircraft would pick them up, they declined, saying it was too small.

The team had been on the road for a month and the players had gone on such a shopping spree that they had too much luggage. At the time, four of the squad played in Saudi Arabia and they brought television sets, video recorders and other electrical appliances, which they were hoping to sell for a profit back home. It was only several days later that the team finally returned to Zambia.

I later had frequent e-mail contact with Ziese, who is said to have earned £12,000 per month as the Zambian coach. He had complained to the world controlling body, FIFA, that he had been wrongfully dismissed and wanted me to send him all the stories I had written, as he needed them as evidence. FIFA ordered the Zambian FA to pay him out his contract, which still had several months to run.

On our sixth day in Bobo - I was still without my bags - something strange happened. We all met in the dinning room for our meal and sat down. As one of the journalists pulled off the sheet that covered the food to prevent flies from squatting on it during the journey from wherever they cooked it to our villa, we were astonished to find that it was not chicken. Since our arrival, we had eaten chicken every day and now suddenly, without any prior warning, our daily routine had been changed. We all eagerly stared at the plate and saw: pigeons. Instead of chicken, we were served pigeon!

Not surprisingly, I decided that I was going to do my own thing for dinner the next day and together with one of the journalists, asked Jacques to drive us into town. He suggested a good restaurant and dropped us there. What he did not tell us, was that it was run by a group of nuns. It was a beautiful restaurant, tastefully decorated with serene music playing in the background. In the middle of our meal (I had steered well clear of anything that had two legs and wings and could fly), a siren rang. Astonished, we looked at the other people sitting around us. They had all put their knives and forks to one side and stopped their conversations. Suddenly, choral music was played over the loudspeaker. This must have lasted for five or so minutes. When it was finished, one of the nuns said a prayer and thereafter, everybody started eating again. We followed suit and enjoyed our meal. And did we enjoy it! The best thing about it was that it had, when still alive, walked on four legs and had no wings and did not even come close to being a chicken.

Back at the villa, there was another surprise waiting for me. One of my bags was standing in my room. I jumped for joy and asked everybody if they knew how this had happened. No, they did not. They had been eating (chicken!) and Jacques had come in with the bag. He said he had been told by Cindi-Anne that it was mine and he should put it in my room. That is all they knew. But what was even more surprising is that absolutely nothing was missing. I tore off my Coca-Cola shirt and changed into a new set of clothes. They made me feel like a new person. It was a wonderful feeling.

In the groups playing in Ouagadougou, there had been quite a few surprises. Ghana, who were considered as one of the pre-tournament favourites, had beaten Tunisia in their first match and seemed well on their way into the next round, before coming unstuck against Democratic Republic of Congo and Togo, thus being eliminated at the first hurdle.

Even more surprising things had happened in group A, where the hosts had benefited from some dodgy refereeing decisions and the support of the vociferous home crowd to finish runners-up to Cameroon.

In two previous appearances at the finals of the Nations Cup, Burkina Faso had played six matches and lost them all, just as they had done the first one against Cameroon this time around. But on their eighth attempt, they finally got it right. They repeated their victory in the very next game and unexpectedly moved into the quarter-finals. There they took on Tunisia and took a surprise lead. Even when Tunisia equalised in the final minute, they did not despair. They pushed forward and in the penalty shoot-out had the luck of the brave. Their success re-instilled an invaluable asset, national pride, and the historic victory against Tunisia unleashed a fervour of nationalism previously unseen in the country.

During the game, I walked around the streets of Bobo, as I had decided to do a feature on football fever in the country. Each and every restaurant or bar that had a television was packed and as many of them were open-air, people crammed the sidewalks to watch the game. When Tunisian captain Samy Trabelsi put his side's tenth penalty wide of the post to give Burkina Faso a well-deserved victory, pandemonium broke loose. People took to the streets, running up and down waving Burkina Faso flags, while motorists hooted their horns. Celebrations lasted well into the night and the victory had - at least in the eyes of local residents - justified the hosting of the event.

South Africa was another team to go through to the semi-finals. They had topped their group after thrashing Namibia and then had gone on to beat fellow World Cup qualifiers Morocco in the quarter-finals in Ouagadougou. I had not watched the match, as I had decided to stay in Bobo to watch the only quarter-final that was being played in the town. It was between Cameroon and the Democratic Republic of Congo whose success in the tournament had taken everybody by surprise. Shortly before the start of the tournament, it was still unclear whether the war-torn country would be able to send a team at all and when they finally arrived, they were certainly the least prepared team in the tournament. But thrown together, the players had grown into a unit and in the game I watched, they even managed to upset the Indomitable Lions, scoring the only goal of the game. What made their victory even more remarkable is that they finished the match with only nine men, after two players were sent off.

That evening, I went to conduct some interviews with some of the Cameroonian players and again I was astonished to see how unfazed they seemed about their defeat. They had been knocked out of a competition that they had started as favourites, but they were quite happy to party well into the night. I joined them! Earlier during the day, my second bag had reappeared just as miraculously as the first, so I felt that I had plenty of reasons to party all night.

The next day I put my life into Jacques' hands again as he drove those of us who had decided to stay in Bobo for the Cameroonian quarterfinal back to Ouga. This time around it did not seem as bad as the first journey. Possibly, I had become resistant to bad and fast driving. It could also have been that the journey was less frightening during the day than at night.

I stayed in the Coca-Cola villa, which by this time was relatively empty, as some of the journalists who had come on the trip had already returned home. One, a youngster for whom the trip to Burkina Faso

had been the first time ever he had been allowed to cover an event outside South Africa, had such a bad case of alcohol poisoning that he was
shipped out on the next flight, while another suffered from malaria and
decided that he would rather take his chances on a plane and in a South
African hospital than being admitted to a clinic in Bobo.

Our trip was rapidly nearing its end, as only four matches remained.
South Africa had luck on their side in the semi's and defeated the
Democratic Republic of Congo 2-1. Their opponents in the final were
Egypt, who had beaten the Stallions in the other semi-final.

Two days before the final, SAFA formally invited all South African
journalists in Burkina Faso to dinner at one of the five-star hotels in
Ouga. As is usually the case at these trips, the officials were staying in
the best hotel in town. This time it was the Hotel Slimande, which was
where we had been invited to join the SAFA executive for a buffet dinner. This was the first time that anything like this had happened, and we
were all very eager to find out what the occasion was.

After enjoying a hearty meal (no chicken), SAFA CEO Danny
Jordaan addressed us. He told us that South Africa was officially going
to launch its bid to host the 2006 World Cup in the next few days. He
said the association had felt it was proper that South African journalists
were told about the situation before the rest of the world knew about
it, and he also wanted to give us an opportunity to ask questions.

None of us were surprised about the World Cup bid, as it had long
been written about and it was a fait acompli that it was going to happen.
What caught us slightly off-guard was the concern about us journalists
and our feelings that the association suddenly had. This was not something that we had previously encountered. Far from it, on many occasions, the media had been treated very much like an irritation that had
to be tolerated.

Jordaan was very forthcoming in his answers. The only question that
seemed to rattle him was the one about crime in South Africa. This
issue was to follow the South African bid around for the next four years
and, as can be seen later, ultimately played a large part in why the 2006
World Cup will not be hosted in Africa.

Back in South Africa, Bafana's progress had generated a lot of inter-
est. Suddenly, fans were sitting up and taking note of the tournament.
A charter plane filled with fans and officials came to Ouga to watch
Bafana play. They were to be disappointed, as Egypt outplayed South
Africa in all departments and deservedly ran out 2-0 winners.

ANYBODY FOR CHICKEN?

That evening I spent partying with the South African players. I am not sure whether they were celebrating having finished second in the competition, or whether it was the thought of leaving Burkina Faso and returning to South Africa that had set them off.

10

MAKING IT BIG

PARTYING WITH THE PLAYERS is something that South African journalists do often, certainly more often than their European counterparts. The reasons are simple. The majority of African football players, be they big-time professional players under contract to a club in Europe or locally based players earning no more than a few hundred pounds or so, retain their friendliness and openness.

This, of course, makes the journalist's job much easier, as getting an interview is, in most cases, no more work than picking up a phone, dialling the player's home number and having a good chat. Most European football journalists enjoy no such luxury. They can count themselves blessed if they are in possession of the home number of one or two players. Very rarely will you see a situation where a journalist has a notebook filled with the home numbers of players from different clubs.

In 1997 I travelled to Portugal to watch an exhibition match between an African XI and a European XI. It was the first time that such a game had been organised and was therefore something that I was not going to miss. It was here that I saw just how much easier it was for African journalists than for European journalists.

Playing for the African side were household names like Taribo West (AJ Auxerre), Nourredine Naybet (Deportivo La Coruna), Sunday Oliseh (FC Cologne) and Tijani Babangida (Ajax Amsterdam). Opposing them were the likes of Matthias Sammer (Dortmund), Rui Costa (Fiorentina), Zvonimir Boban (AC Milan) and Frank De Boer (Ajax Amsterdam). In other words, there was not that much difference between the two sides. Both had internationally recognised players under contract for clubs in the best leagues in Europe in their squad.

But when it came to interacting with the players, they were worlds apart. The European players were generally aloof and not at all interested in speaking to the press. At first I tried speaking to them as a journalist covering the event for the South African magazine Soccer News. No luck! Then I tried wearing my German Press Association (dpa) hat.

It made no difference. All I managed to get from them were the 'normal' statements: "I look forward to the game, it will be tough and blah blah blah."

It was quite a different matter when I approached the African players. They were friendly and eager to speak to me, regardless of whether I introduced myself as a German journalist or as an African one. Another thing that separated them from their European counterparts was that they were also interested in what I had to say. With them, it was not merely a question of me asking something and them giving a short answer. No, it was an interaction in which I was treated as an equal partner.

The contact I had with the players in Portugal was obviously not the first that I had with players from outside South Africa. During travels all over the continent I had met many players - big-name stars and no-name brands. Players who were known to many football fans throughout the world, and players who would probably spend their entire footballing careers in obscurity, known only to a small band of die-hard supporters.

Over the years it was especially interesting to see how players developed as their careers progressed. One such player, with whom I have had quite a bit of contact, is Bayern Munich's Osei Kuffour. The first time I met him was in Mauritius during the African Youth Championship in 1993. He was only 17 years old, but had already been signed by Italian Serie A club Torino. For many players, that would have been enough reason to become arrogant and treat journalists with the contempt that some people think they deserve. Not so Kuffour.

He told me that even though he had won the African Youth Championship, a bronze medal at the Olympic Games a year earlier and the World Junior Championship, and been signed by a club from the strongest league in the world, he still had a lot to learn. "With God's help, I will go far, but I need His help. Without Him I am nothing."

Throughout the years, I was to meet Kuffour regularly. He came to South Africa with his national team and I saw him every two years at the finals of the African Nations Cup. He had not changed and even though he had become a big star in the Bundesliga for Bayern Munich, he remained as humble as he had been when I first met him many, many years ago.

Another player whom I have been able to see often is Egyptian striker Hossam Hassan, who is now recognised as the player with the most number of international caps. He was honoured in 2001 by the world controlling body, FIFA, for this feat.

He, too, had been a frequent visitor to South Africa. The first time I met him was in 1994. His club Al Ahly had won the African Cup Winners' Cup a year earlier, and as their city rivals, Zamalek, had won the Champions Cup, the game for the African Super Cup was an all-Egyptian affair. It was played in Johannesburg and I was one of a handful of local journalists interested in watching the game.

Even though Zamalek won 1-0 I was determined to publish a short interview with Hassan in the next issue of Soccer News. Having received a photographer's pass for the game, I had no difficulty in approaching him. His English was not great (better than my Arabic, though) and we somehow managed to get by. At the end of the interview I asked him if he would like to get some of the photographs that I had taken. He said yes. And then he did something that I will never forget. He took off his jersey that he had worn during the match and gave it to me. "I want you to have this," he said. "You have been good to me and I must be good to you."

I was flabbergasted. Needless to say, I took the shirt. Fearful that he might change his mind or that somebody else would steal it, I quickly hid it in my camera bag.

When I brought him the photographs the next day in the hotel in which they were staying, he thanked me once again and said that it had been nice speaking to me and that I should stay in touch. As he was a regular in the Egyptian side, I saw him whenever I watched the Pharaohs play. And although that was not very often, it was still often enough to see that Hassan, too, had not changed. He had remained as friendly a person as he had been the first time I had met him and even today, the memento he gave me occupies a very special place in the jersey collection that I have built up over the years.

Arguably the most famous African player is Liberian George Weah, who in 1995 was voted as World Footballer of the Year, European Footballer of the Year and African Footballer of the Year. I met him for the first time in 1993, when he was still playing for Paris St Germain in France. I was visiting a colleague who works for France Football and he took me to the 'Black Stars' tournament. This was an annual event at which a team consisting of French-based African players competed against three invited teams. In that year, the organisers had invited a Moroccan club side, the Burkina Faso national team, as well as the 'national' team of the French island Reunion.

Weah arrived at the tournament with French national team keeper, Bernard Lama, to watch some of the games. I went up to them and introduced myself as a South African journalist covering the Black Stars tournament. I asked Weah if I could conduct a short interview with him.

"No!"

That was not the answer I expected. I was stunned and had no idea what to say next. I was about to make a hasty exit when I saw Weah smiling at Lama. He was having me on. "I will interview you," he said.

At first I thought that he was joking, but he was not. For the next thirty minutes, he asked me questions about South Africa, about Nelson Mandela and what the country was like. He said he had never been to South Africa, but would love to visit some time.

The next time I saw him was in 1996 when he finally made it to South Africa. Liberia had qualified for the finals of the Nations Cup for the first time and Weah was in the squad. Watching the side train however, I could see that Weah was much more than just a player. He was mentor and big brother to the younger players and assistant to the technical team. I later found out that he also acted as financier of the poverty-stricken association, paying for airfares for the players and paying the association's debts.

His stay in South Africa was short though as the Lone Stars, as the team is known throughout Africa, were eliminated after the first round of the competition which Bafana went on to win.

In the Bafana side, there were many players who I had come to know well in the three years that the team had played international football. I had seen them enter the international arena, I had seen them being outplayed in their first few competitive matches and then I had seen them develop into an international side. I have also seen several of them being transferred to clubs overseas.

A few years after South Africa's triumph in the Nations Cup, I was sent by Soccer News to Turkey, to do a piece on one of the growing number of African players who had signed contracts with clubs in the Turkish league.

John 'Shoes' Moshoeu had been a big star in South Africa when Turkish club Genclerbirligi signed him. After two successful seasons with the team, he moved to Kocaelispor, with whom he won the cup. This attracted the attention of Fenerbahce, who, of course, are one of the biggest clubs in Turkey. He joined them in 1997 and had made such an impression, that he was made captain of the side. He was still with them when I flew to Turkey two years later.

Istanbul is a huge sprawling city, slightly shabby, but certainly very interesting. There was a marked difference between the Asian and the European parts. My hotel was situated in the European part and was in the centre of town, within walking distance of shops and restaurants.

I had arranged to meet Shoes on the day after my arrival at the Fenerbahce training ground. As the hotel was a long way from the training ground, I had to take a taxi. The driver was very impressed when I told him that I was from South Africa and had come to do an interview with Shoes.

"Are you sure" he asked. "Will they let you in?"

I was not sure what he meant, but said that everything had been arranged. Soon after, we stopped at the training ground. The gates were closed and a security guard stood at the door. I walked up to him and told him that I had come from South Africa to do an interview with Shoes. He answered in Turkish. I spoke no Turkish. I tried again. "Me from Africa. Me speak to Shoes. Shoes know me come."

The guard was obviously not particularly interested and answered something in Turkish again. In desperation I turned to the taxi driver to ask him to translate. Unfortunately for me, he was no longer there and I had visions of myself sitting in front of the ground for two hours, waiting for Shoes to come out.

But as has happened so often during my career, Lady Luck smiled brightly. This time it was in the form of a Turkish journalist, who spoke a bit of English. I explained the situation to him and asked him if he could help me. He spoke to the guard, but even after hearing my story he did not seem particularly interested. It was obviously something that the journalist had come to expect from Turkish guards, as he turned to me and said that he would go to the office and see what he could do there.

A short while later somebody came to the guard and told him to let me in. Grudgingly, he obliged and pointed to a small room at the bottom end of the ground. I made my way to the room, careful not to jeopardise my stay in the ground by stepping off the path he had shown me.

On entering the room, I found out that I was not the only journalist who had come to the training session. There were at least twenty others, as well as three television crews. The man who had earlier come to my rescue was there too. He must have told the others there about the South African journalist, struggling in front of the closed gates, as several of them came to me and introduced themselves. It was only later that I found out that at least a part of their interest had something to do with their hope of being able to find out from me if Shoes was going to renew his contract with Fenerbahce. As I had not yet spoken to Shoes, I could give them no answer.

At the end of the training session, Shoes came over to me. "Hi, nice to see you. I am just going to have a shower, you can wait over there, " he said.

This time around, I was the lucky one as Shoes took me past all the other journalists to a restricted area, where I waited for him.

A short while later he re-appeared and we went to the car park. There were Porsches, luxury 4x4s as well as Mercedes Benzes. There were also a number of smaller cars, no doubt belonging to the reserve team players. But Shoes went up to one of the smaller, less spectacular cars and opened the door for me. He must have seen the expression on my face as he said that he saw no need for a fancy car. "Why should I spend a lot of money on an expensive car? I am going to play here for a few more seasons and then I will return to South Africa. This car will do nicely till then."

He said that he did not live extravagantly and tried to save as much money as possible. "You never know what is going to happen in the future. It is crazy to spend a lot of money. My career is drawing to a close; I am not sure what I am going to do then. I must look after my future. The only big thing that I have bought is a Porsche, that I got when I was in South Africa recently."

His flat, which was in the Asian part of Istanbul, was also not at all what I expected from an international football player. There was no large-screen TV, no fancy hi-fi set and no extravagant furniture. "I have everything I need. This is not my home. My home is in South Africa. I live here and that is all."

For the next two days, I travelled around Istanbul with Shoes. We went shopping together, we had lunch together and he showed me his favourite hangouts. He was obviously as big a star in Turkey as he was in South Africa, as we couldn't go anywhere without him being stopped and spoken to. He spoke Turkish fluently and always made a point of spending a few minutes with people who wanted to speak to him.

Before returning to South Africa, I watched Shoes play in a league match against Kocaelispor. Shoes scored (I like to think that it was for me), but Kocaelispor equalised. This caused the Fenerbahce fans to riot and throw things onto the field. At the end of the match the referee had to leave the field between a dozen or so policemen, who held their shields over him for protection.

Shoes told me later that the scenes at the stadium had been nothing special. "Here in Turkey it is always like that. They are very passionate about their football. Nothing really bad ever happens and one gets used to it."

Moshoeu is not the only South African player to have been given the honour of captaining a top European side. Bafana captain Lucas Radebe is another, having been given the armband at Leeds United.

Rhuu, as South African fans know him, is another of the players who has not let the success he has achieved at club level in Europe change his personality. He has remained as friendly and helpful as he was before moving abroad.

The one thing that has apparently changed is his willingness to play for the South African national team. To understand why this is so, one needs to understand the constant pressure facing African players who are under contract to clubs in Europe. On the one hand, many of them earn good money playing football in Europe; on the other, they face constant call-ups from their national associations. To make matters worse, most international matches and tournaments for African countries are played at the same time as European club matches.

Not surprisingly, many of the African players in Europe are under pressure from their clubs to cut down on international matches. This, however, is not an easy decision as African countries have the right to apply to FIFA to have players banned if they refuse to honour international call-ups. South Africa has used this on a number of occasions. The player has two possibilities. He can either try to reason with the association and be released for most of the games, or he can announce his retirement from international football. Both are tactics that South African players have employed.

In January 2001 rumours were circulating amongst football journalists in South Africa that Radebe was to announce his retirement from international football after South Africa's World Cup qualifier against Burkina Faso. As Radebe was an international star, it was a story that was of interest not only to a South African audience, but also to an international one and I covered it for dpa.

I discussed it with a colleague from Soccer News and he told me that he had just been to the offices of the South African Football Association, where the matter was being treated as top priority. "I did not know that they had something like that," I joked.

"In this case, they do and it seems that they are really worried that Radebe is no longer going to play for Bafana. They think they need him and I tend to agree," he said. "They are blaming Radebe's London-based lawyer Gary Blumberg for the fiasco and said that Blumberg had promised Leeds that Radebe would no longer play for the national team when he signed a new three-year contract at the beginning of the year."

I did not believe that Blumberg would have agreed to something without discussing it with Radebe first. Having dealt with SAFA on many matters, I was also aware that they were always eager to find a scapegoat when things went wrong. And Radebe retiring from international football was things going horribly wrong. But it was not the first time that I had come across Blumberg.

Radebe had been writing a column for Soccer News and his lawyer had been the one who set up the deal. I never encountered any problems with him and respected the professional way in which he handled Radebe's affairs.

After having worked with him for over a year, I was phoned by another lawyer, who said that he had some information that he would like me to have. Always eager to pursue a good story, I accepted his invitation to meet. At our meeting he gave me a bunch of court papers and said that I should go through them as I would certainly find them very interesting.

He said it was a matter between Colin Viljoen, Blumberg and one of his other players, Bradley Carnell. I knew Viljoen. He was a South African who had played quite successfully for Ipswich in the old English First Division before returning to South Africa, where he had a brief stint as a coach in the top division. He had then become an agent and had several promising South African players under his wing. Amongst them was Bradley Carnell, who played for the South African under-23 side. He started playing football in South Africa for a club called Wits University, before moving to Kaizer Chiefs. After only a short stint with Chiefs, he was snapped up in 1998 by Bundesliga club VfB Stuttgart, for whom he still played in 2002.

I took the documents, thanked him and said I would be in touch if I needed any further information. At home I looked at the papers and immediately saw that they were potentially quite explosive. The first document was a letter from one firm of attorney to another in which lawyers acting for Blumberg and Carnell had accepted an out of court settlement. As I read on, it became more and more intriguing.

From the papers it appeared that Viljoen had taken Carnell and Blumberg to court after the player had signed for Stuttgart. Viljoen claimed that he had a valid contract with Carnell, which was due to end on the 30th of October 1998. On the 19th of August of the same year, Carnell had written to Viljoen, informing him that he would not renew the contract after it expired. Viljoen claimed that he had, as a result, suffered damages.

Viljoen demanded damages from Blumberg as he had acted for Carnell whilst the player still had a valid contract with him. From letters attached to the documents, I could see that this was true. Blumberg had written numerous letters to Stuttgart, the first on the 19th of August, which was incidentally the same day that Carnell wrote the letter to Viljoen.

But it was not only that which aroused my interest. There was also a contract proposal that Blumberg had faxed to Stuttgart. In it, Stuttgart were asked to pay an agency/legal fee of US$30,000. This I found particularly interesting, as I had always been under the impression that Blumberg acted entirely as a lawyer to the players, not as an agent. Another thing that caught my eye was a letter that Blumberg had written to Stuttgart in which he said that he had come to an agreement with Stuttgart that the club accept two young South African football players per season for a two-week trial period to be proposed by his company and that Stuttgart pay all accommodation and travel costs associated with such trials. In getting Stuttgart to agree to this, Blumberg had managed to create a brilliant marketing tool for his company. He could now approach young South African players and promise them a trial. This would obviously count heavily in his favour when the players were asked to sign a contract with his company.

Looking at the documents, there was obviously a good story. There was, however, one thing that troubled me. Having covered other court cases, I knew that most out of court settlements were accompanied by a confidentiality clause. I phoned the lawyer who had given me the documents and asked him about a confidentiality clause.

"No, there is no such clause," he said to me. "Their lawyers phoned me after we received our money in terms of the out of court settlement

Following in Mandela's footsteps: A South African media XI taking on the supporters of the South African World Cup Bid Campaign on the Robben Island field. Cameroon World Cup star Roger Milla is in the back row, far left. Terry Paine, a member of England's 1966 World Cup-winning squad, is fifth from the right in the back row. Former African Footballer of the Year, Abedi Pele, is third from left in the bottom row holding on to the author.

From the dusty township fields of Ougadougou in
Burkina Faso (above) to the dusty fields of Mali's capital
Bamako (below) - football is played everywhere.

Why South Africa qualified for France 1998: (above) A juju man in Togo performing his rituals that enabled Bafana to beat the Democratic Republic of Congo. As he creates the voodoo doll, he spits out the names of South Africa's opponents. He then sets fire to the doll and slaughters a chicken, dripping the blood on the doll (right).

Ghanaian footballer Richard Padmore, having finally arrived in Austria after a lengthy delay in obtaining his visa.

The author with former South African president, Nelson Mandela. One of the first delegations to meet with Mandela after his release from prison was a group of football officials - even though Mandela is an avid boxing fan.

When times were good: Former head of South African football, Sticks Morewa, watching South Africa take on Zambia in Johannesburg's FNB stadium. Morewa was soon afterwards sent into the wilderness - disgraced, but much richer having received a huge pay-out after a South African judge found him to have enriched himself while he was in charge of South African football. Sitting to his right is the then Zambian president, Kenneth Kaunda, cheering for his KK XI. Since then Kaunda has fallen into the political wilderness and the Zambian national team received a different nickname.

Africa's passion. South African football fans cheering for
their side during the 1996 Nations Cup.

The man with a price on his head: New Zealand's Charles Dempsey - South Africans blamed him when Germany was given the right to host the World Cup in 2006.

Rudi Gutendorf: One-time world record holder of having coached the most number of teams, sitting next to former Zimbabwean President Canaan Banana.

A Congolese soldier attempts to prevent South Africa
from training ahead of a World Cup match.
South African footballing official Danny Jordaan
tries to reason with him.

and asked for a confidentiality clause, but I told them to forget it." I was in luck!

I then phoned Glyn Binkin, who ran Blumberg's office in South Africa. I had known Binkin for a long time too, as he used to be Bafana team manager before being replaced. At the time, I had spoken to him and offered whatever help he could use. This time around, our discussion was less than friendly, though.

"Hi Glyn, it's Peter Auf der Heyde, I would like to ask you a few questions about…"

But before I could even finish the sentence, Binkin interrupted me: "I have nothing to say to you, I will not speak to you." And with that he put the phone down.

Well, I thought, at least I tried getting a quote. I then sat down to write my story.

Luckily for me though, this was the only time that I encountered such hostility in pursuit of a good footballing story. And even that probably had more to do with Binkin being upset about the lawyers having forgotten to introduce a confidentiality clause than anything else.

All the African players that I interviewed in the course of my work were always more than helpful. And that, regardless of whether they were South Africans who knew me or players from other African countries who had never heard of me.

One of the friendliest players I ever had the chance to interview was Kassoum Ouedraogo of Burkina Faso, whom I interviewed when that country was hosting the African Nations Cup in 1998. He played for a lowly German club, but was obviously considered an absolute star in his home country. And his status, which already was close to being a semi-God by the time the competition had started, increased even further after scoring the only goal of the match in the Stallions' second game against Algeria, which opened their way into the second round.

Ouedraogo enjoyed talking to me because we could speak about Germany and he could practise his German. He seemed to have plenty of time to chat, even though he was involved in such an important competition. He told me all about his country and how important it was for them to do well. He spoke glowingly about their French coach Philippe Troussier and praised him for everything that he had done for the players.

I considered him to be a good example of an African football player. Although the people of his country considered him a huge star, he nevertheless found the time to speak to me and went out of his way to do so. And it was this that separated African players from most of their European counterparts.

After the tournament, I followed his career closely, for a while at least. He did not make the Burkina squad for the 2000 finals in Ghana/Nigeria and without their mentor, Troussier, the Burkinabe failed to impress. They finished bottom of their group and went home early. Ouedraogo's contract with the German club was also not renewed and he is now probably back home in Burkina Faso.

11

THE KING OF AFRICA

PHILIPPE TROUSSIER'S REIGN as coach of Burkina Faso ended immediately after the Stallions had finished fourth in the competition. However, Burkina Faso was not the only country that had to find a new national coach after a continental competition. At the finals of the 2000 African Nations Cup in Ghana and Nigeria, the situation of coaches had become even worse.

Gotlieb Goeller, who was in charge of the Togolese national side, was the first to quit. The 54-year old German's departure came unusually early. Goeller, who led Togo to all four of their appearances at the African Cup of Nations finals, quit before the Hawks' second group game against co-hosts Ghana.

Goeller blamed a lack of organisation by the Togolese Football Federation, which, he said, had hampered his side's preparation for the tournament. He is also said to have demanded salary arrears totaling US$15,000.

The German directed most of his anger at Federation President Gnassingbe Rock, son of the Togolese President, General Gnassingbe Eyadema. "On the day I left, I was fighting with my football federation president. He does nothing and has no idea of what the players need. I asked, where are the vitamins and the minerals, where are the carbohydrate drinks? They said 'Oh we forgot' and I became mad because we only have a few days' recovery between games."

Without Goeller on the bench, Togo was defeated 2-0 by Ghana, thereby losing any chance they had of going through to the next round. The Togolese officials blamed his absence on the bench during the defeat against Ghana on a bout of malaria, but when Goeller was seen leaving the team hotel in a taxi, he looked healthy and fit.

After the tournament had ended, bigger names than Goeller followed. Even Moroccan coach Henri Michel, who had been a successful international player with France before embarking on a similarly successful coaching career which saw him coach his native France before seeking fame and fortune in Africa, resigned shortly afterwards.

Michel, Goeller, Troussier and Sono were lucky. They only lost their jobs. Not so Brazilian coach Walter Da Silva, who nearly lost a lot more. I had come to know him quite well during his stints with various clubs in South Africa. He had come to the country as a player and could look back on a successful career on the field. His coaching career was less illustrious. In 1999, he was in charge of one of the most popular South African clubs, Moroka Swallows. It was a bad season for the club, and the fans called on management to get rid of Da Silva, without much success.

It was then that a group of fans decided that they would take matters into their own hands. On a match day, they waited for Da Silva in front of his house. As the coach got into his car to drive to the game, he was accosted by a group of gun-wielding men. They blindfolded him and he was driven around for several hours. Da Silva was only released, unharmed, once the match had finished. He was told that he should no longer return to the club. He resigned soon afterwards.

Zeca Marques took over from him. He managed to avoid relegation with Swallows and fans were looking forward to a better 2000/1 season. But instead of challenging for honours, Swallows were again in trouble at the wrong end of the table.

Matters came to a head after the team lost a home match against Celtic. A section of the crowd stayed behind after the game and hurled abuse at the coach as he was leaving the field. Marques and his players had to barricade themselves in the change-rooms to escape the mob.

But his troubles did not end there. Some 250 fans baying for Marques' blood converged in front of the change-room. They also confronted Swallows' chairman David Chabeli and told him to fire the unpopular Marques. When things were in danger of getting out of hand, security guards fired several shots into the air. It took some thirty minutes to free Marques and the players from the change-room.

Another coach I have come to know is German-born Reinhard Fabisch. The first time I met him was before South Africa's game against Zimbabwe in Harare in 1992. I had gone to watch Bafana train at the Harare Stadium. Zimbabwe had just finished their own training session and Fabisch was standing around watching South African coach Screamer Tshabalala. I approached Fabisch and asked him in German how his preparations for the match had gone. He told me that things were not looking very good for his side, as a number of promises that had been made to the players had not been kept.

"That is the worst thing that can happen to a coach in Africa. The players are very materialistic in their outlook. They have to be, as all of those who are still playing in Africa do so for very little money. It is not surprising that they want to make money out of playing for the national team. My players are still owed money from their last game, but now the association wants them to do well against South Africa. It is ridiculous."

I asked him whether there was anything he could do about it.

"It is something that I do not like doing, but I have to do it. I will have to give the association an ultimatum and tell them that the team is not going to play unless they receive a guarantee that their money will be paid. And even if they receive a guarantee, they might not accept it, as they no longer believe a word the officials say."

A few days later, I saw him again. He told me that the money matter had been sorted out and that the squad was going to visit Zimbabwean President Robert Mugabe on the morning before the match. He asked me if I wanted to come along, but as I was not sure how my fellow South African journalists were going to feel about me spending so much time with the opposition, I declined.

The visit must have been very inspirational. Zimbabwe completely outplayed the Bafana, the 4-1 score-line being a true reflection of the game! As soon as the referee blew his final whistle, thousands of fans rushed onto the field. They surrounded Fabisch. He was picked up and placed on the shoulders of a group of fans. They carried him around the stadium for close to thirty minutes and even when he had been put down, he could not leave, as there were still so many people wanting to shake his hand. He obviously loved it; his face glowed with joy.

I visited Fabisch again three years later. I was in Zimbabwe to cover a league match between Dynamos and Highlanders and he had offered to put me up for the duration of my visit. As I had already made arrangements to stay with some fellow journalists, I turned him down, but said that I would gladly visit him.

We agreed to meet at a five-a-side football match that he and some of the other expats living in Harare played every Friday afternoon at one of the private schools. Every week the group would meet after work and play for two hours. This usually created some interest amongst the workers at the school and the week I participated in the kick-about was no different.

Fabisch was not yet there by the time I had arrived and I told the others that I had been invited by Fabisch to play. I was assigned to one of the teams and told to play. The standard was not very high and I enjoyed myself thoroughly. I even managed to score a few goals. After a while Fabisch arrived and he joined the side I was playing against. He was not a bad player and his level of fitness made him stand out. After the game we had a quick beer, before he took me to his house.

He lived in a magnificent thatched-roofed house on the outskirts of Harare, which he shared with a dog. Two horses lived in the stables on the huge property. "Welcome to my little house," he said with a grin as I arrived.

"Not bad," I replied.

Fabisch looked back on a very undistinguished footballing career in Germany, having failed to break into the top league. At the end of his playing days, he had attended what is arguably the best coaching course in the world, the German FA coaching courses, and had qualified as a football trainer. This entitled him not only to coach a side, but also to teach coaches.

Armed with his certificates and diplomas, he had joined the Gesellschaft für technische Zusammenarbeit (GTZ). One of the areas in which this developmental agency operates, is on the sporting front. After conducting short coaching courses throughout the world, Fabisch was sent to Zimbabwe to help the country better itself on the football field.

The German developed an instant rapport with his players. Aided by the likes of a world-class goalkeeper, Bruce Grobbelaar, he took the national side to previously unknown heights.

The success he had with the team soon earned him the adoration of the success-starved fans and Fabisch became an instant hero in Zimbabwe. He was one of the most recognizable faces in the country and his popularity had increased with every victory.

I knew that he had many squabbles with the Zimbabwean FA and I asked him if he ever regretted having come to Africa.

"No, never. How could I? Just look at the way I am living here. Do you think I could live like that in Germany? I built this house a year ago. What more do I want? The people love me, the team is doing well and I am earning good money. I live as if I am the King of Africa. What more do I want? Yes, some of the officials are fools and they try to mess up everything, but they do not manage. I know that it is the players who are playing for me and if I treat them well and try to help them get somewhere, they will respect me and try their best."

"What about taking players overseas? Quite a few European coaches in Africa have been accused of doing that. What do you think about sending talented African players overseas?" I asked.

"I know that a few coaches have been doing that. I have no problems with that, even though I do not do it. African players need to go to Europe to reach their potential. Individually they can reach their potential, but as a team, there is still a lot that needs to be done in Africa. I know people have said that an African country will win the World Cup soon, but I can't see that happening unless the officials get their act together. They are all working for their own pocket. They are not interested in the sport."

I asked him how he saw his future; did he think that he was going to stay in Africa?

"I know that at the moment everybody thinks I am the king, because we are doing well. That will change tomorrow if we start losing matches. Then suddenly nobody will want to know me and everybody will scream 'Fabisch must go'. I am not married to the national team and I am not married to Zimbabwe. I like the place, though, and can easily imagine retiring here some time when I am finished coaching. I built the house for that. But I am sure that I will coach in quite a few more countries before that happens."

He told me that he thought the biggest problems facing coaches in Africa were officials. "I know there are many things that are difficult. Facilities are not good, accommodation is often below standard, the diet the players keep would get them fined if they played for a European club and they play for peanuts. But coaches could cope with all of that, were it not for the stupidity of some officials. They are killing the game in Africa."

We continued talking well into the night, before parting company.

I saw him a few times in the next two years. He continued having success with Zimbabwe, but his fights with officials became more and more public and frequent and after having failed to take the southern African country to the finals of the 1998 Nations Cup, his contract was not renewed. Officials also believed he was behind player demands for greater financial rewards.

He briefly took over the coaching reins at South African champion club Sundowns, before becoming national team coach of Kenya. His arrival in the East African country saw a brief revival of the fortunes of

Kenyan football. He assembled a youthful team whose average age was 22 years. The team played extremely well, winning against the likes of Gabon and Guinea while forcing draws away to Cameroon and at home to Nigeria. The team brought brief joy and hope to Kenyan football fans. Suddenly the whole country became football crazy and there were even calls to make him president.

But after a few defeats, the officials no longer tolerated his disputes with them and when the relationship became too strained, he resigned.

He subsequently coached a club somewhere in the Middle East before returning to the country where he was the king: Kenya. In December 2000, he was again appointed as technical director of Kenyan football.

Fabisch was by no means the only King of Africa that I had met. Another was a fellow German, Peter Schnittger, who was in charge of the Senegal national team at the 2000 Nations Cup finals in Ghana and Nigeria. Schnittger, who is considered as one of the true coaching kings in Africa, was born in Hamburg. He graduated from the Cologne Sports School and moved to Africa, where he has been working for over 30 years.

Some of the countries in which he coached included Côte d'Ivoire, Cameroon and Ethiopia. His greatest triumph came in the 1980s, when he took the Cameroon club side, Canon Yaounde, to victory in the African Champions Cup.

A few years ago, he was appointed as technical director of the Senegal Football Association, without being given the task of coaching the national team. But when Senegal lost 1-0 against African minnows Burundi in their first qualifying game for the 2000 African Nations Cup, Schnittger was asked to take over from dismissed national coach Amsata Fall.

Under his guidance, Senegal qualified for the finals, but not before Schnittger had nearly resigned in August 1999 after a dispute between the Senegalese government and the German authorities who sponsor his work in Dakar.

Going into the 2000 Nations Cup finals, Senegal were the distinct underdogs in a group featuring defending champions Egypt and the highly experienced Zambians, as well as the surprise package from the last tournament, Burkina Faso. Faced with such formidable opposition, the Lions of Senegal were expected to be among first-round casualties. In fact, many people believed that the only thing that stood between them and an early flight home was Schnittger.

They played their group games in the Nigerian city of Kano and by all accounts did much better than was expected of them. Their performances in the first two matches were so inspiring that a group of fans travelled all the way to the Nigerian capital of Lagos for their final group match against Zambia. After their side drew two-all to go through, there were wild celebrations in the stands and the Senegalese fans sang, 'Avec Peter jusqu'a la mort' (With Peter to the death).

Just how prophetic those words could have been, they probably did not realise at the time. The next game saw Senegal having to travel to Lagos for their quarter-final clash against co-hosts Nigeria. They took a surprise lead and held on to this until five minutes from the end, when Nigeria snatched a dramatic equaliser. The game then went into extra time. Here Nigeria scored again, causing their fans to run onto the field as they thought the golden goal rule applied. It did not and the game had to be halted for ten minutes while policemen were desperately trying to clear the field. One shudders to think what would have happened to the Senegalese players and Schnittger if the Lions had won.

If Schnittger and Fabisch are the Kings of Africa, then Rudi Gutendorf must be the King of the World.

I met him for the first time during one of my frequent visits to Mauritius. He had just taken over the coaching of the national team and as I had read and heard a lot about him, I was eager to do an interview.

As a player Gutendorf reached the 1948 German championship semi-finals with TuS Neuendorf. He then moved into coaching. Gutendorf had been a successful Bundesliga coach in Germany and is accredited as the man who brought Kevin Keegan to Hamburg. He is a FIFA instructor and had worked on all continents and in more countries than he could remember. At the time, he was listed in the Guinness Book of World Records as having the record for the most number of teams that he had coached. Since 1953, when he started coaching, he had been with over fifty clubs and national teams. I found out later that it was something that he was very proud of.

He lived in the best hotel on the island and I met him there. He suggested we go for a walk on the hotel grounds while we spoke. He told me he stayed in the hotel as they sponsored the local champions, Sunrise FC, and although he was employed by the Mauritian FA, he was also assisting them in their African Champions Cup campaign.

I asked him what had brought him to Mauritius, of all places.

HAS ANYBODY GOT A WHISTLE?

"It is the only country that I have not yet coached," he laughed. "No, seriously, I received an offer from the association and as I wanted to coach again, I accepted. During my three years in Japan, I earned so much money, that I no longer need to be at the beck and call of some club president who knows nothing. They loved me in Japan. I bought a Scottish forward for the club and he was close to two metres. So all we did was to pump high balls into the area. The Japanese were too small to mark him and we were champions two years running."

Gutendorf was excellent in telling stories. And having coached all over the world he had plenty of them. He told me that in 1973 he was national team coach in Chile. "I was very friendly with the president, Salvador Allende. Three days before Pinochet's bloody coup, Allende warned me that it was about to happen and suggested I leave the country, as I was known to be his friend and as such I would also be in danger. I just managed to get out in time.

'That was not the only time that I felt a bit anxious about a situation. In 1981, I was national coach of Tanzania and had to play Kenya in the Nations Cup qualifiers. My assistant came to me and said that 'the old men had decided that Aly would not be playing'. The old men were the witchdoctors and Aly was our best player. But Aly was withdrawn and I never saw him again. Possibly it had something to do with the fact that Aly himself was a witchdoctor and also took part in circumcision ceremonies. Some of the boys are said not to have survived these ceremonies.'

He told me that some of his best memories were of his time in Australia, where he had been national team coach and married a local woman. He had a young son. "I have made Australia my home and I will always return there. But if I receive an interesting offer from somewhere, I would be foolish not to look at it.

"Look at this place. It is like paradise. Beautiful crystal clear water, white beaches with palms. What more could anybody want? There is very little pressure on me, as nobody expects the island to suddenly become world-beaters."

Mauritius had been paired with South Africa in the qualifiers for the Nations Cup and I used the opportunity of my visit in Mauritius to write a few previews of Bafana's matches against the islanders. Gutendorf was under no illusion that South Africa would be easy pickings for his side. "Look at South Africa. They have several European-based professionals, I have one. They have everything they need to prepare for the match, I have very little. It would be foolish for me to expect to be able to produce a side that can beat the South Africans. I need to look at the Indian Ocean Island competition. That is where we need to do well. I hope to be able to win that."

We passed what looked like a wooden pub standing on the beach. Gutendorf smiled and told me to look behind the pub. There was nothing, it was merely a façade. "They use this for a television series that they shoot here. It is about a detective, I think it is called Tropical Heat. You see how good my life is? They even make movies in the place that I stay."

I knew the series. It was not particularly good, but I told Gutendorf that I understood what he meant.

"The only thing that I miss is my wife and child. That is the reason why I will not take a job for a long time. I can't take my son out of his school in Australia and put him into a school here. I might not stay a long time and it would be very disruptive to his life. Because of that, I have decided to come here alone."

It was probably a wise decision. As Gutendorf himself had predicted, his stay with Mauritius was indeed not very long. The island won the Indian Ocean championship and managed to hold Bafana to a more than credible goalless draw in South Africa. He left his little bit of paradise shortly afterwards and returned to Australia, no doubt only on route to somewhere else.

A few years later, as a 73-year-old, he took over the national team in Rwanda after being part of a benefit match for Rwandan war orphans. "How could I have said no?" he asked me when I saw him again.

Being national coach in the central African country might yet be the toughest job Gutendorf has faced. When he took over in 1999, the country was still reeling from the devastating civil war between the Hutu and Tutsi, during which close to a million people were killed. Money for football was not something that the country had and it made Gutendorf's job more difficult. For the first international in which he was in charge, he had to buy boots for the players.

But he remains optimistic. "Half in my team are Hutu and the other half are Tutsi. If a Hutu crosses the ball into the centre and a Tutsi scores, they will celebrate together. That gives me hope for the country."

He was not as hopeful for his first game against Côte d'Ivoire in a World Cup qualifier. "I have a team of amateurs; the Ivorians are all professionals. I do not expect much, though it will count in our favour that our field is like a vegetable patch. My players know where the ball will bounce."

Obviously his players knew where the ball was going to bounce, as a crowd of 16,000 saw his side come back from being a goal down to lead 2-1, before allowing the Ivorians a late equaliser. Gutendorf was happy though, as the two-all draw was a very good result.

Germans are, of course, not the only nationality that wants to become King of Africa. There are French, English, Italian, Russian, Dutch and even Danish coaches.

Dutch coaches seem to specialize in coaching Nigeria. In 1994, when the Super Eagles came within a few minutes of knocking out Italy at the World Cup in the USA, a Dutchman called Clemens Westerhof was in charge. Earlier that year he had won the Nations Cup with Nigeria. His assistant, Jo Bonfrere, who also came from Holland, later replaced Westerhof. Bonfrere made history with the Super Eagles when he coached them to a first-ever gold medal for Africa in football at the Olympics. What made the victory even more special for the Nigerians was that they beat both Brazil and Argentina on their way to the gold medal.

Both coaches have been followed by persistent rumours that they have been involved in transfers of players that they have coached. Former African Footballer of the Year, Victor Ikpeba, for instance, has said that his relationship with Westerhof soured somewhat when he refused to accept Westerhof's 'help' in arranging a transfer. Westerhof, however, maintains that he has never received any payment for such help.

After guiding Nigeria to the 1994 World Cup and taking them to the knockout stage in the USA, Westerhof resigned as national team coach. A few years later he was in charge of South African club Sundowns, but his stay there was short. He reappeared in Southern Africa in 1999 as national coach of Zimbabwe. The country had just been replaced as hosts for the 2000 Nations Cup final by Ghana and Nigeria, and Westerhof was employed to take the team through the play-offs with Eritrea and Senegal. Never before had Zimbabwe qualified for the finals of a continental competition and officials in the southern African country thought that Westerhof was the man to do it. He failed.

He was then given the task to take the national under-23 side to the Olympics and although one of the opponents was Nigeria, Zimbabwe seemed well on course to qualify. They were leading the group by three points with one game remaining. Defeat in Nigeria, however, cost them the ticket to Sydney and ultimately also cost Westerhof his job.

The Dutchman was hoping to take over the position as South African national team coach and left Zimbabwe. After interviewing Westerhof, the South African Football Association gave the national team job to somebody else instead. A furious Westerhof rejoined Sundowns and slapped a £500,000 lawsuit on SAFA, claiming breach of promise.

His stay with Sundowns was even shorter than the first time and four months after signing the contract, Westerhof was told that he had to choose between suing the association and coaching the club. When he said that he was not prepared to drop the lawsuit, he was fired. His first reaction to having been dismissed was to consider suing Sundowns for breach of contract.

Westerhof's former assistant, Jo Bonfrere, has also experienced the ups and downs of being national team coach in Africa. After taking over from Westerhof in 1995, he quit soon after, dissatisfied with his financial rewards and disillusioned with constant interference from various levels of authority, including the right honourable minister of sport.

The promise of leading Nigeria at the 1996 Atlanta Olympics proved too strong, however, and Bonfrere returned. He masterminded a thrilling semi-final victory over Brazil and then did the same against Argentina in the gold medal match.

Bonfrere could have returned to Lagos as King of Nigeria. Instead, he gave up fame for fortune when he signed a lucrative contract with footballing also-rans, Qatar.

Without Bonfrere the Nigerians managed to qualify for Sydney. Officials, however, were scared that the local coaches who had got them there would not be able to do the job and started looking around for a high-profile coach. Their attention soon turned to Bonfrere, who had taken them to their greatest triumph. A reported monthly salary of £22,000 helped convince him to return.

His return evoked mixed reactions. While for some, Bonfrere was the saviour, who was going to bring another gold medal to Nigeria, there were others who were not as pleased. One of the first things that the Dutchman did when he returned to Nigeria was to get rid of the two local coaches, Joe Erico and Bitrus Bewarang, who had taken the side within two matches of qualifying for Sydney. Bonfrere is said to have harboured a grudge against Erico since 1994, when the former national team coach was a member of Westerhof's technical staff at the Nations Cup. He received a gold medal after Nigeria's victory, while Bonfrere did not, as there were not enough.

A Nigerian journalist wrote at the time that 'the word "forgive" is almost non-existing in his dictionary. It doesn't matter who is involved or how long it takes, he always pays back.'

That was obviously something that Erico knew too, as in 1995, when jointly in charge of the senior national team with Stephan Keshi, he resigned after Bonfrere was appointed to supervise the duo. Erico said that the Dutchman did not want him.

After Nigeria's 1-4 defeat against Chile in the quarter-finals at the 2000 Olympics, Bonfrere said he did not believe his players had let him down. "I believe that when you work and you don't get paid, you will definitely get disappointed and when you continue asking to be paid you become a bad boy in the eyes of those in authority. If you do not pay the players £80,000 as they do in Spain or Italy but £4,000, there is a big difference.

"It is not only because of money, we must understand this; the players like to play for their country but also need rewards. Albania is much poorer than Nigeria. The monthly salary for their people is £65 a month. Albania defeated Greece and the President of that country rewarded the players with £8,000 each. If other countries can do this why did Nigeria not promise the players something extra to beat Chile?"

After Sydney, Bonfrere stayed in his position and continued serving the Nigerian FA as technical adviser in charge of the national teams until he was dismissed when Nigeria's 2002 World Cup qualifying campaign went off the rails.

Another coach who has been accused of lining his own pocket is former Peruvian international Augusto Palacios, who had a brief stint as national team coach in South Africa.

Shortly after Simon Kuper's book Football Against the Enemy was published, Palacios phoned me at the office of Soccer News, the monthly magazine where I worked at the time. Even though he has lived in South Africa for many, many years, he has retained an incredibly strong accent, which at times makes it difficult to understand him.

He always called himself by his surname. "Hello, Palacios here, I need to talk to you. I come now, OK."

"Yes, I am in the office, please feel free to pop by whenever it suits you."

Less than half an hour later he was sitting opposite me in my office. "I sue you," he said.

"What?"

"You say bad things about me, I sue you."

"Augusto, I have no idea what you are talking about...what are you talking about?"

"You know, the book, it says bad things about me. This book called Football and Enemy."

I had read Kuper's book and I knew what he was talking about. I had no intention of getting involved in a lengthy argument, so I did the only thing that I could: I lied. "I have not read the book, but I know the guy who wrote it, so I can contact him for you. I will ask him why he is saying things about you."

"So you did not speak to him and say bad things about me?"

"Yes, I did speak to him, but I said nothing bad. But as I said, I will contact the guy and find out."

Palacios must have been satisfied with that answer, as he left. I rushed home to find out what it was that had irked Palacios so much that he wanted to sue me.

Kuper had written that while Palacios was national coach, I had tried to help the Bafana captain Steve Komphela find a club in Europe. I had managed to get a Bundesliga club interested in him. Kuper went on to say, "Komphela was delighted, until Palacios called him in for a chat. The player was given to understand that unless he dropped Peter (in setting up the deal) and took Marcelo Houseman as his agent, he would be out of the squad, captain or not."

After reading what it was that Palacios objected to so vehemently,, I was not concerned at all. Firstly, I would argue 'truth and public benefit' and secondly, I doubted if Palacios was going to take the matter further.

He never did and I had very little to do with him for a few years.

I did, however, have something to do with another football official who tried his best at the art of 'gentle persuasion.' In 1999 a talented youngster moved in with my family. Brett Evans lived near Durban, but wanted to try becoming a professional player in Cape Town. As he was not yet 17, his parents asked me to take him in and look after him. My first step was to find him a club and I contacted John Comitis, who was a co-owner of Ajax Cape Town. An agreement was soon reached and Evans started playing for Ajax Cape Town. Even though he was still so young, he soon established himself in the first team and was called up into the South African under-20 and under-23 side. Everything was going smoothly, until January 2002. That was when Comitis approached Evans and suggested he sign a new contract as his old one was ending in November of that year. He offered Evans the princely sum of £250 per month! Not surprisingly, Evans' response was: "thanks, but no thanks." He then asked me to speak to Comitis on his behalf.

Comitis, who himself had played at the highest level but had not done so with much success, increased the offer by another £50 and then said that Evans would find that he suddenly failed to make the starting line-up if he did not accept the offer.

And this is exactly what happened. Evans, who was one of the best players in the team, was dropped and was benched. I knew that Comitis had done the same to other players, but two of those had persevered and had been allowed to go to other clubs.

Even though Evans knew this, I had a difficult task in keeping his spirit up. He received a tremendous boost though a week after his 20th birthday in March 2002, when he was called-up into the senior national team for a friendly international against Saudi Arabia. This was the big break for which he had been working for his whole life and for it to come a few months before the World Cup was an added bonus.

It was then that Comitis showed his true colours by telling the youngster that unless he signed a new contract, he would not be released for the national team. Legally, Comitis was entitled to do that, as the call-up had been sent to Ajax Cape Town two days after the stipulated deadline. All other players in the squad for the game against Saudi Arabia were in exactly the same situation, but none were denied the opportunity of playing in the national team. When Evans held firm, Comitis sent a letter to SAFA and informed them that they would not release the player, as they needed him. I doubt that he informed SAFA of the real reason!

I approached SAFA and told them of the blackmail attempts that Comitis was undertaking and they advised me to tell Evans that he should get on the flight, regardless of what the club said, as they were prepared to fight Evans' case. When Comitis realised that Evans was not going to give in to his threats, he told the youngster that he was willing to let him go if the player would merely state that he was committed to Ajax. Evans did this and was allowed to go with the national side. He came on to earn his first cap!

Not long before that, I also renewed my acquaintance with Palacios. He was coaching the South African under-20 side and working for a South African club called Orlando Pirates. I heard that he had been asked by an educational institution to do a coaching video. The institution also wanted to enter into an agreement with Orlando Pirates offering discounts for Pirates' fans wanting to enroll in the institution.

Palacios was willing to do both, but at a price! He wanted £50,000 to do the video, and £5,000 just to introduce the managing director to the relevant people at his club. He was promised the smaller amount after the meeting materialised, but his demands for the video were considered so excessive that they did not use him to make it.

He was obviously also still in the business of selling players, as a Zimbabwean striker, Tauya Mrewa, who plays for a club in South Africa, said that Palacios tried to arrange for him to join a top Turkish club, an offer that was declined.

Palacios resigned after only a few months as Bafana coach and took up a more lucrative position in Turkey, where he lasted for an even shorter period before returning to South Africa. His position as national team coach was taken over by Clive Barker, who stayed in the job for two years. After he left, Jomo Sono took over the coaching reins on an interim basis, before making way for a boyish-looking Frenchman called Philippe Troussier. The French coach was given the enormous task of preparing South Africa for their first-ever opportunity to participate in the finals of the World Cup.

Troussier took over at the end of the Nations Cup finals in Burkina Faso in 1998. There he had managed to take the hosts to a credible fourth place.

If many of the foreign coaches in Africa are considered - and consider themselves - as kings, Troussier had no such aspirations. He is known as the 'White Witchdoctor' and has had a 10-year coaching career in African countries, but his unpredictable behaviour saw him move from one state to another. In Côte d'Ivoire, he was dismissed after calling the sports minister a fool.

Troussier started his coaching career at the early age of 28, after an anonymous playing career in the French regional leagues. He was in charge of French minor-league clubs Red Star and Creteuil. From there he moved to Africa and spent four years in Côte d'Ivoire, where he coached the national team in 1993 and was in charge of top club Asec Abidjan for three years. During his three-year stay at Asec Abidjan he never lost a league game.

From Côte d'Ivoire, he moved to South Africa, where he was given the task of coaching glamour club Kaizer Chiefs. He left the country and the club after nine months after clashing with players and officials.

He moved to North Africa where he handled Credit Agricole and FUS of Rabat before Nigeria pulled him from obscurity back into the limelight. He helped the Super Eagles qualify for France '98. But Troussier's tactics, and his stand-offish attitude with various branches of the media, won him few friends among the impatient and demanding Nigerians and he lasted just six months in the job, being dismissed for not 'giving the team enough panache'.

Whatever that means, Troussier does not know. He has said that the situation in Nigeria was a very difficult one. "When I started the job, they paid me £20,000, which was three months' advance salary. From then on things were not going well. I was supposed to get my salary on a monthly basis, but the FA did not honour this. They owed me money up till the time I left, which left me with no choice than to report the matter to FIFA as they had breached the contract I signed with them.

"I think that only a cowboy can manage the Nigerian team. I have never been a coach to compromise on my principles. So when the FA said that I would have to subject my team selections to a technical committee, I knew I wasn't going to be there for much longer. Nigeria, with its pool of top class players in Europe, has a team that can win the World Cup. But without good administration, they will never do it."

That, coming from a Frenchman, was really something. But Troussier was not finished. "A lot of people in Nigeria said I was too small for the job, comparing me to Ruud Gullit, Arrigo Sacchi and Johan Cruyff. There is no doubt that these guys are bigger coaches than I am, but this, and the fact that I managed a second division team in Morocco (FUS Rabat) before taking up the Nigerian job, does not make me an incompetent manager. My players [in the Nigerian team] still keep in touch with me, which I am sure they would not do if I had nothing to offer them."

Arguably more so than any other foreign coach in Africa, Troussier has sought acceptance by the local population. He has adopted many African customs and traditions and his nickname of 'White Witchdoctor' was given to him for a reason.

Prior to leaving for the World Cup in France with the South African squad, he visited the former wife of South Africa's first post-Apartheid president, Winnie Mandela. Together, they slaughtered a cow for the ancestors, asking them for their blessings and guidance in France. As will be seen later though, the ancestors were obviously not satisfied with the quality of the meat, as Bafana's French excursion turned out to be a bit of a disaster. It also heralded the end of Troussier's reign as South African coach.

Troussier has certainly shown that he can achieve results, and perhaps the greatest testament to his wizardry was in leading unheralded Burkina Faso to the Nations Cup semi-finals in 1998 after just three months at the helm.

12

BATHED IN BLOOD

WHETHER TROUSSIER AND Burkina Faso used witchcraft or not, I will never know, although personally I think their initial success had more to do with dodgy referees than anything else. But it was not the first time that I had heard or seen something of muti.

In essence, muti is the belief that external forces - be they ancestors or witchcraft - can contribute towards giving a person or team extra power. Muti can be an actual object, or a ritual which has special powers that can contribute towards playing better or preventing an opponent from scoring.

The most bizarre muti story was told to me by Basil Hollister, who coached Chiltern Park, a club I played for while I lived in Durban. Hollister had been a lethal striker for a number of clubs, including Orlando Pirates and African Wanderers. Both clubs have a rich history and tradition and there is some rivalry between the two about which of them is the oldest professional club in the country. Both have always been very involved with muti.

In 1985 Hollister was winding down his career at African Wanderers. The club was not enjoying a particularly good season and was deep in the relegation zone. In the first round of the Mainstay Cup Competition they were drawn against Durban City, who were not only their city rivals, but were also riding the crest of a wave, perched near the top of the log.

The Wanderers management decided that they needed to do something drastic if the club were to stand any chance of winning. They devised a two-part plan.

Firstly, they told the team that they would have to 'camp' before the match. This, of course, is not an uncommon thing. All over the world professional clubs assemble their players the night before a match. Many clubs do this also for a home game. In Africa, one of the reasons why club camps are held is that club officials believe that unless the players stay together after a muti ritual has been performed, the powers that have been given to them could disappear.

In this case, Wanderers had decided that the Royal Hotel, which at the time was the best hotel in Durban, would be the venue. They wanted to treat the players to a good hotel to ensure that they go into the match fully prepared and in a good frame of mind.

The second part of the plan involved a muti ritual, which the club witchdoctor would perform at the same hotel.

Hollister remembers the incident vividly. "The witchdoctor, who was an important member of the team, probably just as important as the centre forward or the goalkeeper, made a fire on the floor in one of the rooms that the team had booked in the hotel. I could not believe it and looked at the other players, who seemed quite fine with the idea though. They thought there was nothing unusual about lighting a fire on the floor of a five star hotel! We were then told that we had to jump over the fire, run out of the room and jump into a bath in the neighbouring room, which the team had also booked.

"Even though I had been playing football in this league for a long time and knew that these things happened, I decided that I would rather go and see for myself what was going on in the room next door. Brummie De Leur, one of the few other white players in the team, and I decided to walk next door to have a look. The door was open and we looked into the bathroom. The bath was half-filled with a red liquid, that was obviously blood."

Hollister said that he looked at De Leur and shook his head. "This was a very tricky situation. There were less than a handful of white players in the team and we did not want to stand out, but at the same time, I could not see myself jumping into a bath filled with blood, even if it was 'only' ox-blood, as other members of the team assured me. I discussed the situation with Brummie and we decided that we would go to the club captain and say to him that we were comfortable jumping over the fire, we would gladly run into the next room and we would even go so far as to sprinkle some of the blood on us. But jump into the bath was not on."

Luckily for Hollister and De Leur, the witchdoctor said that it would be fine if they did as they suggested.

The ritual obviously worked, as in one of the biggest upsets in professional South African football, lowly African Wanderers beat the more fancied Durban City. The club went on to qualify for the final, which they played against Bloemfontein Celtic. By then the witchdoctor had been fired (the witchdoctor's fate, just like that of the coach, is intrinsically connected to results and a string of bad results will automatically put the witchdoctor, as well as the coach, under pressure) and Celtic won the game.

Wanderers are not the only club in Durban in which muti plays an important role. Another is AmaZulu, which traditionally is the club of the Zulu nation. The Zulus are one of several indigenous tribes in South Africa and are firm believers in tribal traditions and customs, of which muti and witchdoctors are an important part.

A love-hate relationship exists between former Bafana coach, Clive Barker, and AmaZulu. The Durban-born coach has been in charge of the Usuthu, as the club is also known, at regular intervals.

In 1974, AmaZulu made it to the final of the same Mainstay Cup, in which Hollister was involved eleven years later. Their opponents were Orlando Pirates.

The club chairman, Arthur Nxumalo, sat next to Barker on the plane to Johannesburg, where the final was to be played. Barker recalls that Nxumalo was very confident that AmaZulu would win in style. "He dipped into his pocket to bring out a small plastic container which held a fluid resembling olive oil. Inside the oil-like liquid was a piece of string, tied in eleven knots - one for each player in the team."

Nxumalo explained to Barker that he had been to visit AmaZulu's witchdoctor, who had instructed him to drive to the team's home ground and to dig in a certain area. This Nxumalo duly did and with the help of a couple of trusted supporters they dug a hole in the allocated place and found the piece of string in the container!

The team camped in Johannesburg the night before the final and on Saturday morning left for the game in a cavalcade.

All of a sudden, the lead car, in which Nxumalo was being transported, changed direction and they all followed it to an exclusive block of flats in the middle of white Johannesburg. As there were many 'Whites only' signs, the players and Barker climbed the eight flights of the fire escape stairs to the top of the building where they were introduced to another witchdoctor hunched over a primus stove with all his beads and regalia on.

He ordered the AmaZulu players to strip off their clothes and proceeded to prick them all over their bodies with a porcupine quill, which he kept dipping into a strong, mysterious potion. Only one startled and bemused player, Richard Ngubane, questioned this not unusual pre-match ritual.

Barker says that he, very politely, remonstrated with Nxumalo. "But he assured me that this was absolutely in the interests of AmaZulu. Eventually we got the players back into the cars and we made our way to a school building close to the Orlando Stadium. Nxumalo explained that it would be taboo for the players to change into their football gear in the same stadium as the opposition!

"Time was running out and to my great frustration we arrived at the steel gates of the stadium twenty minutes before kick off to find the gates locked! Everybody was inside already, except AmaZulu," Barker said.

Barker warmed up the players in the dusty car park amidst the music, barbeques and people consuming large quantities of alcohol!

"Nxumalo, very enterprisingly, found a stepladder, and in all his AmaZulu finery climbed to the top only to be met by three policemen demanding payment for entry to the grounds. Having gained admittance by paying his 'bribe' he found a league official and implored him to open the gates to enable the Mighty Usuthu to make their entrance. With the aid of Alsatian dogs and the police, we made our way onto the field at 3:20."

It seems though that AmaZulu's muti was not strong enough, as Pirates won by the only goal of the match!

There are those who would argue that Pirates' victory must itself have been secured by muti, as the club is known throughout South Africa as one where the use is widespread.

Former Bafana and Pirates player, Gavin Lane, who joined the club from Johannesburg-based Blackpool, recalls several incidents involving muti rituals. "In 1995, when we played in the African Champions Cup against BCC Lions in Nigeria, our midfielder Helman Mkhalele ran riot along the wing and they didn't have an answer to his penetrative runs.

"Then something strange, yet funny, happened. One of the opposition players sprinkled something at him in an off-the-ball incident. It appeared innocuous at the time but Helman started complaining of itchiness and it affected his performance badly."

Lane is not dismissive of the practice. "Muti is an age-old tradition and is widely used in Africa. There are stories of strange stuff in dressing-rooms. I've also taken part in jumping into baths full of strange stuff."

He said that he had witnessed the power of muti himself when he was treated by a witchdoctor after injuring his ankle four days before

Pirates' African Champions Cup semi-final against Express from Uganda.

"I had been ruled out of the match against Express by our coach, Joe Frickleton. The club took me to Soweto to a witchdoctor, who cut my ankle, then placed my foot into lukewarm water. He produced what looked like a wild cactus flower, heated it on the stove and gently rubbed it around the swollen ankle," recalls Lane.

"I managed to play that weekend."

He remembers a similar incident when he was still playing for Blackpool. "I damaged my ankle badly and one of the officials took me to a witchdoctor in Soweto. It was a wet, cold and overcast Sunday morning and the woman witchdoctor instructed the official to bring me back on Wednesday when the weather was expected to be sunny.

"When we arrived on the appointed day, the official purchased new razor blades which he produced. The witchdoctor made about ten or fifteen incisions on both sides of the ankle - nothing major - just small cuts where the swelling was. Then she produced a tennis ball split in half and kind of sucked the blood out of the wounds.

"And, believe me, thick, black blood clots oozed from the cuts. When we left the place, you could have knocked me down with a feather…the pain was gone."

Many years later, I was to witness another muti incident with AmaZulu. The magazine I was working for sent me to cover a match between them and Moroka Swallows. The game was of significance, because Swallows were at the time top of the table and a victory would have given them all but the championship. A defeat, on the other hand, would see Sundowns pipping them at the post. AmaZulu had little else to play for except their pride.

Throughout the first half Swallows bombarded the AmaZulu goalmouth with shots. They flew in fast and furious, from all angles, but all with the same effect: they did not hit the back of the net! Either the shots were hopelessly off target, or they would fly agonisingly close past the goals. If neither was the case, the goalkeeper, who played as if he was an octopus with eight arms and as many hands, would prevent the ball from crossing the line.

I was sitting in the press box with several colleagues and we all agreed that Swallows was doing everything that was necessary and expected from them, except score. We watched the agony that the substitutes and the coaching staff went through every time their teammates on the field yet again came close to scoring. They would jump up in anticipation of rushing on to the field to congratulate the scorer whenever their forwards came into the Usuthu goal-mouth.

We also saw them get increasingly frustrated as, time and again, their attempts proved futile. It was as if the AmaZulu goal was bewitched and try as they did, they could not score. We all agreed that never before had we seen a team be as dominant as Swallows in the first half but still go into the change-room at half-time goalless.

At the break the Swallows substitutes warmed up in the middle of the field. They were standing in a circle and passing the ball amongst each other. Their AmaZulu counterparts were shooting at one of the goals. They had obviously told the reserve keeper to stand between the poles and were now bombarding him with shots. Possibly they were also showing the Swallows substitutes how it should have been done, as the AmaZulu players had chosen the goal which their side had defended in the first half. Both sets of substitutes were being watched by the groups of security guards that were stationed around the field - a feature of all professional matches. They carried no guns (at least not visible ones), but were armed with knobkerries, pear-shaped sticks normally used as traditional weapons. A blow to the head can quite easily split the skull.

The Swallows substitutes appeared to be no better than the eleven players that had just played as more and more of their passes went astray. I noticed that the whole group was edging closer towards the goals into which their team would be trying to score after the break. The security men too, had noticed that the Swallows reserves were coming closer towards the goal and had moved closer themselves.

Suddenly, there was screaming on the field. The group of Swallows substitutes ran towards the goal AmaZulu would be defending after the break. At the same time the security men, now on full alert, also ran for the goal line.

But if the screaming and rushing towards the goals had been unexpected, the ensuing scramble was not only unexpected, it was also unbelievable. The Swallows substitutes had all turned into forwards and were trying to kick one of the three balls they had been warming up with into the goal. But the security guards got there first and the goal was guarded by five or six bulging men who were doing everything in their power to prevent the Swallows players from kicking the ball over the line. They were even using their knobkerries and hitting out at the ball!

Even though I had been covering football and football matches for close to fifteen years at the time, I had never seen anything like this. I was afraid that a full-scale battle would break out between the two groups. As the one side was armed with traditional weapons and had a weight advantage of at least 35 kilograms, there was no question in my mind who was going to win the war. My next thought turned to Mich D'Avray, the Swallows coach, who would not be able to use any of the substitutes if one of his players was injured during the game.

This fracas must have lasted close to five minutes, during which the Swallows players were unable to get the ball past the security guards who were defending the goal as if their lives depended on it. In the end it was a lucky shot from all of three metres distance that managed to beat the guards and cross the line.

I thought 'the goal' would bring as rapid a close to the conflict as its start. But I was mistaken. Yes, the Swallows players did turn around and walk back towards the centre line, but the guards did not go out of the goal. Far from it!

One of them retrieved the ball from the net. The others huddled around him. The guard holding the ball placed it on the ground, the others knelt down and made a circle around the ball. Suddenly I saw a knife flashing in the hand of one of the guards. Then another pulled out a knife and then another. They were stabbing the ball - slashing it in a frenzy! Now I had really seen everything! A ball being stabbed to death at half-time during a professional football match! What could I say?

I could say nothing, but at least I could find out what had happened. The Swallows players really believed that the AmaZulu goal was bewitched and that that was the reason why their team had not been able to score. They wanted the ball to cross the line during the interval in the hope that this would break the spell. The AmaZulu security guards, on the other hand, decided that by 'killing' the ball, they would prevent the muti that was working in favour of AmaZulu being rendered useless by Swallows kicking the ball over the line.

Looking back at the incident, it would appear that their belief was proved to be correct. The second half continued very much where the first had left off. Swallows pushed forward, created chances and bombarded the goal. The AmaZulu goalkeeper kept everything out. And as time ran away from them, the Swallows forwards were getting more and more frustrated.

Frustration turned to despair midway through the second half when

AmaZulu scored on the break. It must have been their only real chance in the game, but ultimately it cost Swallows the league title. They went down 1-0, while rivals Sundowns won their next league game, thereby winning the championship.

Six years later, in November 2000, very little had changed. Swallows were no longer trying to win the championship; they were desperate to fight off relegation. Things were not going particularly well with the club. They had only won one match so far during the course of the season and they needed three points to prevent them from slipping into the relegation zone. As a result, their league match against Ria Stars had become even more important. In many ways, it was a 'six-pointer', as Ria Stars was a newly promoted side and were themselves not too far off the pace at the wrong end of the table.

On the day of the match a good crowd turned out to see Swallows, but they were disappointed in the first half. Former Bafana striker, Thabang Lebese, had given a shock lead to Ria Stars and even though Swallows pushed forward in search of the deserved equaliser for the last ten minutes of the first half, the Stars goal seemed impenetrable.

Just before the referee was to blow the whistle for the start of the second half, one of the ball boys ran towards the Stars goal. He entered the visitors' goalmouth and ran towards the goal. Once there, he bent down. I am not sure if he placed or removed something from the goal-line.

Unfortunately for him, the Stars goalkeeper, Abram Khwenenyane, saw him. He was obviously not particularly impressed with what he saw and proceeded to chase the ball boy out of his area. With Khwenenyane chasing the ball boy around the field, FIFA referee Ian McLeod, who in 1998 was the first South African referee to officiate at the finals of the World Cup, decided to intervene. He sent the ball boy off the field and told Khwenenyane to return to his goal.

Swallows fans greeted the ball boy's departure with rapturous applause.

Three minutes after the incident, Swallows were back on level terms after one of their strikers had been sent through with a defence-splitting pass. He pounced on the ball and hammered it past Khwenenyane. The home side added a second ten minutes from the end to register only their second victory of the season.

Again, the story could have ended there, but it did not. After McLeod had blown the final whistle, Khwenenyane was seen to remove something from the goal-line he had been defending. Asked to explain what he had been doing, the goalkeeper said that he would not comment.

This practice with muti is not restricted to professional clubs in South Africa or on the continent; it is found at just about any level of football.

Promising South African Brett Evans played his first game in the elite league at the age of 17. Before that, he played for a team in his hometown, Pietermaritzburg. The club was called Mighty Parks and campaigned in the second division. It was a township-based club and drew the majority of its players from the rich reservoir of talent that is to be found in most of the townships throughout South Africa.

Evans was an exception. He is white. But even though rugby and cricket are recognised as the most important sporting codes for South Africa's white minority, a small number of youngsters, like Evans, occasionally opt to play a 'black sport' like football.

For a teenager the step from the tranquil surroundings of 'white' suburbia to the harsh reality of township living must be like stepping into a new and different world. But Evans mastered it. He even mastered the muti rituals his club performed before each match.

"We were given some powdery stuff to sprinkle in our boots and sometimes even on our heads. I had heard about muti and I asked what this stuff was for. They told me that it was not muti; it was merely something that would prevent the opponents' muti from being so powerful that we did not stand a chance to win the game. Looking back, it obviously was muti."

Evans went on to explain that if his side lost, the person who had given them the powder would have said that the opponents' muti had been too powerful to be prevented by his muti. "It was just something that happened before most of our matches and I think those of us for whom it was a new experience just got used to it."

Gordon Igesund played professional football in Austria and has coached both African Wanderers and Orlando Pirates. Both are clubs which are believed to be deeply involved in the practice of muti.

"As coach, I do not actively support the practice. I concentrate on preparing the players for the game and teaching them the tactics that I want them to play. Having said that though, I would be naive to think that nothing else goes on. I do not keep control over my players 24 hours a day."

BATHED IN BLOOD

Igesund is quick to castigate those who ridicule the muti ritual. "Many, many players, even those in Europe, have some form of ritual that makes them believe that they will play better, or score a goal or something like that. There are those who always put on the left boot before the right one, or those who insist on being the last one out of the change room.

"There are coaches in Europe who wear the same shirt after winning a match. What makes those things so much different from some of the things that are conducted during a muti session? Is it so much more rational, for instance, to go to the Pope before a match and ask him for a blessing? In a way asking the ancestors to do the same is very similar. I know it is difficult for people in Europe to understand, but they need to see it in the context of African culture, where the belief and practice in tribal and traditional witchcraft is widespread. If it is viewed in such a light, it is no longer so strange."

There have been several very strange incidents connected to muti rituals, though. The fear of some clubs to change in the stadium in which they are playing an away match has already been mentioned. The clubs fear that the home side has put some muti into the change rooms, which will ensure that the visitors lose.

Many would argue that this was taken a bit too far in 1992, during the final of the African Cup Winners Cup. The host side were Burundi's Vital 'O, their opponents Africa Sport from Cote d'Ivoire. Vital 'O put a huge snake into the visitors change room, hoping that this would not only frighten the Africa Sport players, it would also place a curse on them. The home side, however, obviously did not want to place all their bets on the snake, as they also broke a glass bottle filled with liquid at the entrance of the change rooms. As soon as it broke, a strange smell filled the room.

When the Africa Sport players arrived they took one look at the glass on the floor in front of their change room and turned around, refusing to risk injury by entering. They therefore never saw the snake and entered the field an 'uncursed' side. They held Vital 'O to a one-all draw and convincingly thrashed them 4-0 in Abidjan in the return leg two weeks later to win the cup.

Snakes are not the only creatures that are used for muti purposes. At a major game at FNB stadium in Johannesburg between the two most popular clubs in South Africa, Kaizer Chiefs and Orlando Pirates, a live black cat was once thrown at the Chiefs bench from the Pirates stand in the stadium. The fans hoped that this would bring bad luck to the Chiefs. As soon as the cat touched the ground, a Chiefs security man pounced on it and killed it in full view of some 30 000 people. The Chiefs man believed that by killing the cat he could ward off the spell that would otherwise befall his team.

The incident was captured on national television and the outcry afterwards was so huge that the security man was identified and prosecuted for cruelty to animals. He received a suspended sentence and was ordered to do community work.

In another professional match the goalkeeper noticed that he had difficulty in judging the bounce of the ball when it came close to the penalty spot. On closer examination, he found a fresh mound of sand and it was apparent that somebody had been digging in the ground. He informed the referee and started digging himself. After digging for a short while, he triumphantly held up an object that he had taken out of the ground. It was the severed head of a goat, which had been buried in the ground in the hope that it would bring bad luck to the visiting side.

Often goalkeepers bear the brunt of many of the muti rituals. I remember watching a game between Wits University and Kaizer Chiefs at Wits's ground a few years ago. The stadium was packed and even though it was Wits's home game, virtually all the fans in the stadium were Chiefs supporters.

South African national team goalkeeper, Steve Crowley, stood between the sticks for Wits and he was having an absolute blinder. As he thwarted more and more of the Chiefs attacks, a section of the crowd sitting immediately behind him became restless. They started murmuring amongst themselves. And as Crowley pulled off more breathtaking saves, the crowd was becoming louder. Now and then, one or two would break free from their seat and rush towards the fence that separated them from the field. They would point to something that was lying in Crowley's goal and then return to their seat. The situation became tenser as time was running out for Chiefs to score.

I, and I am sure most other neutral spectators and the handful of Wits fans, were becoming a bit nervous. I could sense that tension was not only in the air, it was rising rapidly.

The players could presumably feel it too, as one of the few black players who was playing for Wits at the time went to speak to Crowley. He told me later that the player had told him that the fans thought he carried muti in the small bag in which he had a second pair of gloves and which he had thrown into the back of the net - as he always did.

Crowley had the sense to turn around to the fans and show them the bag. He opened it and took out the gloves. Then he showed them the bag again and turned it inside out, showing that it was empty. The crowd were obviously satisfied knowing that Crowley was just a good goalkeeper and that it was not muti that was preventing their beloved Chiefs from scoring. In fact, a little later, Crowley joined Chiefs!

Muti remains one of the most controversial and taboo subjects of African football. But without it, South Africa might not have qualified for the World Cup finals in France in 1998!

13

HOW I HELPED BAFANA QUALIFY FOR FRANCE '98

AFTER THE DISASTER DURING THE WORLD CUP qualifiers for US '94, which saw South Africa lose against Nigeria's Super Eagles, the local association was more determined than ever to ensure that the country was one of the five that would represent the continent at the next finals in France in 1998.

This journey began promising enough. A 4-0 aggregate victory over two legs against Malawi in the preliminary round ensured South Africa a place in the final round, where the Bafana were grouped with Congo, the Democratic Republic of Congo (which at the time was still called Zaire) and Zambia. As none of the three countries were considered as major powerhouses in African football, South African fans were hoping for a first-ever appearance at the finals of the World Cup.

The first match was at home against Zaire and even though South Africa failed to impress, Chippa Masinga's late goal was good enough to earn three points. The next game was away to Zambia, who had not lost at home in a World Cup match since 1974. A goalless draw ensured that Zambia kept their proud record, but at the same time earned a valuable away point for Bafana. Equally important, it kept them at the top of the group with four points - tying with surprise team Congo, whom South Africa faced away in their next match.

The stadium in Pointe Noire held good memories for South Africa. The Bafana's first away victory was against Congo in Pointe Noire, in an African Cup qualifier six years earlier. Few in the travelling party believed that this time around would be any different.

I had travelled with the team in 1993 and did so again in April 1997. The first time around our first stop was Brazzaville, the capital of Congo, from where one had an incredible view of Kinshasa, the huge sprawling capital of the neighbouring Democratic Republic of Congo (DRC). Across the Congo River one could see the shanty towns, which were home to the hundreds of thousands who were living perilously close to the line that separated life from death in Africa. Not only did they have to contend with poverty and starvation, they had, starting some time around the beginning of the 1990s, also had to deal with political upheaval that had led to the worst possible kind of violence. Tens of thousands had decided to escape this despair by crossing the crocodile-infested Congo River seeking a new life in Congo.

And as the situation had not become much better in the four years since South Africa's first trip to Pointe Noire, I was quite happy to book myself on a charter plane that was to fly non-stop to Pointe Noire, rather than having to go via Brazzaville.

The South African team had been booked on the same plane. As usual, players were seated in the back, officials in the front. But as players were used to officials looking after themselves before looking after anyone else, it did not upset them. The mood in the squad - and therefore on the plane - was generally upbeat. The draw in Zambia had been a good result and coach Clive Barker was able to call on his strongest team, including the ever-increasing number of players who had signed lucrative contracts overseas. More importantly, however, the players had not only benefitted financially, their on-the-field performance had improved too and that made the Bafana a force to be reckoned with - at least in Africa.

The airport in Pointe Noire was tiny. A small building standing in the middle of nowhere. 'Bienvenue à Pointe Noire - Welcome to Pointe Noire' was written on the side of the building. The players were ushered through the passport control in no time. Journalists and the handful of fans that had made the trip took much longer. But in the end we, too, had been cleared, followed by the usual wait at the conveyor belt for luggage, which might or might not arrive. In this case it did arrive - in many instances during my footballing travels throughout Africa it did not.

The bus trip from the airport to downtown was short. Pointe Noire really was more like a small town than the second largest city in the Congo. The buildings, few of them higher than two or at the most three stories, were reasonably well kept and there was certainly not the kind of atmosphere of decay one sensed in many other large African cities.

We - that is, the journalists and fans - stayed in the Hotel Azur. Situated in the centre of town, there was nothing wrong with it. The rooms were clean, there was hot water in the shower and cable TV. One could really not ask for much more, or could one?

I had decided not to make my way to the first team training session, opting instead to walk around town. I therefore did not see for myself the training facilities that had been offered to the South Africans for their first training session. In continental competitions such as this, the host nation has to make fields and facilities available to the visiting side to enable them to train for the match. The Congolese had taken the South Africans to a field that had no grass, no goals and no change-rooms. The coaching staff had decided that they would rather not train than risk injury on such a field.

They returned to the hotel and after a quick inspection of the sur-roundings decided that they had found a more suitable venue than the 'official' training pitch: the hotel grounds. No sooner had the players returned to their rooms when they were summoned to the next training session, which took place in the garden behind the hotel. An outsider watching would have thought that it was a bunch of holidaymakers hav-ing a kick-about in front of their hotel. Admittedly, they were very ath-letic-looking holidaymakers, but the goals were still made out of track-suit tops and there were neither markings nor change-rooms. But at least there was grass!

That evening a few of the other journalists and I decided to put football aside and enjoy some of the nightlife Pointe Noire had to offer. Our first port of call was the Nganda Ku-Kel bar, which was just oppo-site the hotel. The glass on the floor as we entered suggested that it was not an establishment catering for the well-heeled. That was probably just as well, as anybody who has ever spent an evening in the company of a group of journalists will know that it is not for the faint hearted.

As Ngoks (as the local beer is called) flowed freely, we became more and more festive and engaged the locals in friendly banter. They were convinced that their side, the Diables Rouge or Red Devils, were going to win. We told them in turn that there was little chance of that hap-pening.

It was well past midnight that we left, but there was still plenty of nightlife to be enjoyed. In the Basar du Kouilou, which seemed to be at the centre of things, old men were sitting in small bistros, eating pois-son (fish) and safu (fruit) and playing draughts. They were smoking Fine and Sprint cigarettes.

We also saw the down-side of life in Pointe Noire. Next to the Fortunes Nightclub (which was closed) and where red and white strips on the windows promised riches, a group of hawkers were sleeping next to their tiny stalls. As a blanket they used a pagne, which is similar to a sarong. Not an easy life, I thought to myself.

We ended the evening in the Club Le Pieuvre dancing a local dance called Le Musepe. The dance floor was packed and huge speakers were vibrating from blaring music. The air was heavy with the smell of sweat, cigarettes and alcohol, but none of that seemed to discourage those swaying to the music. The only time they stood still was to salute, which seemed to be an important part of the Le Musepe. I never did find out whom it was that we were saluting, but we did so until the early hours of the morning, when we finally returned to our hotel.

The South African team management had decided to visit the local market with the players the next day. They hoped to woo some of the local fans by going where the locals went. It was - like many decisions taken by South African footballing officials - a decision that was to backfire. Just about everything could be bought in the Marche de Tie-Tie. Small wooden stalls selling food, clothing and curios lined narrow paths that were filled by locals and tourists alike. As Pointe Noire was hardly a favourite destination for tourists, locals far outnumbered the few backpackers that had lost their way to the city. And it seemed that each and every one of these locals wanted to be able to go home having touched a Bafana Bafana player. They were literally swamped and the expression on their faces by the time they had fought their way back to the bus clearly showed how relieved they were to have returned - unharmed - from the misguided public relations exercise.

But if things were bad in the morning, they got worse in the afternoon. International footballing regulations stipulate that visiting teams are allowed to conduct at least one training session on the field on which they are to play the match and the Bafana had decided to do this on the afternoon before the following day's kick off. Not wanting to miss this, I jumped into a taxi and followed the team bus that took the players, who had already changed, straight to the stadium. There an unbelievable sight greeted us.

Congolese soldiers, their semi-automatic weapons lying on the grass in front of them, prevented the players from entering the field. Heated arguments followed, which were probably worsened by the lack of anything but rudimentary French spoken by all members of the South African travelling party. As the arguments progressed, the situation became more and more tense. One of the members of the South African Football Association (SAFA) management team was Irvin Khoza, who, under normal circumstances, is quite a likeable fellow. But he is certainly no graduate of the South African diplomatic school and started screaming at the Idi Amin-type head soldier who was the only one willing to engage the South Africans in any form of communication.

"You have to let us train, it is a FIFA ruling," Khoza, who was obviously used to getting his own way, screamed at Idi Amin. He answered in French and judging by his facial expression and the tone of his voice, he did not regard the world controlling body as something important in his life.

"You people here are shit," Khoza went on. "We will complain to FIFA and we will get you kicked out of the World Cup." The situation was becoming ugly now and Khoza and Idi Amin were heading towards a shootout, which the khaki-clad soldier was obviously going to win, as he was the only one armed with a gun. It was at this stage that Danny Jordaan decided to intervene.

Jordaan was the exact opposite of Khoza. A former Member of Parliament for the ruling African National Congress, he had resigned from mainstream politics to become involved in the politics of football. He was the SAFA Chief Executive Officer and he obviously knew when to be diplomatic and when to use force. Not surprisingly, he realised that faced with a group of some twenty gun-wielding soldiers in a foreign land, the best approach would be a conciliatory one. He tried to pull Khoza away. Khoza, who has a reputation of having made plenty of money, the origins of which never surfaced, had obviously smelt blood, but was unaware of the fact that it was his own blood he had been smelling.

The former MP was not a man who gave up easily, and after a while he managed to get a fuming Khoza away. During this whole fracas, which lasted more than half an hour, the players were sitting in the stands. Those who already had some 'Africa' experience watched bemusedly while Khoza and Idi Amin screamed at each other. Those for whom the trip to Pointe Noire represented their first foray into Africa were more alarmed.

It was then that the football gods decided to end the stalemate before the dispute over the field had claimed its first victim. They sent an official of the Congolese association to the stadium and he managed to convince Idi Amin and his henchmen that, whether they liked it or not, Bafana were going to have to be allowed to train on the field.

It was obvious though that the coaching staff did not entirely trust the peace that prevailed and conducted only a very short session - barely long enough to give the players a feel of the field on which they were going to play an important World Cup qualifier the next day.

On match day, Bafana's problems continued. Although Idi Amin was nowhere to be seen, he had obviously sent his twin brother and it was now his job to make South Africa's life as difficult as possible. This time around it was not the field that the players were prevented from entering, it was the change-rooms that were out of bounds for the Bafana. Again, gun-wielding soldiers stood between the team and the place they would like to be. And given the intolerable heat in the stadium - it must have been close to 35 degrees centigrade, it was hardly surprising that the players were eager to get into the change-room as fast as possible.

Idi Amin's brother stood firm though, speaking in French which obviously was something along the lines of, 'No bloody chance at all, you will not get in here.'

Again, tempers were getting heated, voices became louder, but luckily for all concerned, Khoza was nowhere to be seen. Instead, Fannie Malope led the attack for South Africa. Now Fannie was not just anybody. Weighing at least 140 kilograms with muscles bulging from just about every part of his body, he was a policeman seconded to take charge of the security of Bafana Bafana. I am not exactly sure what his job entailed, but more often than not it was good enough that he just stood around and looked menacing. This normally resulted in previously shut doors opening rather miraculously.

Not so this time around. Even though Malope had a weight advantage of some thirty kilograms over Idi Amin's brother, the rifle the soldier cradled in his arms swung the pendulum back in his favour.

No pleading seemed to work and again the players had to stand around while South African officials and Congolese soldiers shouted obscenities at each other. This continued for twenty minutes and the players looked more and more uncomfortable.

It was probably the look in the eyes of George Koumantarakis that made Malope decide on the path he took. Koumantarakis was a relatively unique phenomenon in South African football: not only was he in his final year at university studying towards a law degree, he was also white. He was a tall lanky striker, similar to the former Arsenal player Alan Smith, and had been banging in goals for his club, Manning Rangers. Even though he was not popular with the fans (which, in

HAS ANYBODY GOT A WHISTLE?

South Africa, is often a prerequisite for a successful career in the national team), he had been called up for national duty. But this was obviously his first trip into 'darkest Africa' and the fear in his eyes showed quite clearly that it was not something that he would like to repeat soon.

Malope must have taken pity on the youngster, because he looked at Idi Amin's brother, pushed him aside and entered the change-rooms. Before the soldiers had realised what had happened, Malope was out again, a white bench under his huge arms. He placed it on the floor in front of the players and told them to sit down. He then fetched another bench and another, until all of the players had a place to sit. The team then changed into their strip.

When the players finally made the field, the intimidation continued, as the capacity crowd in the Stade Municipal made them feel very unwelcome, which they probably were.

South Africa started slowly. As attack after attack from the Red Devils rolled towards the South African goal, it soon became apparent that it was going to be one hell of an afternoon. Things got worse midway through the first half when Mark Fish, who is one of South Africa's best defenders and at the time was playing in Italy's Serie A with Lazio, had to be taken off with a bad cut above his eye.

Even though Bafana managed to go into the change-rooms goalless, they were clearly a side under pressure. This pressure mounted when the Congolese coach, David Memy, brought on German-based Macchambes Younga-Mouhani in the second half. Younga-Mouhani, who had only arrived in Pointe Noire that morning from Germany, was obviously the local hero as the crowd erupted the minute he started warming up.

The crowd went absolutely wild a few minutes later when Younga-Mouhani, who had just entered the field of play, opened the scoring for the home side. After adding a second four minutes later, he could do no wrong and his every touch of the ball was cheered. South Africa had very little to offer in terms of coming back into the game and when the referee blew the final whistle, one could see that most of the players were happy to just get off the field and back to South Africa as soon as possible.

The defeat put Bafana under tremendous pressure, as they were trailing Congo by three points and still had a difficult away match in Zaire to play.

It was thus clear that the game against Zaire was going to be one of the most important in South Africa's short international footballing history. A defeat would end all hopes South Africa had of making it to France.

Zaire had gained independence in June 1960, when it was still known as Congo. Patrice Lumumba of the Congolese National Movement served as the new country's first premier. He chose Joseph Desire Mobutu as his private secretary and soon afterward named him chief of staff of the army. In September 1960, Mobutu intervened militarily, deposing Lumumba, who was murdered the following year. Evidence later emerged implicating Mobutu and the U.S. Central Intelligence Agency (CIA) in Lumumba's death.

In 1965, Mobutu seized power permanently, declaring himself president. In 1971, he changed the name of the country, its major river and its currency to Zaire. He decreed that all European names were banned along with western-style suits and ties. He changed his name to Mobutu Sese Seko Kuku Ngbendu wa za Banga (officially translated as 'the all-powerful warrior who, because of his endurance and inflexible will to win, will go from conquest to conquest leaving fire in his wake.').

Zaire is one of Africa's most resource-rich countries. Gold, diamonds and precious minerals such as uranium are plentiful. Yet, the average Zairian income is no more than £120 a year.

Not so for Mobutu. Reportedly stealing billions of dollars from export earnings and Western aid, officials of the International Monetary Fund are said to have estimated that his personal fortune had peaked at £2.5 billion in the mid-1980s. He owned palaces and luxury residences in Zaire, Morocco, South Africa, France, Belgium, Switzerland, Spain and Portugal. A wine collection at his castle in Portugal was worth an estimated £1.6 million.

Mobutu himself once gave an indication where his huge fortune came from when he told citizens at a public rally, 'Go ahead and steal, but don't steal too much, or you will get caught.' So everybody stole. Zaire was an unofficial 'kleptocracy,' where soldiers looted, policemen mugged and hospital nurses would not admit patients without a bribe.

He stayed in power by sharing the wealth with his political allies and controlling their access to sources of government revenue. However, political rivals whom Mobutu regarded as a threat were often executed or murdered.

It was clear, however, that changes throughout the world would not go unnoticed in Mobutu's personal fiefdom, and by the mid 1990s the people of Zaire had decided that they had had enough. A bitter civil war ensued and it was this instability that had forced FIFA to instruct the Zairian association to move the match to another country. They had chosen Togo and in April 1997 we all boarded a flight to Togo's capital city, Lome.

Lome was once described as the pearl of West Africa. However, that was before political turmoil in the country during the 1990s had reduced Togo from a favourite destination for tourists to a country that was best avoided during a trip to Africa.

We stayed in the Hotel du 2 Fevrier, which was centrally located. It was within easy walking distance of the national stadium in which Bafana was to play. Independence Square and the Museum & Palais de Congres, were also close by. The latter was previously the headquarters of the political party of Togo's despotic ruler, President Major-General Gnassingbe Eyadema.

As Eyadema, who had come to power in a bloodless coup in 1967, had then spilt plenty of blood in an attempt to stay in power, I decided to steer clear of his former headquarters, restricting my sightseeing to a walk to the Place de I'Independence. Eyadema had put up a gilded bronze statue of himself with his mother there, but in 1991 during riots in Togo, the statue, which had been carved by North Koreans, was pulled down.

Togo is best known as the home of voodoo. From there slaves who were taken from Africa to other countries introduced it all over the world. In Lome there is a special market dedicated only to the sale of items that one needs for this practice. The Marche des Feticheurs (fetish market) is a few kilometres from the city centre in an area called Akodessewa. There one could immediately see that animals had a particularly difficult time in Togo. In the market they sold monkey and bird skulls, porcupine skin, warthog teeth and all kinds of bones. The fetish priests (also called juju men) would flock to this market to buy these goods to use them in their voodoo rituals.

I had travelled to Togo with a colleague, Julian Drew, and we had decided to share a room to keep costs down. During one of his frequent walks into the city, he had met a young Togolese who had struck up a conversation with him. He had asked Julian if he was from South Africa and connected to the football team. Julian replied yes to both questions.

The youngster, who had introduced himself as Hubert Polo, said that he could help Bafana reach France. This, of course, had grabbed Julian's attention as he realised that Bafana needed all the help they could get. Hubert said he knew that Zaire was using juju to secure a victory against the South Africans and unless Bafana did the same, they would lose.

Julian said that he was very interested and would discuss it with somebody else. He asked Hubert if he could come to the hotel the next day to see what could be done.

After returning to the hotel, Julian spoke to me about his strange meeting. He was more convinced than I that Hubert was for real and could help South Africa.

He told me that I should be less critical. "After all, what is there to lose? We all know that the game is very tough and we are in Africa. Such things not only exist here, they also work. I know!"

Of course, I wondered how he knew. I certainly could have told him what we had to lose - pictures of my hands and head being sold somewhere on the Marche des Feticheurs came to mind. But I pushed that aside and said that I was willing to give it a try.

Early the next morning, Hubert arrived at the hotel. He came to our room and said that he had spoken to a juju priest and he was willing to help us. He added that the priest was expecting us and we should not keep him waiting too long.

Julian and I looked at each other. I shrugged my shoulders, but then said that we should go and try it out.

Hubert had obviously expected that answer. When we arrived at the entrance to the hotel, he already had a taxi waiting for us. We drove down so many side roads that I was certain I would never find my way back to the hotel.

After about twenty minutes, the taxi stopped in front of a huge white wall. A door, big enough for two cars to go through, stood open and as we entered, I saw that it was like a compound. On either side of the entrance there was a long row of rooms - there must have been at least three rooms on each side - and straight ahead, there were another two rooms as well as one that was slightly separate from the other two. A group of small children was playing in the sand in the middle of the compound and two or three women were sitting around a small fire that was burning next to where the children were playing. A dozen or so chickens were running around.

Hubert took us to one of the rooms at the top end of the compound and asked us to enter. It was pretty dark inside, which was hardly surprising as the only light came from a small paraffin lamp that stood on top of a wooden table. We sat down on a rickety bench and waited. Hubert told us that his brother, who was the one we needed to speak to, would be with us soon. 'Soon' turned out to be a much longer wait than anticipated and only after an hour or more had passed did Epiphani Komi Polo enter the room.

As Epiphani was a juju priest, I had expected him to arrive dressed in spectacular robes. It was nothing like that though and the blue jeans he was wearing looked as if they needed a good wash.

Hubert must have been reading my mind, as he started telling us about his brother, who spoke not a word of English. Epiphani was not just anybody. He was, Hubert assured us, considered one of the top juju priests in Togo and had been entrusted with bringing success to the Togolese football team. I became worried, as Togo was not exactly an African-beater, let alone a world-beater. In fact, a World Cup qualifier between South Africa and Zaire was probably as close as they were ever going to get to the world's greatest sporting event.

Hubert proudly told us that Epiphani had travelled with the Togolese team to Zimbabwe three months earlier for their World Cup qualifier. After 49 minutes the home team had been leading 3-0 and by all accounts they had then relaxed and sat back easily holding the score until the end. But Hubert told us that it had nothing to do with the Zimbabweans holding back. "It was my brother. He was good. Without him, Zimbabwe would have scored six or even more."

I wanted to believe him and as nothing but a victory for Bafana would do, I had very little else to believe. Having supported clubs like Werder Bremen in the Bundesliga and Santos in South Africa, I had come to accept that winning a football match was far too important an event to leave it completely in the hands (or should I say feet) of eleven players. And thus, somewhat reluctantly, I decided that it was going to have to be Epiphani who was going to take us to France.

Hubert conducted negotiations for us. It soon became apparent that it was not simply a case of a quick prayer and South Africa was going to win 4-0. Hubert, who had become our confidante and therefore a pivotal part of South Africa's attempts to reach France, was engaged in very serious discussions on our behalf. We sat there, not understanding a word. Now and then he would turn to us and tell us in English he was just telling his brother what it was that we wanted.

Negotiations took longer than anybody expected. An hour later we were still sitting on our wooden bench, while Hubert and Epiphani were chatting away. They had been joined by another man, whom Hubert assured us was also a juju priest but not as high-ranking as his brother. He was introduced as Kuma. As it was getting dark, I was a bit worried that things were not going as fast as they should.

Again, it was as if Hubert could read my mind, as he said that we could now go. "We must come back tomorrow and then everything will be sorted out. My brother has asked the High God Mawu, the ancestors and trowo, who are intermediaries of Mawu to help. They have agreed and they will help South Africa and you will beat Zaire," he said.

"Thank you very much, we appreciate that," I said as I got up, thinking that matters had been settled for the day.

Hubert and the two juju men made no attempts to get up and looked expectantly at me. I, in turn, looked expectantly at Julian.

Sensing that neither Julian nor I had any idea why they were not all getting up, Hubert told us that the ancestors needed a gift from us before we left.

"What kind of a gift?" Julian inquired.

"The best thing is money," Hubert answered. The ancestors obviously also held little faith in the African economy as he added that American dollars would be much better than the local currency, CFA.

We went through our pockets and together managed to come up with some US$100. For journalists like us, who were not on huge expense accounts, that was quite a bit of money and as I could hardly go to my publisher and tell him that I had spent US$100 on a juju man, I realised that I would have to cough it up myself. But then 100 dollars was a small price to pay for something as important as World Cup qualification and we gave Epiphani the money. He took it, his face remaining as expressionless as it had been during the entire time we spent in his company.

Having finished our business for the day, Hubert organised us a taxi and we returned to our hotel - content with the knowledge that South Africa's participation in France was guaranteed, without having to rely on such unreliable activities as 90 minutes of football.

Hubert fetched us early on Friday morning and took us to the same compound. We entered the room and sat down on the same rickety bench that we had sat on the day before. And then we waited. And waited. And then we waited just a little bit more. This time around we must have sat there for at least two hours before Epiphani arrived, again accompanied by Kuma.

They sat down in front of us and started talking among themselves. Hubert joined the conversation.

After a while he looked at us and said we should wait while they prepared everything. Epiphani left the room, but returned a few minutes later. He had a wooden sculpture and some string in his hands. He sat down and started talking to the other juju priest. Hubert turned to us and said that the sculpture - which looked just like a wooden doll - would help us win the match. He asked us what score we wanted and told us that we needed to give him the names of some of the Zairian players who were likely to play in the match.

Julian - greedy as ever - said 3-0. I looked at him and said that 2-1 would be fine, as we also wanted to see an exciting match. On the issue of the names we had no disagreement. He suggested Botende Eshele, a goalkeeper who had spent some seasons playing in South Africa before going AWOL from his club. He had reappeared in goals for the Zairian national team. I came up with Michel Dinzey. He was one of an increasing number of players born in Europe of African parents, who were then co-opted to play international football for the country in which their parents had been born. He had been born in Germany, played in the Bundesliga, and spoke neither French nor any local Zairian dialect. I had interviewed him a year earlier during the Nations Cup and now felt a bit guilty giving Epiphani his name. The other player we felt confident would be in the starting line up was Emeka Mamale. He, too, had played in South Africa.

Once Epiphani had the names, he started winding the string around the doll, spitting at it each time he mentioned one of the players. Emeka Mamale swish, Botende Eshele swish, Michel Dinzey swish, Emeka Mamale swish, Botende Eshele swish, Michel Dinzey swish, all the time winding the string around the doll. It was as if he was chanting himself into a trance-like state.

While Julian and I sat silently, watching in amazement as Epiphani was preparing the doll, the other juju priest was chanting something else. This went on for some twenty minutes.

When they were finished, the two priests left the room and Hubert told us that they needed some chicken. "That should not be too much of a problem," I thought to myself, "after all, there were plenty of chickens running around in the yard."

But Hubert got up and followed his brother. Julian and I looked at each other and then we followed Hubert.

Epiphani was sitting on a bench in front of one of the rooms. A few metres from him at least half a dozen chickens were pecking in the sand, unaware of the danger that I thought they were in. They obviously knew something that I did not know, as Hubert turned to us and said that he needed some money to fetch the chickens.

We pointed at the chickens that were in the yard and looked at Hubert. "No, my brother needs special chickens, we can't take those."

I asked Hubert how much money he needed. "How much have you got?"

Julian and I dug deep into our pockets and came up with another US$50. We showed it to Hubert and he took it. "That should be enough," he said. "You wait here, I will be back soon." And with that he left the compound.

Having played the waiting game long enough the day before, I had come well prepared this time around. I had brought a trashy novel! I sat down in the shade of a tree and started to read. It was nothing earth-shattering, but reading helped to pass the time and was certainly much better than sitting around doing nothing. And just as well that I had brought it. The wait turned out to be even longer than I had anticipated - which seemed rather strange given the fact that everywhere one looked in Lome a bunch of good-looking, healthy chickens scrounged around in the dirt. Hubert was obviously looking for a very special kind of chicken, which he must have found a good few hours later, as it was past midday when he finally returned.

"We have got everything now," he said, clutching four chickens under his arm. They were still very much alive and were making their disapproval of being stuck under his arm apparent by emitting piercing screams. They tried scratching too, but as their feet were tied together, they were unable to do so. "Please come with me," Hubert said.

This time we did not go into the room in which we had conducted all previous consultations. Instead, we went into the room at the top of the compound that was slightly separate from all others. It was even darker than the previous one and filled with all sorts of artefacts, including what looked like an altar in one corner. Epiphani and Kuma were already in the room and I noticed the wooden doll that they had prepared the day before standing on the floor.

Hubert beckoned us to sit on a bench against a window and we sat

173

down. He gave Epiphani the chicken and sat down next to us. His brother took the chicken and threw them on the ground in front of the altar. He and Kuma turned their backs to us and faced the altar and started talking to each other. Their voices were soft and monotonous. We watched spellbound, not daring to say anything. After a short while they turned around. Epiphani was holding a huge knife in his hand, the blade glistening in the light of the candle. Kuma had the wooden doll in his hand and placed it next to the chickens, two of which he picked up. He took them back to the altar and threw them on the ground in front of it. Epiphani picked one up and turned towards the wall, the knife still in his other hand. He pressed the body of the chicken between his chest and his arm and placed his hand around its head. Then he bent the neck backwards and with the other hand made one clean cut across the neck. He moved to the centre of the room and held the chicken over the doll.

I expected blood to come spurting out. It did not; instead only a few drops trickled out, which he sprinkled on the doll. The chicken struggled under his grip, but he held it firmly, not allowing it to move. After a few minutes it stopped struggling and he threw its lifeless body on the ground next to the other two. He turned towards the altar and fetched the second one, which was still lying there. It suffered the same fate as its predecessor. Neck pulled back, a quick turn of the wrist, blade cutting across the neck and blood dripping.

When Epiphani had finished with both, he and Kuma started talking again. This time it was more like a repetitive chant. They knelt down in front of the doll. Epiphani lit a match. He moved his hand with the match down towards the head of the doll. There was a sudden flash and smoke filled the room.

Julian and I looked at each other, unsure of what was going to happen next. Epiphani and Kuma continued chanting, Hubert watched them motionless. After a while, Epiphani took the wooden doll and went outside. Hubert told us to follow.

Epiphani took the doll and walked to a second fire that was by now burning in the courtyard. He sat down on a small rock by its side and placed the doll next to the fire, his rhythmic chanting continuing as he did so.

We watched some wood in the fire go up in flames. Once it had been burnt to ashes, Epiphani scooped up some of the hot ashes and walked back to the room in which the initial offering to the ancestors had been made. Again we followed.

"The ancestors said that you have to put the ash into the boots of the players and then your team will win," Hubert explained to us as we were again sitting on our bench.

We looked at each other. I am sure Julian and I had a similar picture in our minds. That of going to ask a seasoned European-based player like Lucas Radebe, who, after all, was the captain of English Premier League club Leeds United at the time, whether he would have a problem with us sprinkling ashes into his boots before an all-important World Cup qualifier. I thought I knew what his answer was going to be and rather than risk myself being labelled as a mad-cap journalist, I asked Hubert to ask his brother to ask the ancestors, whether it would be good enough to merely sprinkle ash on the boots of the players before the match. Hubert translated for his brother, who in turn asked the ancestors. Their reply was - Hubert assured us - positive and Epiphani sprinkled some of the ash into a small piece of cloth for us and gave it to me.

Hubert said that he would meet us the next day at the hotel with the doll and that we would have to ensure that he was allowed onto the pitch to make sure that the spell worked. Not quite sure of how we were going to make all of this happen, we returned to the hotel.

Luckily for us - and, of course, if unbeknown to the Bafana - we devised a plan. Being a football journalist in South Africa is very different from being one in Europe. Most African players, regardless of whether or not they play in Europe or are still playing in the domestic leagues, remain just as much the friendly guy from next door that most of them were before they started earning their living by kicking a ball around. It was not at all uncommon to see journalists enter the change-rooms, even before a big match. I was just going to linger around the South African dressing room before the kick off and then sprinkle some of the powder on the boots as the players came out.

To get Hubert onto the field was going to be a bit more difficult, but there, too, we came up with something. We were just going to make him into a photographer for the day! Julian approached one of the South African officials and managed to secure another photographer's pass, which would enable him to sit behind the Zairian goal during the match.

Together we made our way to the stadium.

It was Julian's task to make sure that Hubert was well positioned, while it was mine to ensure that the players' boots received the proper preparation to ensure a South African victory. We managed to successfully complete both tasks. Julian ensured that Hubert stood as close to the Zairian goal as was possible, while I stood in front of the South African dressing room. As the players came out, I knelt in front of the door and sprinkled some of the powder on their boots as they made their way to the field. Luckily for me, they were far too psyched-up to notice what I was doing.

The ancestors were obviously happy with what we had done, as South Africa surged forward from the first whistle. Urged on by the local Togolese fans, Bafana mounted attack after attack against Eshele Botende's goal. After only twenty-one minutes they broke the deadlock. Doctor Khumalo, who was possibly South Africa's best known player, latched onto a cross and slammed the ball into the back of the net. Confident that Bafana were well on their way to victory, I sat back to enjoy the game. Unfortunately, I had forgotten that I had told the ancestors that Zaire, too, could score a goal and within five minutes they had drawn level through Zico Tumba. Even though South Africa enjoyed the majority of play for the rest of the first half, the sides went into the change-rooms a goal apiece.

I was a worried man. During the interval I went to Julian who was standing next to Hubert. I looked at Hubert. "Are you sure this is going to be OK?" I asked.

"Not to worry, everything is right," he said.

The second half began as the first, South Africa piling on the pressure and again breaking the deadlock after twenty-one minutes. This time around it was Italian-based Chippa Masinga who did the damage, scoring his second goal of the qualifying rounds. The ancestors were back in favour!

Zaire knew that a defeat would end any hopes they had of making it to the finals for the second time since 1974 and it was now their turn to go forward. But the ancestors stood firm. Bafana's defence was as solid as a rock and withstood even the most promising attack. However, with a minute to go, a Zairian forward broke through the defence and raced towards goalkeeper Andre Arendse. He struck a fierce shot that easily beat Arendse who had come out to meet him. The ball rocketed towards the South African goal and...hit the upright and bounced back into play. Shortly afterwards, referee Emmanuel Dada Obafemi from Nigeria blew the final whistle and the South African players started celebrating.

In a post-match interview Clive Barker, the South African coach, said that he was happy with his side's performance. "But I must admit that we were a little bit lucky. And when your opponents hit the post with only a few minutes to go, then you know that somebody is on your side."

I smiled when I heard him say that and wondered if he knew something.

Julian and I decided to return to Epiphani and thank him personally. We convinced Danny Jordaan, who headed the SAFA delegation in Togo, to accompany us. The four of us - Hubert was with us - drove to the house and went to sit in the room in which the ritual had taken place.

Jordaan, who had been briefed by us on the way, opened the conversation. He thanked Epiphani for having helped us with the victory and asked him to pass South Africa's thanks on to the ancestors. Familiar with customs all over Africa, he pulled his wallet out of his pocket and gave Hubert US$200 to pass on to his brother.

His brother took the money, turned to Kuma and spoke to him. Then he looked at Hubert and told him something. He looked at us and said that the ancestors had told Epiphani that they were happy that South Africa had won, but they were not happy with the offering they had received.

"That is all we can give at the moment," Jordaan said. "If South Africa qualify for France, I will gladly pay more."

Once Hubert had translated, Epiphani made it known in no uncertain terms that he was not particularly pleased with the explanation. He and Jordaan continued arguing for quite some time before Jordaan looked at Julian and myself and said that it was time to leave now, as he still wanted to get back to the hotel in time for dinner.

The ancestors could not have been too upset about the offering, as they did not prevent South Africa from beating Zambia 3-0 in Johannesburg in the next game. The victory ensured South Africa top place in the group and all they needed to qualify for France was a draw in their final match at home against Congo.

Again it was Masinga who got the all-important goal. His long-range shot in the second half, which gave South Africa a historic 1-0 victory, caused wild celebrations all over South Africa. Bafana were on their way to France!

14

EARLY EXIT

HAVING PLAYED A PART in helping Bafana reach the World Cup finals in France, I had made my World Cup plans. I was determined to be at their opening match against the hosts France in Marseillé on 12 June 1998. The idea was that I would leave a week or two before the match to be with the team for their final preparations. That, at least, was the plan as it stood on the day in September 1997 when my wife Andrea said she needed to talk to me.

"Sure, what about?"

"I've got something to tell you, I am pregnant."

I was ecstatic, over the moon and jumped up and hugged her. "That's wonderful, well done. That's the best news I have had for a long, long time. When?"

"Sometime at the end of May," she said.

"But what if it is a little bit late, what then?"

"Then it is late, that's not a problem" she replied, not knowing about my World Cup plans. I decided that it was probably not the best time to talk about them. It might spoil the moment.

What was important, though, was to ensure that South Africa did as well as they could at the World Cup. And for that, they needed a strong team. One of the weak links in the team was the goalkeeper. One of the best South African goalkeepers, Andre Arendse, had gone to England and signed with Fulham, where he had not made enough of an impression to command a regular place. He was then handed on to Oxford. There, too, he spent most of his time on the bench. Locally, the best goalkeeper was a youngster who played for Kaizer Chiefs, but he lacked the experience necessary to compete at this level. Something needed to be done.

I had read somewhere that a South African-born goalkeeper called Hans Vonk was playing in the Dutch first division for a club called Heerenveen. I spoke to my colleagues at Soccer News and we decided pursuing the story for two reasons. Firstly, it was a damn good story and like any half-decent footie mag we were always looking for a damn good story. And secondly, we thought that it would be in Bafana's interest to have a good goalkeeper and anybody who played regularly at the highest level, which the Dutch first division certainly is, must be pretty good.

I had no difficulty in obtaining Heerenveen's number and they had given me Vonk's number. I phoned him. He told me that he was sitting in the canteen at his club and was having lunch, but he would gladly speak to me. I said that I was from Soccer News and was writing a story about his eligibility to play for the country of his birth. I asked him whether he had ever played international football and whether he would like to play for South Africa. He replied yes to both questions. I thought that would probably be the end of the story, as FIFA had strict guidelines that nobody who played international football for one country, could ever play for another country. Or could they?

"When did you play for Holland and was it a friendly or a competitive game?" I asked him.

"It was a friendly match and was many, many years ago. I can't even remember the exact details anymore," he replied.

"I'll contact the Dutch Football Association and get all the information from them. That should not be too difficult, and then I'll contact you again."

It was not at all difficult to get the information from the association. I phoned them and within a few hours, I received a fax. Vonk had played once in a friendly for the Dutch under-20 side. That was his only taste of international football to date. I phoned him and gave him the good news.

"I am not sure if you are allowed to play for South Africa though. I will phone FIFA and find out," I told him.

He thanked me and said that he looked forward to my next call which hopefully would bring him good news.

FIFA was as helpful as the Dutch FA had been. A spokesman for the organisation said that the rule states that players who have played for one country are not permitted to play for another, unless they played only in a friendly.

Immediately after having heard from FIFA I phoned the goalkeeper and told him the good news. He was very happy and said that he would gladly play for Bafana. I asked him whether he was also keen to play in the World Cup, as I thought there would be a good chance that he could become the South African number one. Nothing would give him a greater thrill, he said.

"In fact, if I am chosen for the World Cup, I will invite you to France and pay for you."

"Not to worry, I will definitely be there with my magazine. But I would gladly accept a jersey, as I collect them."

"That's a deal," he said.

I then contacted Bafana interim coach, Jomo Sono, who was busy assembling a squad for the African Cup of Nations, which was to be held in Burkina Faso at the beginning of the year. I told them that there was an excellent goalkeeper in Holland who not only was eligible to play for Bafana, but was also willing to play for the team.

Sono's reaction was lukewarm. "Can you organise some videos of him playing and send them to me?"

"Sure Jomo, I can do that." Not that I had any intention of doing it, as I knew that once the story appeared in our magazine, it would be too big a story for any national team coach - interim or not - to exclude Vonk.

And that is exactly what happened. Vonk did not play for South Africa at the Nations Cup, but new coach Philippe Troussier, who took over from Sono, called Vonk up for his first friendly. Vonk not only played well, he played so well that he kept his place for the following friendlies and was an automatic choice for the World Cup squad.

In the run-up to the World Cup there was tremendous local hype around South Africa's chances. South African football fans had great expectations for the team and a national Sunday paper even predicted that Bafana would make it all the way to the final (and they were not even joking!).

I also made it to the World Cup in time, as my son, Marc, was born on 9 May. As usual, my first port of call was the press centre, where I picked up my accreditation. Having suffered days of frustration trying to organise accreditation at various African competitions, I was pleasantly surprised when I received my World Cup accreditation on the very same day I went to collect it. The next day, I took a train from Paris to Marseillé.

The hotel that I shared with other South African journalists was in the centre of Marseilles, near the harbour and not too far from the stadium. I loved the city, as it was buzzing with activity. It was as if the city was divided into two worlds though. On the one hand you had the Marseilles, which was a part of France and Europe and on the other hand you had the Marseilles, which was home to hundreds of thousands of immigrants from North Africa and gave it a very different flavour.

On match day, I made my way to the Stade Velodrome and took my seat in the press box. I sat next to a colleague from a rival publication and we started talking about the importance of this game not only in terms of football, but also in much more general terms for the country as a whole. By playing our first game at the finals of the World Cup, South Africa was firmly entrenched amongst the league of nations. There was nothing that said South Africa was different from other countries in the world. We played at the finals of the World Cup, just like Germany, England, Croatia and Argentina.

But that is were the similarities ended, as all of the above did well in their first match, whereas Bafana lost. From the first whistle it was apparent that South Africa would not achieve much that afternoon. The World Cup hosts pushed forward and could have scored more than the one goal they did before half-time. The goal came when substitute Christophe Dugarry, who had been on for less than ten minutes, made a great leap in front of the South African defence before latching on to a Didier Deschamps corner and heading home.

The second half began as the first had ended, with France pushing forward in search of more goals. Dugarry had the ball in the back of the net eight minutes into the second half, but the goal was disallowed for offside.

Shortly afterwards, France was rewarded for their enterprising game when Bafana defender Pierre Issa deflected a Youri Djorkaeff shot past Vonk into the goal. In injury time, France added a third when Thierry Henry burst through the defence and slotted the ball past the goal-keeper.

For South African journalists, the result was a disappointment. Although Bafana had played with great commitment, they had been completely outplayed by France. I decided to drown my sorrows by going out with some colleagues after the match.

I was obviously not the only one who felt like that, as several of the players did the same - much to Troussier's irritation. The French coach, who is known to be a strict disciplinarian, told South African journalists that he was furious that at least ten players decided to go to a discotheque after the France game and had partied there until the early hours of the morning.

"I do not expect the players to love me. I have tried to do my best.

My job is to get results and for this I have my rules and my discipline," he said.

One of the players who was involved in the early-morning session, Mark Fish, said they had wanted to have some fun to get over their loss to France.

"We don't mind losing, but the way we lost was so disappointing. We wanted to go out and relax. We went to a restaurant for dinner and came back a little late.

"The coach had a big thing about it, but after he had his tantrum we decided that, coach or no coach, we wanted to perform for South Africa and do our best at the World Cup."

The players had to apologise to Troussier, who accepted their apology and even said that he believed some good had come from the whole affair. "After we had talked, I wasn't angry anymore. I realised that, from then on, I could rely on them to respect my rules. It is important to give the players a break and I can trust them now."

After the game against France, I began a hectic 'match a day' routine. FIFA had asked all the journalists to submit a list of games they wished to cover. As some of the stadiums had fewer press seats than journalists requesting accreditation, FIFA posted all the names of journalists who had been granted press tickets on the local web site. This did not prove too much of a problem though, as unlike the last African Nations Cup that I had covered, there were enough computers. Not only that, there were also no local helpers sending greetings to their loved ones all over the world on the official computers.

I had been granted tickets for all the matches that I had wanted to see. My next problem was getting to the games, which were scattered all over southern France.

Going through the Internet site to see whether I had been granted tickets, I noticed that a certain Sammy Adelman had been granted tickets for virtually every match that I wanted to see and I decided to contact him about the possibility of travelling together.

Adelman was registered as a South African journalist, although none of the other South African journalists knew for whom he worked. I recalled a South African student leader called Sammy Adelman, who had been president of the student representative council of one of the country's top universities in the late 1970s. He had invited Jane Fonda and her then husband Tom Hayden to come to South Africa to address the students. This, as well as his outspokenness against the system of

Apartheid, had made Adelman unpopular with the government and they had banned him. In essence this restricted his movement, the people he could be with and speak to, and he was no longer permitted to leave the country. Adelman had decided that life in exile was preferable to being banned and he had fled the country. I remember reading an article about him in a Sunday newspaper shortly after he had left. The newspaper alleged that Adelman had been invited by Fonda to visit her in Hollywood and he had lived it up there. That was the last I ever heard of him and I had no idea whether this Adelman was the Sammy Adelman.

I tracked him down after the Argentina-Japan match in Toulouse. By his accent I could immediately hear that he was South African. I asked him if he was the man who had invited Jane Fonda to South Africa and had been banned as a result. I had obviously got the story wrong as he reacted rather harshly.

"That is not why I was banned, I did a lot of other things. The media just liked that one, so they blew it up," he said.

Having gotten that out of the way, I asked him whether he would be interested in working together for the next two weeks, as we had both received tickets for the same matches. He agreed.

That was lucky for me, as I had made my travel arrangements for France with a South African travel agency, for whom this was obviously a first. Virtually everything that I had been promised - and I had paid for - did not materialise. Rooms had not been booked, flights did not take off and I must have lost close to £1,000 in the process. The man in charge of all arrangements was called Robin Ball and a bit later I found out that I was obviously not the only person who had been hard done by as I read an article in another football magazine titled: "What a Balls-Up". In it, the journalist shared the experiences he had made with the same company.

After frequent complaints to Mr Ball he promised me that he would compensate me later. I am not sure what he meant by later, as four years down the line, I am still waiting. I also noticed that he later changed the name of his company and was offering tours to Japan and South Korea for the 2002 finals, probably continuing to cause havoc for South African football fans.

Under the circumstances, I was very lucky that Adelman was around and the next two weeks I spent travelling with him in his red Opel. We drove from city to city, shared hotel rooms and spoke about South

Africa and football.

He was in his early forties, smoked too much, snored louder than I had heard anybody snore before and thought he was going to be the next Michael Schumacher. His tendency to try and break all speed records en route was bad enough, but he had also decided that spending time in a car was wasteful unless doing something else at the same time. Which he then did. He shaved, read, filled in his diary and did anything else that needed doing. I normally sat next to him, thinking of Marc, who had not even turned two months. I had visions of me dying somewhere in France in a mangled car and him growing up fatherless. I tried to discuss it with Adelman and he would always drive a bit slower, for at least twenty kilometres before pumping the gas again.

Adelman was a good guy and we had a great time (apart from the fact that he smoked too much, drove too fast and snored too loudly, the last of which was not his fault). Even though we had chosen most of our games in southern France, we still spent an awful lot of time on the highways, driving to and fro between Marseillé, Toulouse, Bordeaux, Montpellier, St Etienne and Lyon. Luckily for us, the tellers at many of the toll roads had decided to strike during the World Cup and as we normally used a toll road a day, which were all very expensive, we saved quite a bit of money. We must have done thousands of kilometres in pursuit of our goal to watch a game a day. We spent hours in the car debating football, South Africa and children.

He told me that yes, he had been invited by Jane Fonda and yes, he had visited her. But the rest of the story that had been published in South Africa did not reflect what had happened. He had continued his studies and was now working at a university. I asked him why he had not returned to South Africa after Apartheid had been eradicated. He said that he would have loved to have come back, but as his son would have had to stay behind in England, he was not going to return to the country.

I had decided that I wanted to get as wide a perspective of the World Cup as possible by watching as many games as I could. The first one was, of course, South Africa's first-ever match at the finals of the World Cup. Thereafter, I was in Stadium Municipal in Toulouse on 18 June to watch South Africa play their second match against Denmark. As the Scandinavians had won their first encounter against Saudi Arabia, Bafana knew that anything but victory or at least a draw would in effect rule them out of the competition. But then anything but a victory for the Danes would be an upset.

The game began as the last one had ended for South Africa. The opponents pushed forward looking for an early goal and they got it. After only 13 minutes Allan Nielsen crashed a volley past Vonk after Brian Laudrup picked him out at the far post with a perfectly weighted cross.

South Africa's defensive naivety was repeatedly exposed in the early stages and Michael Laudrup came close to extending the lead three minutes later with a fierce 20-yard shot, which was only inches too high.

The Danish offensive continued with Martin Jorgensen's curling corner hitting the far upright and Vonk was glad when Brian Laudrup's follow-up diving header flew straight at him.

Troussier must have spoken stern words to his side in the dressing room, as Bafana came out a changed side. They were back on level terms within eight minutes of the re-start. Benni McCarthy, who at the time played for Ajax Amsterdam, rounded off a marvellous move involving John Moshoeu and Shaun Bartlett. To add insult to injury, the 20-year-old managed to score by slotting the ball through the legs of goalkeeper Peter Schmeichel. It was South Africa's first-ever goal at the finals of the World Cup.

The goal spurred Colombian referee John Jairo Toro Rendon into action. He must have been worried about being upstaged by players from both sides, as he tried desperately to regain centre-stage. He did so by unleashing a colourful orgy of red and yellow cards on the players.

The first player to be sent off was Danish substitute Miklos Molnar, who presumably did not even have to shower as he had been on the field no more than eight minutes when he was shown the red card. Bafana's Alfred Phiri, who had come on for Brendan Augustine at half-time, was the next to go. Rendon obviously had a deep-rooted hatred for substitutes, as Morton Wieghorst, who had come on with only seven minutes to go, was sent off again three minutes later. The third substitute to be sent off in a fair game!

Playing against only nine players, Bafana realised they were in with a chance and pushed forward. In the dying moments of the game, the cross bar denied them a historic victory, which in fairness would have been an undeserved win. With Schmeichel well beaten, Quinton Fortune took a long-range shot, only to see his effort bounce back into play.

The point was enough for Bafana to at least retain a theoretical chance of making it through to the next round. They needed to beat Saudi Arabia, while France needed to beat Denmark. Bafana also needed to make up three goals against the Danes by scoring at least twice. I thought that South Africa was still in with a good chance.

What happened first though, was that Bafana made international headlines. And all for the wrong reasons!

Two South African players, midfielder Naughty Mokoena and striker Brendan Augustine, were sent home after breaking the curfew that Troussier had set. What made their offence more serious was that they had broken the curfew for the second time.

The aptly named Naughty Mokoena and Augustine went out for a night on the town, returned at curfew time and then sneaked out to a nightclub once again for more fun. They only returned to the team hotel at 5am.

Understandably, Troussier was far from amused. He told journalists after a training session in Bordeaux's Stade Lescure, where the game against the Saudis was going to take place, that he had reached his limit. "I've been given an important mission, which is to prepare a team for a World Cup. There are rules which are linked to organisation and discipline ... and then there are the expectations of the people of South Africa, who expect preparation to mean something other than players going to nightclubs until 5am in the morning. The players have a responsibility to the team and the country and they have to respect that."

The Frenchman went further and criticised the attitude of the players. "Sometimes, the players seem more like tourists, here to shop and discover France. Sometimes, I feel like I'm in charge of a group of holiday-makers rather than a football team."

Troussier was so disappointed with the players that he told the journalists that he would no longer coach South Africa after the World Cup, irrespective of the outcome of the game against Saudi Arabia. "What South Africa needs is a much stricter coach, not me. I'm not that type of coach. They must look for a coach perhaps like a Franz Beckenbauer, not a Troussier."

Not surprisingly, most of the players differed with Troussier. Turkish-based Shoes Moshoeu, who was one of the most senior players in the side, said that these things were bound to happen. "I firmly believe it is not acceptable to send them home. It will not solve the problem. They should've been kept and the issue dealt with differently.

Perhaps they could've been fined. Sure, they made a mistake, but I would like to think that we are being judged on what we do on the pitch and not how many drinks we have had."

With all that was happening off the field, many of the players themselves did not think they stood a chance of going through. Some did not even want to go through!

A day before the match against the Saudis I spoke to German-based Delron Buckley, who said he had not enjoyed working with Troussier or the World Cup. "Thankfully everything will be over after tomorrow."

With that attitude, it was not surprising that Bafana failed to get the result that they needed in Bordeaux. Bartlett opened the scoring for South Africa early in the first half. But instead of pushing forward in search of more goals that would take them into the next round, most of the Bafana players were just going through the motions.

On the stroke of half-time, Youssef Al-Tunian, recalled to captain the Saudi's, was brought down by Issa in the penalty area. Sami Al-Jaber, who had been the Saudis' best player during the first half, made no mistake from the spot.

They went ahead in the second half after being awarded a second penalty, when Ibrahim Al-Shahrani was bundled over in the area. Al-Tunian stepped up and made it 2-1.

Bafana seemed resigned to their fate, but in the dying moments the referee awarded a third penalty. Bartlett, South Africa's only inspirational player during the game, stepped up and shot accurately into the top left corner of the net.

After the match, I went down into the mixed zone, where journalists could meet players, and spoke to Vonk.

"I have something for you," he said. He bent down and took something out of his tog bag. It was the shirt and pants he had worn against the Saudis.

"I wanted to swop with Barthez and Schmeichel, that's why I have only got this one. I hope that's OK and thanks for getting me here."

Of course that was OK, I said, grabbing the jersey like a child who had just been given a whole bag of sweets. He told me a bit more about the mood in the camp and said that unfortunately reports that the attitude of some of the players was bad were true. "It has still been a wonderful experience, one that I shall remember for the rest of my life."

And thus ended South Africa's first participation at the finals of the World Cup. It was an early exit and many would argue that it was a fiasco. The spirit in the squad was not conducive to doing well and officials did little to change the situation.

Troussier, who is undoubtedly an excellent coach and showed that clearly by winning the Asian Cup with Japan two years later, was not given enough time with the team and he had players in his squad who were unwilling to work with him. The early exit was certainly not only his doing.

My participation in the World Cup did not end after the defeat against Saudi Arabia. Adelman and myself continued driving around southern France watching matches. Germany against Iran, Japan versus Jamaica's Reggae Boyz and then the second round match between Italy and Norway. Thereafter, we too parted company, as Andrea and my sons Marc and Alexander arrived in France.

During the six weeks that I had not seen him, Marc had turned from a tiny infant into a healthy baby and it was wonderful seeing him. Football ranked a distant second to spending time with him and I was quite content to sit in the house we had rented in a tiny village called Rouillac and watch the matches on TV.

Now and then I would jump onto a train and travel to Bordeaux and watch more live action, only to look forward to returning to the tranquil surroundings of rural France.

The final, of course, was something that I did not want to miss. The scramble for tickets was huge, but as FIFA took geographical representation into consideration when allocating tickets for the final, I knew I had a good chance as I was one of only a handful of African journalists remaining in France. I was extremely happy when I saw my name amongst those whose request for a ticket had been successful.

As I had promised to take my older son Alexander to Disneyland, I left Rouillac the day before the final. We arrived in Paris early enough to go through to Disneyland and spent the rest of the day riding in teacups, flying on elephants and eating junk food. Having done all of that, we returned to Paris, where we stayed with France Football journalist Frank Simon in Putteaux.

Simon is an African football expert like no other. He had spent days in the African embassies in Paris and had built up such a vast knowledge of African football that he reminded me of a walking football encyclopaedia. He knew everything there was to know about African football even before he had set foot on the continent for the first time.

But there was one thing that he did not have, which I had: and that was a ticket for St Denis for the World Cup final the next day. As France Football had so many journalists working for them, only a handful of their journalists had been lucky enough to get tickets for the final and he was not one of them. I was rather grateful for that though, as it solved my baby-sitting problem. I also knew that Alexander, who had become quite a football expert himself, had a knowledgeable viewing partner for the final.

Even though the final was only to be played at 8pm, I left early to make sure that I could savour as much of the atmosphere before the game as possible.

It was well worth it. Everybody behaved as if they were going to a carnival and I noticed none of the hostility that is so often found at international matches.

I entered the stadium, and made my way to the press centre to pick up my ticket. I had also applied for a pass to the mixed zone but had not been given one. I was also not among the lucky ones whose name was drawn for the few unclaimed passes. But as I had not seen the name of a single African journalist on the list of journalists to have been given a pass, I decided to go to the FIFA press officer and ask him for a mixed zone pass. I explained to him that it would be wrong if Africa were not represented in the mixed zone. He agreed and managed to somehow find a spare pass, which he handed to me.

The final itself was a fantastic game. First there was the secrecy surrounding Ronaldo's non-appearance on the team sheet. Then, of course, there was the miracle of France winning the cup and for me there was the joy of seeing France win with an Algerian and a Ghanaian in the side.

At the end of the match I made my way to the mixed zone. I was less interested in conducting interviews than I was in seeing all these great players face to face. I also decided that I was going to get the French players to sign my match ticket as a memento of the final. I still have it and it is the centrepiece of my football memorabilia collection.

After all the players had left the mixed zone and been whisked off in their bus escorted by police with blaring sirens, I too made my way to the journalist bus. Unfortunately, there was no police escort with blaring sirens for us. The victory had turned Paris into a hive of activity and even though it was well into the early morning already, the streets were filled with people walking and cars from which the French flag was flying. Everybody was making as much noise as possible. As the streets were so full, the trip from the stadium to somewhere near Putteaux took over three hours. I am not quite sure if this was really necessary or whether the driver just enjoyed being part of the victory celebrations, as I did notice that we passed some landmarks more than once.

I finally arrived back at Simon's place at 3am, totally exhausted. He was still awake and we sat chatting about the World Cup and the Final for another hour.

The next day I returned to Rouillac. I had another day there before we all travelled back to Paris for our return flight to South Africa.

Even if Bafana had made an early exit and had not really achieved much, the World Cup had still been a wonderful experience for me.

15

MR DEMPSEY, I PRESUME?

FOLLOWING THE DISASTER IN FRANCE, South African football officials returned to their next venture, that of bringing the World Cup 2006 to the country.

The right to host the World Cup is awarded by the executive committee of the world controlling body, FIFA, which comprises 24 members. Of these the largest block, namely nine, come from Europe. Asia and Africa each have four members, while the two Americas have three members each. The final member of the committee comes from Oceania. Each member of the executive has one vote, which he can freely dispose of. The continental associations do not have to vote as one block. In the event of a tie, the FIFA President has the deciding vote. The bidding countries have to achieve a clear majority and there are as many voting rounds as it takes to achieve this. After each voting round, the country with the least number of votes falls by the wayside.

Before the actual voting process, FIFA appoints a World Cup inspection committee which visits all the bidding countries. After these visits, the inspection committee compiles a detailed report on the strengths and weaknesses of the respective bids. These reports are handed to the members of the executive committee to help them make up their minds to decide on which way to vote.

The idea to bring the World Cup to South Africa was first mooted sometime in the mid-1990s, by the then South African Football Association (SAFA) Executive President, Sticks Morewa. He said that he wanted to bring the World Cup to South Africa. Even though Morewa had been forced to resign from the association after a judicial commission of inquiry found him unfit to hold any office in football, SAFA decided to continue pursuing the dream of hosting the World Cup on African soil for the first time.

Wisely, the association seconded its Chief Executive Officer, Danny Jordaan, to head the South African World Cup Bid Committee. Jordaan was, without a doubt, not only the hardest-working official in South African football; he was also by far the most able.

HAS ANYBODY GOT A WHISTLE?

A former schoolteacher by profession, Jordaan had been involved in organizing the unification of South African football. He had then briefly become a member of parliament for the ruling African National Congress before taking over the reigns at SAFA. After Bafana returned from France, Jordaan had been relieved of his SAFA duties and told to concentrate on the World Cup bid.

The South African bid was to run under the motto of 'Laduma, it's Africa's call.' One of the main arguments the bid committee put forward was that it was Africa's turn to host the event, as the continent had not yet been granted the right to do so. 2002 was Asia's turn and four years later it should be Africa's.

For South African journalists the bid campaign, of course, opened up exciting possibilities as the South African attempt to bring the World Cup to the country was recognised worldwide as a serious one.

It was not the first African bid for the World Cup. Morocco had already twice attempted to persuade the FIFA executive committee to stage the world's biggest sporting event in Africa. They failed both times, but at their last attempt - to host the 1998 finals - they had lost only by a single vote to France, which not only went on to host the World Cup, but also won it.

Internationally, there was growing interest in the South African bid and the German press agency, dpa, requested an interview with Jordaan, who was confident of South Africa's chances.

"It simply is Africa's turn. One can't talk of a world event if it has never been held in Africa. But we are not expecting anybody to vote for us just because it is the correct thing to do. People must vote for us because our bid is the best. We do not want a sympathy vote, we want people to say we can host the World Cup because our bid is the best," he told me.

I asked him about the high level of crime in South Africa. Surely that was a factor that would weigh heavily against the country, I said.

South Africa's most popular tourist venue, Cape Town, had been hit by a spate of bombings over several months and the police seemed unable to do anything to prevent them or find the perpetrators. Car hijackings and violent robberies are part and parcel of life in most South African cities. Hotels in the bigger cities warn their guests not to walk in the city centre or at least not to take any valuables with them. Not only tourists are affected by this unlawfulness. Most houses in the suburbs are surrounded by high walls with iron spikes at the top of them to protect residents.

During the All Africa Games, which Johannesburg hosted in 1999, the organisers went to tremendous trouble to ensure the safety of all participants. But even a huge police contingent could not prevent a few nasty incidents from taking place.

The question of safety and security was the only one that the bid committee dreaded. I felt sorry for Jordaan. It was a question that politicians and policemen should have been answering. The Bid Committee had no influence over the crime issue, but it was what the international media focused on. Jordaan tried his best to answer. "Other countries have similar problems, it is not only South Africa. We are also hosting the cricket World Cup in 2003 and nobody is speaking about the issue there. So why should it prevent us from getting the football World Cup, which will be staged three years later?"

South Africa was not the only country bidding to host the event. To make matters worse, they were not even the only country from Africa bidding. Two-time losers Morocco put in a bid, as did Nigeria. There was even a pan-African bid proposed by Ghana. Brazil bid on behalf of South America, while Germany and England were the countries bidding from Europe.

Jordaan said that he felt confident that when FIFA took the vote in July 2000, South Africa would be the only African country bidding. He was certain that the other three candidates would withdraw in favour of South Africa. "I think Germany and England will be our main challengers, with Germany probably having the edge over England."

Most observers would probably have agreed with Jordaan. England and Germany had entered into a "gentleman's agreement" over the 1996 European Championship. Germany had backed England's bid to host the championship in return for an English undertaking that it would back the German bid for the 2006 World Cup. Unfortunately for Germany, this had not been agreed to in writing, and the English felt that they were not bound by it. But as the Association of European Football (UEFA) knew about the agreement, it did not look very favourably on the English bid. As a result, seven of the nine European votes (excluding that of FIFA President, Sepp Blatter and Scottish delegate, David Will) were considered safe ones for Germany.

Jordaan's prediction that South Africa would be Africa's only candidate proved partly right. Nigeria was the first to withdraw and did so in favour of South Africa. Ghana's pan-African bid was scuppered by

FIFA's announcement that it would not consider a joint bid until they had seen whether the World Cup, hosted by Japan and South Korea in 2002, had been a success. The only thorn in South Africa's flesh remained Morocco, and they were like a niggling sore that would simply not go away.

Most of Jordaan's work was done out of the country and I would have given anything to get just one tenth of his frequent flyer miles. Jordaan and his team spent months travelling from country to country, canvassing support for the South African bid.

During one of the first trips, the committee travelled to Cannes to the International Football Expo. There they wanted to introduce the South African bid to the world. One of the South African delegates to the Expo was a man named Cyril Kobus, once one of the most influential men in South African football. He had then conspired with the former Public Relations Officer of the National Soccer League, Abdul Bhamjee, to defraud the league of huge amounts of money. Kobus had been sentenced to jail for his involvement and had only just been released. It seemed that nobody on the Bid Committee questioned whether or not he was a suitable candidate to present South African football to the world!

As the date for the voting drew near, the campaigning became more vigorous and, in some cases, more vicious. The South Africans accused the English of launching a smear campaign, the English said the South Africans were making statements about the English bid that were inaccurate.

The question of crime and violence was a recurring theme that plagued the South African bid. At the official handing-over ceremony of the bid document to the Ministry of Sport, which took place in Johannesburg at the end of 1999, the Director General of the Ministry, Mthobi Tyamzashe, addressed this question.

He said that crime statistics in South Africa were greatly exaggerated. He said that his department had, for instance, looked into the statistics on rape and had come to the conclusion that all the figures that were being quoted had in fact come from one source, which had got it wrong. "The biggest problem is that most of these horror stories come from South Africans themselves who want to speak badly about the country. They are enemies of South Africa," he said.

As he said this, virtually everybody at the ceremony broke out in tumultuous applause. I looked at Arnold Lampert, the publisher of the

South African monthly magazine Soccer News, who had accompanied me to the function. I noticed that he did not clap either.

Shortly afterwards, we left. Arnold offered me a lift to the house of friends where I was staying for the duration of my visit to Johannesburg. They lived in a leafy suburb, not far from the enormous mansion, which housed the World Cup Bid Committee.

As we turned into the road in which my friends lived, I noticed an old Ford Cortina that seemed to be following us. As we slowed down to find the house number, the Cortina also slowed down. I told Arnold not to stop in front of the house, but to continue down the road. As he increased the speed, the Cortina increased its speed. We drove to a traffic circle and drove back the way we had come. With screeching tyres, the Cortina made a U-turn in the road and followed us. By now it was clear that the occupants of the car wanted to hijack us. Car hijacking is one of the most serious problems in South Africa and several are reported each day.

"Arnold, don't stop. Just drive faster," I said.

As we sped down the street, the Cortina was still following us. We were both scared. "Just follow the road and at the end of the street, turn left. There is a police station nearby. I think we should be OK there," I said.

The Cortina followed us all the way. It was only at the police station that it raced past us. We reported the incident to the police and they immediately sent out a patrol car to inspect the area.

Arnold then took me to my friends. Both of us were pretty shaken by the incident, but as neither of us wanted to be classified as an enemy of the state, we decided not to say anything about it.

As the momentum of the South African bid grew, so too did the number of prominent supporters. Edson Arantes do Nascimento, arguably the best-ever footballer and known throughout the world simply as Pelé, put his name behind the South African bid, as did former World Footballer of the Year George Weah, and three-time former African Footballer of the Year Abedi Pele. Another supporter of the South African bid was the never-aging Roger Milla, who in 1994 at the age of 42 had become the oldest player to score a goal at the finals of the World Cup.

Jordaan was also confident that FIFA President Blatter supported South Africa, although I was not as confident as Blatter had come out at various stages in support of Brazil, Germany, South Africa and

England. The World Cup 2006 had become a political football between him and Lennart Johannson during the FIFA presidential elections a few months earlier. The two had become embroiled in a bitter campaign, during which Blatter had promised that the 2006 World Cup would be held in Africa if he were elected. This had secured him enough votes to beat Johannson. The South African Bid Committee was therefore confident that Blatter would cast his vote in favour of South Africa.

In March 2000, the much awaited FIFA inspection committee arrived in the country. South Africa was the last stop for the group whose members had already been to the other bidding countries, Germany, England, Brazil and Morocco. According to them all of the contenders - with the exception of Brazil - were in a position to host the World Cup.

They were received with as much ceremony as any visiting head of state would have been received. They were wined and dined, met South African President Thabo Mbeki, and were shown just about every tourist attraction there is to see. In terms of FIFA rules, they were not permitted to speak to the press during their visit, except for one major press conference that had been scheduled in Cape Town.

The Mother City, as Cape Town is called, was the last leg of their whistle-stop tour. There they were welcomed by the most famous African face, Nelson Mandela. The former President told them how important it was that South Africa gets the World Cup. He said that it would do a lot towards nation building and that it could play an important part in healing wounds left over from the days of apartheid.

The Bid Committee held the press conference on Robben Island. Now a museum documenting South Africa's struggle for liberation, Robben Island had been the world's most notorious prison. During the apartheid era hundreds of opponents of the regime, including Nelson Mandela, were imprisoned there. The committee must have been hoping that the venue would induce some sympathy - which was something they needed if South Africa wanted to be granted the right to host World Cup 2006.

For Jordaan, the venue was a very symbolic one. "This used to be a place of despair, now it is a place of hope. Hope that we have been able to convince the inspection group that not only are we in a position to host the World Cup, we should get it."

I was one of countless journalists who made their way to Robben

Island for the press conference. The Atlantic Ocean island is some 40 minutes south of Cape Town and is reached by boat or hovercraft.

On arrival, the members of the inspection group were taken on a quick tour of the prison, while the journalists were whisked away by bus to the island's small hotel, which was the venue for the press conference. As soon as we arrived, it became clear that the venue was much too small. Photographers had an area of no more than five square metres from which they could take their photographs and television crews had an even more difficult task finding space for their tripods. There were also not enough chairs for the many journalists, who had been accredited for the event.

As befits such an eminent group, the journalists were made to wait. It was hot and packed. The waiting was only made bearable by watching an argument between one of the organisers of the press conference and a bid committee member. The Bid Committee member was saying that somebody or other had to sit upfront with the dignitaries, while the organiser said that there was no space. The Bid Committee member won. I wondered, however, why people working in such high profile positions seemed so ignorant in their dealings with journalists.

After waiting for about half an hour, the group finally arrived. They sat next to Jordaan. Heading the FIFA inspection committee was Alan Rothenberg, who had chaired the organising committee of the 1994 USA World Cup and had made himself a cool few million dollars in profit share at the end thereof.

He outlined his group's visit to the country and said that they had been impressed by what they had seen. He particularly had liked the atmosphere and capacity crowd that the group had experienced at a league match in Durban. I did not know if he was aware that the Bid Committee had arranged for the match to be played in Durban as it feared a low turn-out for the match in Johannesburg, which was not only several hundred kilometres away, but was also home to both of the clubs that were playing.

Rothenberg diplomatically sidestepped all negative questions and made it very clear that he was not prepared to talk about any of the other bidding countries. He did say though that they had been very impressed with the professionalism of the bid.

The American did not want to answer the question whether he believed the country had the capacity to host the World Cup. "We came to South Africa to look into that and I am certainly not going to inform the world before we give our report to the FIFA Executive."

Having said, in essence, nothing, the conference was closed and all the journalists were invited to have some snacks in a room that was even smaller than that in which the actual conference had been held. By the time I had fought my way through all the hangers-on, most of the snacks were gone.

I was not unduly worried though, as I still had an important football match to play. The Bid Committee had organised a game between itself and the media, which was to take place on the gravel pitch in the prison grounds. The Bid Committee's side was strengthened by some of the ex-footballers who supported the bid.

I had, as soon as I found out that a game had been scheduled, staked my place in goals for the media XI. The opportunity to play on the same field as some of the heroes of the South African liberation was too important to miss. As nobody else was mad enough to volunteer to jump around on the gravel and risk serious injury, I played.

Lining up in attack, and therefore playing against me, were: Roger Milla (three times a World Cup finalist participant and the oldest man to have scored a goal at the finals of the World Cup), Abedi Pele (European Cup winner and three-time former African Player of the Year), Terry Paine (member of the winning England World Cup squad in 1966) and Jomo Sono (former New York Cosmos player, where he starred with Franz Beckenbauer and Pelé). So what that their combined age must have been close to 220 years and they were carrying a few kilos too much. I still felt as if I was playing in an international match.

Unfortunately for me, most of my teammates were also carrying a few kilos too much. Consequently, we were completely outplayed by our opponents. Abedi Pele scored in the first half, Milla and Sono added two more in the second and we were beaten 3-0. In between, I managed to palm a Sono pile-driver against the bar and stop a powerful Milla shot. My best save of the afternoon was reserved for an Abedi Pele breakaway. It was him against me. It was Olympique Marseilles against TuS Schwachhausen second team. It was Ghana against South Africa. And I/TuS Schwachhausen/South Africa won. The three-time former African Footballer of the Year (I apologise for bringing this up again) had been put through by a defence splitting pass (which was not particularly difficult as two of my defenders were standing on the middle line, chatting to each other). He feigned going to my right. I wanted to go to my right too, but slipped and fell to my left, just as Abedi Pele pushed the ball to my left. I fell right onto the ball. The crowd cheered. Even Abedi Pele gave me an encouraging pat on the back. With my honour intact, I left the island.

Once the FIFA inspection group left the country, all that remained was for Jordaan and his team to travel the globe in search of the 13 votes the country needed to bring the World Cup to South Africa.

They tried desperately to get the other non-European bidders to withdraw from the race. Brazil finally agreed to do so a few days before the voting, but Morocco tenaciously clung to its chance of hosting the 2006 World Cup.

Of the nine European votes, South Africa firmly believed they had Blatter on their side. Of the remaining eight votes, only that of Joseph Mifsud from Malta was considered worthwhile chasing.

A hastily arranged friendly against Malta gave the Bafana a historic first-ever win on European soil, but ended in a public relations disaster when several high-ranking South African officials failed to make the trip.

Votes in the bag, so to say, for the South African bid were obviously the four from the African Confederation (CAF). One of the voting members, Ismail Bhamjee (Botswana) was born in South Africa and retained strong ties with the country, so there was little doubt which way he would vote. Mali's Amadou Diakite and CAF President, Issa Hayatou from Cameroon, were other votes the South Africans were bound to pick up. Only Slim Aloulou (Tunisia) was said to have favoured the other African bid, Morocco, but once they were out of the running he was sure to switch allegiance to South Africa.

After Brazil's announcement that it would withdraw in support of South Africa, the three votes from the South American Confederation, Nicolas Leoz (Paraguay), Ricardo Teixeira (Brazil) and Julio Grondona (Argentina), were votes that South Africa could count on.

Similarly, the three delegates from North and Central America, Chuck Blazer (USA), Jack Warner (Trinidad & Tobago) and Isaac Sasso Sasso (Costa Rica) indicated that they would like to see the 2006 World Cup in Africa. Warner, who is the President of the North and Central American Confederation, said during a visit to South Africa a few weeks before the voting that he was sure that the South Africans would be very happy with the news they got after the voting.

Going into the final stretch, the situation surrounding the four Asian and the lone Oceanic delegate was unclear. Thailand's Worawi

Makudi, Qatar's Mohamed Bin Hammam, South Korea's Mong-Joon Chung and Saudi Arabia's Abdullah Al Dabal as well as Charles Dempsey from New Zealand could sway the vote either way.

South Africa was banking on Dempsey, a known supporter of the English bid, to vote in their favour once the English had been eliminated. Jordaan was also hoping that at least one or two of the Asians would support their bid.

If they did, Jordaan was hoping that they would ensure the necessary majority, without having to use Blatter's decisive vote. Jordaan realised that this would put the FIFA President in a very awkward spot.

Jordaan also thought that the inspection group, which had ranked South Africa's bid on a par with that of Germany, ahead of all others, had given South Africa the final boost it needed and he was optimistic when he arrived in Switzerland, where the FIFA headquarters is situated.

Switzerland is beautiful in summer. The leaves are green, the sun shines and a feeling of holiday is in the air. That is, when it is not raining. When it rains, it becomes dark and gloomy. And that is what it was like in the days before D-day, the day when the FIFA executive committee was going to vote. It was pouring with rain!

Jordaan should have seen the signs when he arrived in Zurich.

Hundreds of journalists from all over the world had assembled at the exhibition centre where the announcement was going to be made on 6 July.

Of course all the action started a few days earlier - much of it probably unbeknown to the various bid committees. What is known is that Sepp Blatter convened an urgent meeting with both African bids, explaining to them that things did not look as rosy as was thought at first and that one of them needed to withdraw from the race, even at this late stage, if the other was to prevail. Though Blatter did not say it, it was clear that he meant Morocco had to withdraw.

At that stage there were already rumours that Germany was going to win by a single vote. That, so everybody thought, was impossible as there were 24 voting members. It would either be a tie, or a two-vote margin or more for one of the candidates.

The final presentations were made on 5 July, and then the waiting began. But much more than waiting, the lobbying began. There were a few votes that could possibly still be swung this way or that. The four Asian votes were those that South Africa sought to get. But the Asian countries remembered the snub they received from the African Confederation over the question of an extra place at the World Cup in 2002. FIFA had decided that it would give them no extra place in the finals, even though co-hosts Japan and South Korea automatically qualified. This had resulted in a situation whereby all the remaining Asian countries were to compete for only one place at the finals. The dispute had threatened to split FIFA. Africa had stayed neutral. Not so the Europeans; they had offered a compromise and had even gone so far as to suggest a play-off between one of the European countries and an Asian one for a place in the finals. The Asians had gladly accepted this offer. They now owed the Europeans a favour, which they could repay by voting for Germany. That gave the 1974 hosts 12 votes, enough to tie, but not to win without Blatter's deciding vote.

That left 78-year-old Charles Dempsey from New Zealand as the man wielding all the power. He became the focus of all the attention. He had already played golf with Franz Beckenbauer, the chairman of the German Bid Committee, now he was courted by the President of UEFA, Lennart Johannson.

Jordaan was a worried man. He had worked tirelessly for the past two years, flying all over the world and spending endless hours arguing the merits of the South African case. All that could now be in vain, if he did not do something fast. Jordaan, who has always been an astute politician, played his trump card. South African President Thabo Mbeki phoned New Zealand Premier Helen Clark and explained to her how important it was for the country to get the World Cup. She replied that South Africa had the backing of her country. Unfortunately, she had no say in the matter. It was Mr Dempsey who had all the say. It was at this stage that Nelson Mandela was asked to intervene by speaking to Charles Dempsey directly. Mandela, who next to Princess Di and the Pope must rank as the most well known public figure in the world, was put through to Dempsey's hotel. Presumably Mandela had wanted to speak to Dempsey about the nice things that were happening in South Africa. From one octogenarian to a near-octogenarian, so to say. But the man from New Zealand refused to speak to Mandela and thus when he voted the next day, he did so without having been given a glowing report about the rainbow nation by its first post-apartheid president.

No wonder then that he voted for England in the first round - the round in which Morocco was eliminated with only three votes. No wonder then, that he voted for England in the second round, one of only two members to do so. But what happened then took everybody by surprise. Mr Dempsey took a taxi to the airport and flew home, leaving behind a stunned press corps. Well actually, they were not stunned at that stage, as they only found out that Dempsey had done his Houdini-like disappearing act much later when Sepp Blatter said that the winner had won by a single vote. He then took the envelope, opened it and read to a worldwide audience, who were watching the proceedings on television, 'And the winner is: Deutschland.'

16

STADIUMS OF DEATH

NEEDLESS TO SAY, SOUTH AFRICANS were devastated. All, of course, blamed Dempsey and within the course of a few days he had gone from being an unknown pensioner to heading the South African most-wanted list. But it was not only Dempsey who bore the brunt of the South African attacks. Some said it had been a racist decision, others claimed that Europe had grouped together to deny South Africa what was rightfully theirs. Few, if any, looked at the way in which the Bid Committee had done its job or sought to place any blame at South Africa's own door.

Luckily, a few days after the disappointment in Switzerland, the country had an opportunity to shift its focus onto the field of play. The draw for the African World Cup qualifiers for the 2002 World Cup had seen Bafana being grouped with Burkina Faso, Guinea, Malawi and Zimbabwe. And it was South Africa's northern neighbour, which played host to Bafana in the first game.

Having neglected my domestic duties during the unsuccessful bid campaign of the previous few months, I decided to stay in Cape Town and not travel with the team to Zimbabwe's capital, Harare. Instead, I was going to watch the game at home on television and file a short match report from there.

The first half was without incident. Bafana had more of the first 45 minutes, but failed to score, while the home side looked dangerous on the break. Both sides obviously wanted to start their World Cup campaigns on a winning note, as they pushed forward after the break.

Germany-based Delron Buckley opened the scoring for South Africa midway through the second half and added another eight minutes from the end. It was then that all hell broke lose. As Buckley ran to the side of the field to celebrate with his teammates, he was pelted with a barrage of objects, including bottles.

As Buckley fell to the ground, police facing the stand from which the bottles were being thrown shot into the crowd. I saw immediately that it was teargas that they were firing indiscriminately into the stands.

HAS ANYBODY GOT A WHISTLE?

As I was watching the whole drama unfold on television, I could see that the police kept on firing into a section of the crowd, who were picking up the teargas canisters and throwing them back onto the field.

Soon the air over the field was thick with smoke, and the players, obviously overcome by the fumes, fell to the ground. Members of the Bafana coaching staff rushed onto the pitch, handing the players water to pour over their faces and urging them to keep low. The referee had no option but to abandon the game.

While this was happening, fans tried to rush out of the packed 60 000-seater stadium, eager to escape the burning sensation teargas causes.

At this stage it was clear that the story was no longer the game, but the chaos around it. This made it difficult for me, as I was witnessing events several thousand kilometres away. Having travelled to Zimbabwe on many previous occasions, I had enough contacts there and I frantically started phoning all over Zimbabwe to get the full picture.

As the story unfolded, I became more and more upset. At least 12 fans had been killed in the stampede and as far as I was concerned, each and every one of those deaths could have been prevented had the police not fired teargas into the crowd.

Often enough during my time in Grahamstown with the XI Attackers, police there had fired teargas onto the field while I was playing. But this was merely to intimidate me and they shot one, at most two or three canisters on to the field. But each and every time this happened, it caused a mad rush to escape the fumes.

In Zimbabwe the police had not fired one or two rounds of teargas, they had kept on firing until the stadium was engulfed with smoke and scores of people lay injured and dead all over the Harare Independence Stadium.

A first body count revealed that 12 people had been suffocated or crushed to death in Zimbabwe's worst sporting disaster. A 13th victim was added a day later.

The government reacted swiftly, blaming the political opposition Movement for Democratic Change (MDC) for the mayhem. President Robert Mugabe, once one of the champions of the African liberation struggle but who became more and more erratic in the late 1990s after holding on to power for some 20 years, said that he found it "disturbing to hear that the people who sparked off the disturbances were members of a planted group that had been taking advantage of the huge crowd to sloganeer and exhibit their symbols". He also ordered a police inquiry into the tragedy.

The world confederation, FIFA, was not particularly interested in the internal bickering that characterised Zimbabwean politics and immediately banned the stadium for international matches until further notice. They also ruled that the three points be awarded to South Africa.

Irrespective of FIFA's decision though, the inquiry continued and it took less than two weeks to be completed. Not surprisingly, its findings were more or less the same that the police's political master, Mugabe, had found a few hours after the incident.

Police commissioner Augustine Chihuri accused the opposition MDC of recruiting 300 hooligans to "disrupt the match". He said spectators who waved the party's open-handed salute and brandished small plastic squares to symbolise "giving the red card" to President Robert Mugabe and his ruling Zanu-PF party, had created a "politically-charged atmosphere at the match".

Chihuri, a former guerrilla fighter in Mugabe's Zanu/PF party and appointed to his post by Mugabe, admitted, however, that the police performance "leaves a lot to be desired" and that the police response was "not coherent".

"Truly there was too much teargas, and perhaps it should not have been applied, but it is wrong to totally blame the police."

One person who blamed the police, though, was former England and Wimbledon player John Fashanu, who was in the stadium when the mayhem started. "I blame the police for this disaster. Some bottles were flung onto the pitch, but there was no need for such a heavy-handed reaction."

He went on to say that enemies of African football would pounce on the incident as a justification for not taking the 2006 World Cup finals to South Africa. "Once again South Africa will take the blame for something that happened beyond its borders. I have been to South Africa many times and this incident would not have happened there."

Tragically, it took just eight months for Fashanu to be proved wrong - horribly wrong!

South Africa's biggest and most popular clubs are undoubtedly Kaizer Chiefs and Orlando Pirates, both of whom are based in Johannesburg and derby matches between the two are always highlights on the country's football calendar. Both teams draw support from all over South Africa and many of their fans travel hundreds of kilometres to watch the two teams play against each other

In April 2001 the teams met in Johannesburg's Ellis Park Stadium in a night match that could determine the outcome of the league that season. At the time Pirates were heading the table, but were being challenged by Chiefs.

In most African countries, there is no tradition of pre-buying of tickets for football matches and fans merely arrive at the stadium on the day, buy their ticket and enter. This night was no different. And shortly before kick-off, the 65 000-seater stadium was filled to capacity, while tens of thousands of fans were still standing outside, trying to get into Ellis Park.

Unaware of the explosive situation that was developing outside the gates, league officials decided to start the match. As it was in progress more and more people streamed into the stadium, pushing those who were already seated forward.

Outside the situation was even more chaotic. Both sides scored within the first 15 minutes and as their respective fans cheered, the crowd outside became even more eager to enter the stadium and tried to force their way through one of the gates, which at this time had been shut to prevent more people from entering. The security officials were not only hopelessly outnumbered, they were also totally ill-equipped to deal with such a situation. Unfortunately, they had not learnt from the tragic mistake their Zimbabwean counterparts had made a few months earlier and shot teargas at the crowd.

Much later, at an inquiry into the disaster, both police and the private security company commissioned to provide security at Ellis Park denied shooting teargas at the crowd. However, it seems very unlikely that members of the crowd had brought teargas canisters with them to the game!

The teargas fired at the crowd standing outside the locked gates had the effect - I don't know if it was the desired effect - of making the situation even more chaotic. People were running around, trying to escape the fumes, others were trapped against the security barriers erected before the match to control the crowd. Within minutes, it became apparent that people were being injured - badly.

Inside the game was continuing, but there, too, people were being injured as supporters kept on surging into the stadium. Some of those in front became entangled in barbed wire as they were pushed by the stampede. The injured were being taken onto the field and laid on the grass. It was clear that something had to be done and officials decided to abandon the game. It was a wise move, as the horror of the situation only became clear once the players had left the field. Bodies and seriously injured fans were being pulled out of the tightly packed stands.

Coaching Orlando Pirates at the time was my friend Gordon Igesund. I had known Igesund for many years and had helped him in some dealings with German clubs. He was also godfather to my son Marc. When I saw him, he was totally shocked.

"I have never seen anything like this. It is just terrible. I was sitting on the bench, trying to concentrate on the game, but we were all realising that something terrible was going on behind us. I am just glad that they stopped the match; hopefully that has prevented even more injuries and deaths from occurring. It is like a nightmare."

Igesund's description of the situation as a nightmare proved to be just right. As the body count began, the enormity of the tragedy emerged. The death toll stood at 43, the number of injured - many of them seriously - came close to 100. Paramedics and ambulance workers struggled to resuscitate some of the injured and then get them to hospital as the roads were congested with people trying to get home after the game had been called off. Even ambulances called to the stadium struggled to enter, and only once a helicopter landed on the field and the stadium announcer said that all those in the stadium were to please stand in their seats and not move, did the situation get better.

The stunned crowd stood for another 30 minutes while the emergency services used advertising boards in lieu of stretchers to carry the injured. Many fans did not realise the seriousness of the disaster until the telephone number for the local mortuary was read out in the stadium.

The South African government the next day ordered a judicial commission of inquiry to look into the causes of the disaster. This commission was to hear later that security guards manning the gates had allowed people who did not have tickets into the stadium after receiving 60 Pence from them. This had obviously led to serious overcrowding and ultimately to the deaths that occurred within the stadium.

The commission also heard from the stadium manager that there were several problems in the planning stages prior to the tragic April 11 game. These included the fact that although the stadium only had a seating capacity of 60,000 many more tickets for the game were printed. He also admitted that when the game started, the situation outside was not under control. This was in direct contravention of the rules and regulations of the South African Football Association (SAFA), which stipulated that there should be no kick off until the situation outside and in the stands is under control.

In the days following the tragedy in South Africa, many asked how something like this could have happened. But it was not a question on everybody's mind. Agence France Presse's Africa football correspondent, David Legge wrote that he was not at all surprised. "Perhaps the only surprise was that it took so long for the Ellis Park stampede to happen. There have been numerous close shaves with tragedy being averted through pure luck. When Chiefs and Pirates met at Ellis Park two years ago, fences were broken, the stadium's capacity was exceeded, but swift police action averted the loss of life.

"An estimated 100,000 spectators saw South Africa defeat Congo at the 80,000-capacity FNB stadium near Soweto to clinch qualification for the 1998 World Cup finals in France. Every pathway was occupied, every exit blocked and security officials later admitted that one fight or one misplaced cigarette butt could have left hundreds dead.

"As South African soccer continued to skate on rapidly melting ice, it ran out of luck at Ellis Park when thousands of locked-out fans smashed every obstacle that prevented them gaining entry. This is the way it has always been: a free-for-all with no respect for pre-booked tickets or seat numbers. Faced with vast numbers of fans demanding entry, security personnel are often powerless to intervene."

And while Legge was certainly right on virtually every point that he raised, he was wrong when he said that the only surprise was that it took so long for an incident like this to happen in South African football. It had happened before!

Ten years earlier, at a game between the same sides, 42 people were killed in a stampede. Eight years later, a potentially explosive situation at Ellis Park during a match between Chiefs and Pirates was miraculously defused without the loss of any life. After that incident, the Chief Executive Officer of the Premier Soccer League, Trevor Phillips, ruled that games between the two most popular sides in South African football should not be played at Ellis Park, as it was too dangerous.

Unfortunately for the 43 victims of the stampede, Phillips had in the meantime resigned and returned to England and his successors obviously felt no need to heed his warning.

If they had taken him seriously, FIFA might not have had to make another statement about the deaths of football fans in an African stadium.

FIFA president Sepp Blatter said it was necessary to examine the causes of the disaster. "Priority then must be to obtain complete and exhaustive findings by the competent authorities on the causes of this latest tragedy in our game so that lessons can be drawn for the future. Football must do everything in its power that such disasters do not occur again."

But just like Fashanu before him, Blatter was to be proved wrong. And that, just over two weeks later!

This time around it happened in the Democratic Republic of Congo (DRC) at a match between southern DRC's top teams, Lupopo and Mazembe. The game was played in a packed stadium in the southern city of Lubumbashi.

Reports said that fans started throwing bottles when Mazembe tied the game at 1-1, with just 10 minutes to go. The police did exactly the same that had contributed to the loss of life in South Africa and Zimbabwe: they fired teargas into the crowd, causing a wild stampede.

As people tried to run away from the teargas, they knocked over steel barriers in the stand and several fans were crushed to death. A doctor at the Lubumbashi morgue later said that ten people had died.

Tragically, Africa's football stadiums had not yet finished claiming lives for the year 2001.

On the 9th of May, in the Ghanaian capital of Accra, the country's two most popular football clubs, Hearts of Oak and Ashanti Kotoko, faced each other in a league match played in the 45 000-seater Accra Stadium. The game was a sell-out and Kotoko were leading 1-0, when Hearts of Oak scored twice in rapid succession to go into a 2-1 lead with only five minutes to play. This irked a section of the Kotoko fans, who started destroying plastic seats at the Accra Sports Stadium and throwing them on to the running track surrounding the pitch.

The police did what police throughout Africa have been doing whenever an unruly crowd confronts them - they shot teargas. This is said to have resulted in bottles being thrown at the police, who, in turn, continued shooting teargas. As the gas spread, panic ensued and the fans scrambled for the exits. These were locked shut and several fans were suffocated and crushed to death against the gates. While this was happening, police apparently kept on shooting teargas.

As only a few minutes of the game remained, most of the ambulance men and Red Cross officials had already left the stadium and, as a result, a squad of volunteers had to sort out the bodies as well as take those who were injured to hospital.

Reporters said afterwards that hospital corridors were crowded with the dead and wounded, along with relatives frantically searching for loved ones. "I personally counted over 100 dead in one of the hospitals," said Komla Dumor, a presenter on a local radio station.

Unfortunately, the reporter was not exaggerating and 126 people were smothered or crushed to death in the stampede.

Once again the government was fast to react, announcing not only a three-day period of mourning, but also a committee of inquiry. However, unlike those in Zimbabwe and South Africa, the commission in Ghana came out with a critical report within a few weeks of the tragedy having occurred. Before issuing the report, the commission held 17 public hearings, heard 102 witnesses and visited seven sites in Ghana and two stadiums in England.

The report placed most of the blame squarely on the police and urged the government to charge six of the policemen on duty that night with manslaughter. Although more policemen were involved in the firing of teargas, no more faced prosecution as the commission accepted that junior officers were acting on orders from more senior policeman. The police were also accused of 'lax procedures' in investigating the disaster. These procedures included improper records of police ammunition and falsified entries on officers' comings and goings at the stadium. The report went on to say that no ambulances were on standby at the crowded stadium, the stadium clinic was closed and there were no security guards at the exits.

The report also recommended that the award of the contract involving the supply of plastic chairs in the stadium must be thoroughly examined with a view to instituting legal proceedings against the contractor. Safety measures, first aid posts and ambulance services, adequate sanitary facilities and proper supervision by officials of the Ghanaian National Sports Council and police officers were also recommended.

Following the deaths in Accra, FIFA was once again called upon to make a statement. But this time around, Blatter did not mince his words and blamed officials and match organisers directly. He said, "there is disturbing evidence to indicate" that the lessons of previous disasters "are not being learnt".

STADIUMS OF DEATH

In an editorial in FIFA News, Blatter said: "The stadium disasters at Johannesburg's Ellis Park and in Ghana brought chilling reminders of incidents in recent years, not least the Hillsborough tragedy of 1989."

During the Hillsborough tragedy 95 people were crushed to death at the FA Cup semi-final between Liverpool and Nottingham Forest. There were striking similarities with the African tragedies, particularly the Ellis Park one. Both were high profile games with fans arriving late and trying to get into an already crowded section of the ground. In each case the games had started and were halted when it was realised what had happened in the crowd.

While bodies were laid out on the field at Hillsborough, the same happened behind the goal at Ellis Park, as the stadiums became temporary morgues.

Blatter warned though that while "Hillsborough led ultimately to changes in stadium design and a trouble-free Euro 96 in England, there is disturbing evidence to indicate that the lessons are apparently not being learnt everywhere."

Blatter claims "basic directives" have not been adhered to, such as issuing the correct number of tickets in accordance with a stadium's capacity, stemming the flow of spectators into a stadium by setting up ticket control cordons and delaying kick-off until the overall security situation is under control.

Needless to say, these tragedies made headlines around the globe and placed the continent firmly on the lead pages of most major newspapers throughout the world.

17

WORLD CUP 2002
- THAT'S WHAT FRIENDS ARE FOR

THANKFULLY, DISASTERS, STAMPEDES and deaths were not the only things that I could write about during 2001. The other thing of interest was the race to the 2002 World Cup finals in Japan and South Korea.

The football gods were, once again, incredibly kind to South Africa when the draw for the African qualifiers were made. Bafana's opponents, Burkina Faso, Guinea, Malawi and Zimbabwe are not exactly considered heavyweights of African football and South Africa were favourites to advance to their second consecutive World Cup finals.

Their task was made even easier, when the 'wise men' of FIFA - otherwise known as the FIFA Executive Committee - decided that they would suspend Guinea from all footballing activities following that government's decision to disband the local football association. Presumably it was a case of professional jealousy, as FIFA does not like anybody but the organisation itself interfering in the footballing affairs of any country.

After the tragedy that occurred at the first qualifier in Zimbabwe, it was plain sailing for South Africa. Victories over Malawi, Burkina Faso and Zimbabwe meant that South Africa needed only three points from their two remaining matches to qualify for the finals. Victory in the first of these two matches in Ouagadougou against Burkina Faso would have given Bafana the honour of becoming the first country to have qualified for the 2002 World Cup finals (apart from defending champions France and co-hosts South Korea and Japan, who qualify automatically)

Even though the one-all draw against the Stallions meant that the champagne would stay on ice a bit longer, South Africa secured the points they needed in their next match against Malawi.

Bafana did not have the honour of becoming the first country to have secured their place in the finals. That honour went to Cameroon's

Indomitable Lions, who qualified for the finals some 30 minutes before South Africa did.

The same football gods who had smiled upon South Africa had extended their benevolence to Cameroon when the draw was made. The West African country faced Togo, Zambia, Angola and Libya en route to the finals and only Zambia was considered a worthy rival.

Right from the start it was apparent that nothing would stand in the way of Cameroon, as the team rushed from win to win. Surprisingly, as the side was going from victory to victory they were also going from coach to coach.

Frenchman Pierre Lechantre took the team through the preliminary matches against Somalia and the first two group matches against Libya and Angola. In between, he also took the Cameroonian under-23 side to glory at the Sydney Olympics. He then decided that the time was ripe to discuss new employment terms and conditions with the Cameroonian football authorities.

Had he asked me, I would have told him that there are three things that African football officials do not like. The first is paying money, the second is losing and the third is paying money. The officials of course could not fault Lechantre on losing matches, but he certainly expected them to pay more money. The officials reacted like football officials all over the world have reacted: they told Lechantre to pack his bags and go.

In his place, they hired local coach Jean-Paul Akono, presumably because he was willing to work for much less than Lechantre had been paid. And Akono continued where Lechantre had left off: winning. Under the new coach, the Indomitable Lions won in Togo and in Libya and at home against Zambia. After five matches they had a perfect record of having won all five. They came unstuck in their sixth match though, losing 2-0 to Angola. That evening the officials sat down again and discussed Akono's fate. After all, the coach had broken the second rule: don't lose. He too was told to pack his bags and go.

What now, they must have wondered? When in doubt, revert back to the tried and tested, which is exactly what they did when they offered Lechantre his old job back. Obviously not being a very proud man, he jumped at the chance, went back and unpacked his bags.

But if Lechantre was hoping for a smooth ride, he was sadly mistaken, as he had the misfortune of having to coach the side at the Confederations Cup in Japan. His job - which was already pretty difficult as Brazil and France were two of the other countries participating - was not made any easier when one of his players, Pensee Billong, was arrested for theft.

Billong, who had represented his country at the World Cup finals in France in 1998, joined a South Korean team after the tournament. During the preparations for the Confederations Cup, Cameroon played a friendly in South Korea against the local national team and after the game Billong was arrested by the police and placed in custody.

The defender was accused of stealing 7.4 million Won (about £3,700) in bank cheques from his former club, Sungnam Ilhwa, a few months earlier. In his defence, Billong told the police he had taken the money as part of his overdue payment from Ilhwa and that he had to leave the team because he had been badly treated by them.

Cameroon arrived in Tokyo without Billong and went on to lose their opening two matches against Brazil and Japan. Even though they managed to beat Canada 2-0 in their final match, it was not enough to prevent the officials from having another of their regular meetings at which the position of the coach was discussed. At the end of the meeting Lechantre was told - for the second time in less than a year - to pack his bags and go!

Robert Corfu was given the coaching reins instead. Also from France, Corfu was already in Cameroon at the time, where he was employed by the association to oversee youth development.

Needing only a point from Cameroon's two remaining matches, Corfu knew that he would have little difficulty in ensuring a fifth appearance at the World Cup finals for the Indomitable Lions.

A 2-0 victory over Togo gave Cameroon the point they needed, thereby becoming the first country to qualify. The final game in Zambia was of academic interest only and the players obviously knew that, scrapping to a 2-2 draw. As Corfu was always meant to be a short-term solution, the familiar meeting was held. Having been in charge for only a few weeks Corfu, who presumably had not yet even unpacked his bags, was told to go. In his place, the association hired a German coach, Winfried Schäfer, and put him in charge of the Indomitable Lions at the World Cup.

Cameroon was not the only country that changed coaches midway through the qualifying campaign.

One of the favourites for one of the five African places at the World Cup was Tunisia. Twice before the North Africans had qualified for the showpiece of world football and after being drawn into a group with Congo, Madagascar, the Democratic Republic of Congo (DRC) and Côte d'Ivoire, few doubted that they would make it for a third time.

In charge of the team at the start of the campaign was Francesco Scoglio, an Italian whose home club was Genoa 93. He was well-liked in Tunisia and enjoyed quite a good reputation. His stature grew as the World Cup qualifiers progressed. His team quite easily brushed aside Mauritania in the preliminary rounds, dropped two points in a draw against Côte d'Ivoire and then went on a three-game winning streak against Madagascar (1-0), DRC (6-0) and Congo (2-1).

But while this was happening in North Africa, the picture in Italy was very different. Genoa 93 was once one of the most successful and competitive clubs. It had won nine Scudetti and one Coppa Italia. By all accounts, not a bad record! Unfortunately for their fans though, and for Scoglio, the last triumph was during the 1936/7 season, when they won the cup. Since then, they have been in and out of Serie A and while Signore Scoglio was making waves in Africa, his beloved Genoa 93 was in danger of sinking even further. Seeing his club in danger of relegation, Scoglio approached the Tunisian Football Association and asked them if they would be prepared to allow him to coach both the Tunisian national team and Genoa 93. Not surprisingly, he was refused permission.

He then decided that he would put club before country and told his bosses in Tunisia that he was going home.

Having obviously grown very fond of Tunisia and Tunisians, he asked five Tunisian players to accompany him to Genoa and he managed to convince his new club to sign goalkeeper Chokri El Ouaer, defender Khaled Badra, midfielders Hassen Gabsi and Raouf Bouzaiene, as well as striker Imed Mhadhbi. El Ouaer left after playing only a handful of games for the Serie B club, but the four outfielders became regulars under Scoglio. The coach's reign at Genoa did not last very long and within a few months he was out of a job, leaving behind a very distinct Tunisian flavour at the club.

But if Scoglio had any hopes of returning to his old job in Tunisia, it was no longer available. Not willing to wait for Scoglio to have a change of heart or of Genoa firing him, the Tunisian association hired Eckhard Krautzun.

Krautzun had coached several German Bundesliga clubs, five national teams (Canada, Japan, South Korea, Philippines and Kenya) as well as a club in Tunisia, with whom he won a continental cup. With a CV like that, he was the man they were looking for and the Tunisian FA employed him to finish the job Scoglio had started.

It was not a particularly difficult task, as Côte d'Ivoire was really the only opposition. Krautzun's first game ended in a 2-0 win against Madagascar. The next game was at home against Côte d'Ivoire and a victory for Tunisia would practically have guaranteed them a place in the finals, with two games to spare! It was not to be, as a one-all draw kept the group alive. The two final matches were against the two Congos and after thrashing Congo 6-0 in the penultimate game, Tunisia faced the DRC in Kinshasa. Krautzun was not permitted to sit on the bench in the former Zaire, as he had been suspended after insulting an assistant referee in a previous match. Instead, he sat in the stands, armed with a mobile phone, which he used to give instructions to his assistant coach.

One of Scoglio's Genoa-boys, Khaled Badra, opened the scoring for the North Africans early in the game. This, of course, did not go down too well with the local fans and they turned their attention to the German sitting in the stands and influencing the game. At first they merely pointed fingers at him, then they grew a bit more vociferous and then one of the fans tried to grab the mobile phone from him. At that stage Krautzun decided that he would rather sit in the comfort and security of the VIP enclosure, even if it meant not having the best possible vantage point.

From his new seat, Krautzun continued directing proceedings on the field and must have done a pretty good job, as the Tunisians added another two goals. More importantly though, the three points ensured Tunisia a place in the World Cup finals.

For Krautzun, the victory was like a dream come true. As a 60-year-old, he was nearing the end of his coaching career and before taking over the coaching of the North Africans, he said that he was hoping to take a side to the World Cup finals as the cherry on top of a successful career, so to say. And to ensure that the World Cup campaign developed just as successfully as the qualifying campaign, Krautzun started working on a programme of action within a few weeks of having qualified.

He did not, however, get very far with his programme of action, as on 18 August 2001, press reports announced the end of Krautzun as Tunisia's coach. He was either fired, or resigned - depending on which report one read. In his place the Tunisians hired French coach Henri Michel, who was given the honour of taking the side to the World Cup finals.

Tunisia was not expected to be the only North African country to qualify for the finals as the draw had practically set up a two-horse race between Morocco and Egypt in group C. The third North African team in the group, Algeria, was given only an outside chance to top the group and qualify for the finals, while Namibia and Senegal were considered cannon-fodder for the others.

After the first three matches, Senegal had not exactly come across as cannon-fodder, but nor had they seemed like world-beaters. The Lions of Teranga, as the team is called, drew at home to Egypt and away to Algeria and Morocco. In their fourth game, they started turning on the heat and trounced Namibia 4-0 followed by an equally impressive 3-0 victory against Algeria. Although a 1-0 defeat in Egypt meant that Morocco needed only a draw in Dakar to qualify, Senegal kept on track by beating the favourites 1-0 to set up a nail-biting finale to the group.

Ahead of the last round of matches, Egypt, Senegal and Morocco still had a chance to go through. A 5-0 victory in Namibia and Algeria's draw against Egypt ensured a fairy-tale ending to the Senegalese qualifying story, even though they had to wait for a while after Egypt protested against the result of their match in Algeria.

The two North African countries have long been bitter rivals and in 1990 Egypt won a controversial World Cup qualifier against Algeria to qualify for the 1990 finals in Italy. During the match a fight broke out between the two sides and criminal charges were laid against Algerian star Lakhdar Belloumi for an alleged attack on an Egyptian after the game.

The Pharaohs retaliated by deciding to withdraw from the 1990 African Nations Cup finals, which were held in Algeria five months after the World Cup qualifier in Cairo. But after lengthy negotiations, they decided to send a weakened side instead. This did not go down very well with the Algerian fans, who attacked the Egyptian players after the hosts beat them in the group stage at the Nations Cup.

Since then, relations between the two countries have been somewhat strained and it was not surprising that Algeria had not given Egypt an inch in the crucial World Cup qualifier in 2001. FIFA dismissed the protest and finally Senegal was assured of their place in the finals.

Credited with much of Senegal's success is French-born coach Bruno Metsu, who took over the coaching reigns in October 2000 from popular German Peter Schnittger.

Metsu, who at the time was 47, could look back on an unspectacular playing career with teams such as Nice, Anderlecht and Valenciennes, followed by coaching stints with unglamorous club sides that included Beauvais, Lille and Sedan. He then moved to Africa, where he had a short stint as coach of the Guinean national team, before taking over Senegal.

If Metsu directed proceedings from the outside, Elhadji Diouf was certainly the man who controlled what was going on on the field. The striker, who started playing in France as a 17-year-old prodigy in 1998, scored back-to-back hat-tricks during his side's 4-0 win against Namibia and 3-0 victory against Algeria. Like his national teammates, defender Ferdinand Coly and midfielder Pape Saar, Diouf plays his club football for French team Lens.

Arguably the most important strike of his career was the goal he scored during Senegal's 1-0 victory over Morocco in a match that the North Africans only needed to draw to be guaranteed first place in the group and a place at the finals.

The speedy striker scored his eighth goal of Senegal's qualifying campaign during the West African's 5-0 drubbing of Namibia - a result that secured them their first-ever appearance at the World Cup finals.

Qualifying for the finals caused scenes of wild celebrations throughout the West African country and even President Abdoulaye Wade, who is known to be a keen fan of the national side, joined in.

He welcomed the team on their return from Windhoek and wore a No 11 jersey as a tribute to striker Diouf, whose eight goals were pivotal to the Senegalese success. Wade also richly rewarded the players for their efforts - something they can also expect if they do well in South Korea/Japan.

The Senegalese players were not the only ones who were rewarded after a game in the World Cup qualifiers. The same happened to the Ghanaians.

Rewarding players for their winning performances is practically a daily occurrence in international football and is not considered as something out of the ordinary.

However, there was something distinctly out of the ordinary about the rewards paid to the Ghanaian players. For one, the money was paid to the Ghanaian players by Nigerian authorities. Secondly, it was paid only a few hours after Nigeria had beaten Ghana 3-0 to qualify for the

World Cup finals.

Nigeria's Super Eagles were always considered the overwhelming favourites to advance from their group, which included Sierra Leone, Liberia, Sudan and Ghana. But surprisingly, they did not have things their own way. After beating Sierra Leone 2-0, they crashed to Liberia, beat Sudan, drew with Ghana and lost the return leg to Sierra Leone. At this stage their World Cup aspirations were in total disarray and they were in serious danger of not making it to the finals.

As a first step, they fired the coach. It was a decision not taken lightly, the President of the Nigerian Football Association, Brigadier-Colonel Dominic Oneya, told me a few weeks later. "I looked at the situation and I realised that we would be in trouble if I did not act swiftly. It was not a nice thing to do, but I had to do it, so I fired Jo Bonfrere and gave the job to Amodu Shaibu."

Shaibu had been in the same situation before and as a Nigerian, he knew all the players and they trusted him. Shaibu's first game was at home against Liberia and anything but a win for the Super Eagles would have given Liberia's Lone Stars a first-ever appearance at the World Cup finals.

But the chance of playing at the World Cup finals was something that the Super Eagles did not want to give up too easily. For the first time during the qualifying campaign, they performed to their potential and ran out 2-0 winners. In the next game, Sudan was the opponent and they were brushed aside 4-0. As Liberia had surprisingly lost at home to Ghana, the Super Eagles suddenly found themselves in a situation whereby they could, after all, qualify for Japan/South Korea, provided they beat Ghana's Black Stars in their final qualifying match. On paper, that looked like a fairly straightforward and simple task. In practice though it was not that simple, as Nigeria had not beaten Ghana for 17 years.

This time around, Nigeria won 3-0 and qualified for the World Cup. It was a result that did not please the former World Footballer of the Year George Weah, who happened to be a Liberian and missed out on an opportunity of playing at the World Cup finals.

Weah, who was 35-years old at that stage, was probably pretty upset about missing out on his one and only chance of making it to the World Cup and his accusations that Ghana had been bribed to lose the game were seen in that light.

The story should have ended there, but it did not.

HAS ANYBODY GOT A WHISTLE?

Several months later a newspaper in Ghana reported that the chairman of the Ghana Football Association, Ben Koufie, had accepted U$ 25 000 at a reception held after the match and organised by the governor of the province in which the game was played. The newspaper said that Koufie had at first rejected the money, but had then changed his mind after discussing the issue with the 31 players and officials making up the delegation.

The vote was 31-0 that Koufie should move back to the high table and return with the offerings. Knowing that he was only bowing to public opinion, he went and collected the money and was coasting to his bench when one of the people in the travelling party pointed out to him that he had forgotten to take several other gifts offered to the Ghanaians, so he had to return again.

The money had been shared between the 31 members of the delegation who had travelled to Nigeria for the game. The handful of journalists in the travelling party had at first not received a share of the money, but after complaining had been given some cash, which probably goes a long way towards explaining why the story only broke a few months after it had happened.

The Ghana Football Association was quick to react, issuing a strong statement in which Koufie was exonerated from any wrongdoing. They said the allegation of bribery was both unfounded and without merit.

Nigerian officials were equally quick to react. "To the best of my knowledge, I don't think any money was given out to any team. This is a grave allegation," a spokesman for the Nigerian sports and youth development department said.

"The money was a personal gift from the provincial governor, freely given and freely received," a Nigerian diplomat in Ghana said.

With such contradictions, it was not surprising that FIFA launched their own enquiry, which cleared both Ghana and Nigeria of any wrongdoing. The organisation did, however, warn both countries of the "considerable ethical problems and legal uncertainties over such gifts." They were told that there should be no repeat.

The FIFA disciplinary committee ruled the cash was not bribery as it was offered after the match at a public event. They said that gifts for opposing national teams seemed to be a local custom.

This is something that was confirmed by a provincial politician, who said that his government had, "as it is usual, organised a public banquet at which the Ghana team, friends of Nigeria and the international media attended after Nigeria had won the ticket for the World Cup.

"Everybody was entertained because it was a joyous occasion at which modest gifts were extended to Nigeria's national team, the Ghanaian team and Nigeria's Supporters Club."

For the players and officials in the Ghanaian touring party, it might really have been a modest gift, but nobody will ever know for sure if the modest gift led to a far greater gift for Nigeria - that of making it to the World Cup!

18

CHAIRMAN MAO'S
DISAPPROVING LOOK

BUT BEFORE THE FIVE TEAMS packed their bags and flew to South Korea and Japan, they had a much shorter trip to Mali to compete in the 23rd finals of the African Cup of Nations.

I embarked on the same journey - only just though!

The first stage was pretty easy. Phone a travel agent, book a flight and off I go, I thought. Cape Town to Johannesburg, Johannesburg to Abidjan, Côte d'Ivoire's capital, and from there directly to Bamako, the capital of Mali, on Air Afrique. That would get me there well in time for the start of the tournament on 19 January 2002.

At least, it would have got me there had Air Afrique not followed many other airlines in the wake of the World Trade Center bombing and run into financial problems and stopped flying - a few days before I was to leave. By the time I had managed to make alternative bookings, the competition was well under way. Thanks to satellite television and good friends who had made different travel arrangements, I was able to make the best of a bad situation and filed my stories on time. Hopefully nobody noticed that I wasn't yet in Mali.

My next confirmed flights were with Air Cameroon. Cape Town to Johannesburg, Johannesburg to Douala and from there to Bamako. But again it was not to be, as Air Cameroon cancelled the flight. I however was determined to make it to Bamako to see at least some of the matches. Finally, on 30 January 2002, I arrived at Johannesburg International Airport for my Air Cameroon flight to Douala, connecting to Bamako. The only problem was that there was no flight to Douala listed amongst the departures. The only Air Cameroon flight scheduled for that day was to Kinshasa. By then I was so desperate that I was prepared to take any flight, as long as it was going north, and I joined the queue.

As I checked in my baggage, I asked the Air Cameroon official why the flight was going to Kinshasa instead of Douala.

"It is not going to Kinshasa, it is only going to Douala," he answered.

"But the sign says Kinshasa. I thought the flight is supposed to go to Douala, but now it seems that it is going to Kinshasa."

"No, the flight is to Douala, it goes via Kinshasa, but today it is going directly to Douala. Why, I don't know."

Satisfied that I did not have to go via Kinshasa, I proceeded to the departure gate and boarded a bus. There were only a handful of people on the bus and three of them were uniformed policeman who were standing around a man sitting on one of the benches. A man standing next to me started a conversation, asking me if I had even been to Kinshasa.

"No, but the plane is not going there today," I said.

"What do you mean the plane is not going there."

"Well, the guy at the check-in counter told me that the plane is going directly to Douala today. Why, I don't know."

With that, the man suddenly became very quiet, obviously trying to figure out how he was going to get from Douala to Kinshasa. I turned my attention to the man being escorted by the policemen. I later found out that he was an illegal immigrant being deported from South Africa.

The flight to Douala was very pleasant. We were only 20 passengers and I managed to catch up on some much-needed sleep.

We landed in Douala soon after midday. The airport in Douala was not a particularly inviting place. A moist, sticky heat made the temperature almost unbearable and as I had no local currency, I could not even buy something to drink. The departure time to Bamako was scheduled for 4pm and I thought that I could probably survive till then.

4pm came and went and at about 5pm I asked somebody at the Air Cameroon check-in counter what time the flight to Bamako was leaving. "Maybe at 6pm," the woman behind the counter answered. She must have seen the disappointment in my face, as she gave me a meal voucher. "Here, you can have some supper with this. The restaurant is upstairs."

I went upstairs and sat down. A waiter brought me a plate of chicken with rice. He asked what I wanted to drink. "Sprite, with lots of ice."

Just as 4pm had come and gone, 6pm came and went without much movement in the airport. When darkness descended over Douala a short while later, I was still sitting in the airport restaurant and reading. Suddenly I, too, was sitting in the dark, as a power failure caused all the lights to go off. After about ten minutes they went on again, only to go off again a short while later. This kept on happening for the next two hours before we finally were told that our flight was ready to leave.

We left Douala at 9pm, but my hopes of a quick flight to Bamako were dashed as I found out that we were flying via Lagos and Abidjan.

The flight finally arrived in Bamako shortly after three in the morning. The visa formalities did not take any time and within ten minutes of disembarking I was standing in the arrival hall waiting for my luggage. But even though it took a long time to come, it did finally arrive and I was on my way out of the airport building.

I had arranged to share a hotel room with a Nigerian journalist living in London. James Coker worked for the Treasury, but dreamed of publishing an African sports magazine. He had been in Mali for two weeks already and had given me the address of the hotel he was staying.

The minute I set foot outside the building, I was surrounded by a group of youngsters. "Taxi, hotel," they asked.

Being a French-speaking county, I should not have been too surprised that the majority of those surrounding me spoke only French. Surprised I was not, but having spent over 18 hours travelling, I was slightly irritated and tried to shoo them away. One of them, however, was very persistent and ended up coaxing me to a yellow taxi that had obviously seen better days - many, many years ago.

I gave him the name of the hotel and got in. Even though I had none of the local currency, CFA, I said: "Five thousand CFA, OK," I asked.

He stared at me blankly. "I will pay you five thousand, that is what it costs from the airport to the Hotel Maxim. Do you know where that is?"

The same blank expression, only this time it was followed by a longish outburst of something or other, which I presumed to have been French. I decided that I was just too tired to try to make myself understood and sat back, hoping that he had understood me.

He obviously had, but just as obviously he had no idea where the Hotel Maxim was. After driving around for nearly thirty minutes he stopped the car and mumbled something to some people sitting on the side of the road. The only thing I could understand was 'Hotel Maxim.'

The Hotel Maxim must have been a tiny establishment, as it was only after the fourth time that he had stopped and asked for directions that we pulled up in front of a sign that said: 'Hotel Maxim.'

As I had thought earlier, the hotel was very small - little more than a house with a tiny garden and a pool in front. But not only was it small, I also discovered that it was locked and for the next ten minutes I knocked on windows and doors, hoping to find somebody to let me in.

After banging on numerous windows, somebody finally switched on a light and opened the door for me. He showed me to James's room.

Not surprisingly, James had been sleeping. "Hi, I was waiting for you for hours, but then fell asleep. Welcome to Mali."

We chatted for a while before turning off the light.

After having slept for a few hours, we got up for breakfast. In the morning I discovered just how small the hotel was. There were four rooms, each with two beds that had mosquito nets hanging over them. There was a lounge-cum-dining room, as well as two bathrooms. In the small garden, there was a swimming pool with refreshingly cold water. On that day, the pool was being used for a photographic shoot of a bridal couple. The bride was very beautiful, the blackness of her skin highlighted by the whiteness of her dress.

Breakfast, consisting of tea and coffee, jam and rolls was served on the veranda. Once we had finished our breakfast, we took a taxi to the 'Palais de Congrés' to sort out my accreditation. Surprisingly, it took only a short while and within thirty minutes I had in my possession the badge that separated me (and the other journalists) from the mere mortals who had to stand for hours in the sun queuing for tickets to allow them to sit in the sun waiting for a game to begin.

My first game was the quarter-final clash between Nigeria and Ghana in the March 26 Stadium in Bamako on Sunday afternoon. As I had to also write a match report of the earlier game between Mali and South Africa that was being played in Keyes, we decided to leave early for the stadium and watch the game in the quiet and comfort of the press centre at the stadium. Our plan might have worked had it been any other day, but as the hosts were themselves fighting for a place in the semi-final, the press centre had become the centre of the universe for all those working in the stadium and the handful of working journalists needing a clear vision of the television and a desk to work from had to compete with dozens of hostesses, soldiers, security guards and technical people for these scarce resources.

It was a battle I was certain I would not be able to win and in desperation I sought the help of those responsible for the press centre. I found an official-looking man in a T-shirt with the logo of the organising committee on it. "Excuse me, I am not trying to be difficult, but I really need to work. For that, I need to be able to see the television and work at a desk. Surely this is the press centre and should be for journalists."

"Yes," the official-looking man agreed with me, "but I am not going to tell the soldiers that they can't watch television here. If it is a problem, you tell them."

A quick glance at the soldiers: six foot two, guns hanging from their hips and built like oxen, convinced me that I should not try what he was not going to try. Instead, I took a chair from one of the adjoining offices and pushed my way past the soldiers, past the security men, past the hostesses and past the technical people and put my chair next to one of the handful of working journalists who were watching the game.

It turned out to be a pretty exciting match, as the hosts made full use of their bonus of playing at home. Inspired by a capacity crowd, they ran out 2-0 winners.

In the second quarter-final- the one I was watching in the stadium - Nigeria left it late, but fully deserved their victory. The most significant moment of the game occurred late in the first half, when Nigerian goalkeeper Ike Shorunmu was badly injured and stayed down after a Ghanaian attack. The Ghanaian player who had the ball at the time did not do what many other players would have done and shot for goal, he kicked the ball out of play allowing the badly injured 'keeper to be taken off the field and rushed to hospital.

After the game we took a taxi back to the hotel. The drive nearly ended in a fistfight after the driver dropped us off. As we gave him the deux mille fare we had agreed upon before getting into the taxi, he did not want to accept it, saying he wanted more. Even after we doubled the money we placed before him, he did not seem satisfied. In desperation, I went into the hotel and looked for one of the other guests, who I knew spoke French. Luckily for me, Bharat Amarnani was there. He came out and spoke to the driver. He turned to me: "He says that you told him that he said to you that it would cost ten thousand CFA and that you agreed."

"No we did not, he said two thousand, deux mille and that is what we said we would pay." I held up my two fingers and stuck them under the driver's nose. "Deux mille."

The driver opened both hands and showed me all ten figures. "Dix mille," he said.

And with that, I suddenly realised what the problem was. We had mistaken dues for due and that is why the driver was so unhappy. He felt we were short-changing him by eight thousand CFA! I gave Bharat five thousand and told him to tell the driver that was two thousand more than one normally pays for the trip and he was not going to get more. I then went inside.

I watched through the window as Bharat gave the driver the money. Although he was obviously not very happy, he went back to his car, still muttering to himself.

That evening we went out for supper with Bharat. He was a real character. Originally from Bangalore in India, he moved to Liberia's capital of Monrovia as a teenager and started his career as a trader. By all accounts, he must have done pretty well for himself and was living a comfortable life with his wife, whom he had married in an arranged marriage.

He was not at all embarrassed to talk about arranged marriages. "Today, there is so much dishonesty in the world. I have been happily married to my wife for more than 10 years and I am very eager to have my own daughter married in such a way. Look at the high divorce rate. The divorce rate amongst arranged marriages is much lower than it is for other marriages."

The civil war in Liberia had not passed him by. "My house and everything we owned was burnt down and I sent my family to Togo's capital of Lomé. I thought that president Samuel Doe would step down and that Charles Taylor would take over and that things would calm down. They did not and in 1991 everything was burnt down for the second time. I was evacuated by the American marines, who took us onto a boat. We were not allowed to take anything with us. They asked us if we wanted our lives or our possessions. On the boat, we were debriefed for days. They wanted to know everything about the war. They even wanted to know things like whether the attackers wore shoes or not, and what uniforms they had."

As the drinks flowed freely in the Le Campagnard - James assured me that they served the strongest Bacardi with Cokes that he has ever been served - we found out more and more about Bharat. Although his family had moved back to Bangalore after his house had been burnt down for the second time, he still did all his business in Africa. He imported African print material from China to various countries in Africa and spent several months each year on the continent.

He obviously came from a very close-knit family, as by the time we finally left the Le Campagnard and stumbled across the road to Asia Restaurant for our meal, Bharat had told us about cousins and sisters who lived in Spain, Jamaica, Hong Kong and the Philippines.

The next morning Bharat took us to the market to buy some textiles. He had all the contacts and not only managed to secure the best prices and qualities, he also showed us the stalls selling rip-offs of famous brands. You could buy Adibas and Reedbuck shoes, as well as my personal favourite, the 'Air Shoes', which not only had the Nike swoosh, they also had the three stripes of Adidas. Also on sale were thousands of Osama Bin Laden souvenirs, like pictures and T-shirts.

The next game in Bamako was the quarter-final between Senegal and the Democratic Republic Congo (DRC), which was played in the small Modibo Keita Stadium. We arrived there about thirty minutes before the kick-off and already it was packed. There must have been several thousand flag-waving Senegalese fans, who had come to see their side advance into the semi-final. And they were certainly not disappointed, as Alassane Diou scored in the first half. El Hadji Diouf added a second shortly before the end and the World Cup finalists were safely through, joining Mali, Nigeria and Cameroon, who had earlier disposed of Egypt.

As I had to file my stories immediately after the game, we were amongst the last to leave the stadium and this unfortunately meant that we had a very limited choice when it came to deciding how to get home. We could either walk, or take the lone taxi that was still standing in front of the stadium. We opted for the latter and walked towards the yellow taxi. As we drew closer, we had an inkling why the car was the only vehicle left behind.

It had four wheels, four doors and windscreens, but that just about was the only thing that justified calling it a vehicle. "This is like a taxi from hell," James said. "I am not sure that it would not be better to walk, even if it takes a few hours."

"Don't be so spoilt," I replied, as I opened the back door and sat down. I noticed two huge holes in the back, through which I could see the road.

"Bloody hell, the guy does not even have a key to start the car," James sounded somewhat panicky.

I looked in front and could just see the driver brush two wires together. There was a huge spark and the car spluttered into action. I needn't have rushed to look as in the course of the short trip home, the rusty car stopped several times. The driver would then brush the two wires together, the spark would appear and the car would jerk forward. Surprisingly though, we managed to make it all the way to the hotel and were dropped off.

Our trip in B 9865 MD was not the only experience we had with taxis of a somewhat dubious nature. The very next day we wanted to visit the Cameroonian side, who had arrived in Bamako.

As in most major cities throughout Africa, in Bamako there is no difficulty in catching a ride in a taxi, and the driver of the taxi we flagged down assured us that he knew exactly where the CAN Village deux was. So we got in and started our journey to see the Indomitable Lions. A few minutes into our ride, James suddenly pointed to a sedan parked on the side of the road. "Look at that, there is a cow in the back of the car and it is not even a van."

I have travelled in many, many African cities, but even for me this was a first. "At least the cow is not tied to the roof," I answered.

Shortly afterwards I was to encounter another first. This time in the form of a goat, tied to the front of a bicycle weaving in and out of the traffic. The poor goat, however, was a huge thing and therefore had to be perversely disfigured to fit around the bicycle.

My immediate reaction was to consider living a life without rare to medium fillet steaks or pork chops smothered in a garlic sauce and becoming a militant activist for vegetarianism, but on second thoughts I thought that animals probably preferred being eaten than being driven around the streets of Bamako tied to a bicycle or in the back of a sedan.

As we continued our search for the Cameroonian squad, it soon became apparent that the driver - contrary to what he had assured us - had no idea were they were staying. At first it was just a hunch I had, but the third time we passed the same juvenile detention centre, I realised that we might be spending the rest of the day driving around Bamako looking for the Indomitable Lions. And we probably would have, had the driver not ran out of petrol - not once, but twice!

When it happened the first time, he opened the bonnet, unplugged the pipe that fed the engine with petrol and sucked on it. After getting a good mouthful, he connected the pipe again, spat out the petrol and managed to start the car again. He then drove a few hundred metres down the road to a tiny wooden stall that sold petrol in bottles on the side of the road. He bought one and poured it into the tank and drove on.

A few minutes later I heard James muttering something along the lines of: "This does not look very good." His voice sounded very anxious and I looked up. A Landrover was driving on the wrong side of the road and was heading directly for us. A few metres before he hit us in a head-on, he took a left turning, leaving us gasping for breath. We turned around and looked back, just in time to see how a moped was sent sprawling to the ground by the Landrover. Its driver did not seem particularly interested though and continued driving.

Shortly afterwards, we ran out of petrol again and I suggested that this was a sign that not only would we not find the Cameroonians, we should also see it as a sign that we should get out of the taxi while we still could. James, who normally is rather argumentative, agreed immediately!

For supper, we went with two Swiss, who were also staying in the Hotel Maxim, to a Chinese restaurant, which we had already used twice for take-aways. What puzzled me about it was that there were always plenty of cars parked in front of the building, but never any people inside.

As we entered the restaurant, I noticed that it was empty again. We sat down at a table and I chose a seat in line with a huge photograph of a very stern-looking Chairman Mao.

Gianpaoplo Amado, whom we only called JP because we had at first believed his name to be Jean-Paul, and Orlando Scheuber had taken leave from their jobs in Switzerland and travelled to Mali to watch football. James told me that JP was the original Trainspotter or Anorak (both terms I did not know). He worked for worldstadiums.com and knew the most obscure stadiums in obscure cities in obscure countries. He also knew obscure clubs throughout the world and any conversation with him was punctuated by references to clubs like Dangerous Darkies (Nelspruit/South Africa), Eleven Men in Flight and Peacemakers (Mhlume/Swaziland) or Mighty Jets (Jos/Nigeria).

Over sweet and sour pork JP, who was like a walking encyclopaedia of football stadiums, told us that he had been to at least 100 stadiums in 18 different countries. He was hoping to add at least two countries and a couple of stadiums during this trip, but was having problems confirming a flight to Côte d'Ivoire, as Air Cameroon had cancelled the flight they had booked for and Air Mauritania had no seats for them, even though they had confirmed bookings.

James asked him if he preferred to visit a stadium when it was empty or if a game was in progress. "To be honest, if I had a choice between going to a stadium when it is full and when it is empty, I would always choose to go when there are no people."

When I wanted to know from him if he actually enjoyed football, or just the stadiums, he replied with a line that I think is worthy of making any list of 100 top footie quotes. He said: "Players come and go, but stadiums stay."

We spent the evening speaking about football and stadiums and I was extremely pleased to have finally met somebody who seemed even more 'football mad' than I was.

A few hours later we had covered stadiums throughout the world, finished our supper and were ready to go. Before leaving, I needed to make a trip to the bathroom and left my seat, walking past Mao, who was looking just as fierce as he had when we entered the restaurant. To get to the bathroom, I had to go past the kitchen and a number of rooms that I had not seen earlier. There were about four rooms; each had a double bed, a red bulb hanging from the ceiling and a shower. In front of one of the rooms a young woman stood, leaning against the wall. As I passed her on my way back to the restaurant, she winked at me and said something in French, beckoning me inside. I declined, but finally realised why there were always cars in front, but never any people in the restaurant: the building housed a Chinese restaurant in front and a brothel in the back!

JP and Orlando also accompanied me to the second semi-final between Cameroon and the hosts. James had decided to also go to the earlier match between Nigeria and Senegal, in the Modibo Keita Stadium. As there was only an hour or two between the two matches, I decided to head directly for the March 26 Stadium. We had decided to treat ourselves to the comfort of a Mercedes taxi, instead of the 'normal' battered old car.

To get to the stadium, one had to cross the Niger river. There were two bridges over the Niger. One was practically a highway, while the other was a single carriage lane. But as the width of the river was so huge, there were three areas on the bridge, where cars could pull off to let others pass.

The main problem with the bridge, though, was that not only was it used by cars, it was also used by goats and sheep that were being herded across the bridge. This caused huge traffic congestions. On our way to the semi-final, we were lucky though, as there were no animals using the bridge. Instead, there was an accident that resulted in a huge line of cars, stretching virtually the entire length of the bridge. We had visions of being late for the kick-off and only felt better when we looked behind and saw a bus transporting the Cameroonian side to the game.

For the Indomitable Lions, that was not to be the only problem they faced during the day. Shortly after we finally made it to the stadium, I heard a huge commotion outside the press centre. I rushed to the window and saw four soldiers manhandle one of the Cameroonian squad. Cameroon's coach, Winfried Schäfer, was also there, yelling at the soldiers in German. I rushed outside to get a better look.

Schäfer told me that he and his assistant coach, the former international goalkeeper Thomas Nkono, had been on the field to watch the last few minutes of the other semi-final between Nigeria and Senegal that was being broadcast on a large screen TV in the stadium at the time.

"Suddenly these idiots appeared and pulled Tommy off the field. They handcuffed him and started pushing him around. I pleaded with them, but they would not listen. It was only when some people from the organising committee came that they let him go. I wonder where their sense of fair play is."

Intimidation, harassment and a strongly partisan crowd were not enough to help the home side to a second major upset. Salomon Olembe scored twice in the first half and Marc-Vivien Foe added a third shortly before the end to give Cameroon a second successive final at the Nations Cup. But as Senegal had continued with their fairy-tale football season in beating Nigeria in the other semi-final, Mali 2002 did not provide a repeat of the 2000 final, instead pitting Cameroon against Senegal in the Championship match.

After the semi-final we decided to go and eat at a restaurant in a place called Luna Parc. This was an amusement park with several rides. These rides were priced between 500 and 3,000 CFA and not surprisingly, Luna Parc was virtually empty, as very few people in Mali could afford to pay such prices for an evening's entertainment. One of the cashiers selling tickets told us that the park had only been open for three months. I wondered why they had managed to finish an amusement park three months before the start of the Nations Cup, but had failed to complete the villages in which the players were meant to stay, forcing them to live in hotels.

CHAIRMAN MAO'S DISAPPROVING LOOK

The food was good and after spending the evening talking about obscure stadiums and obscure clubs, we walked back to the Hotel Maxim, passing hundreds of goats that were standing on the side of the road. I later asked Bharat why there were thousands of goats all over Bamako and they seemed to be getting more each day.

He told me that there were three Muslim festivals. Ramzan, or Ramadan, was one, the other was Moharan. The next festival was Bhakrid, or Tabaski, and that was the one which was just around the corner. During Bhakrid Muslims slaughtered goats and Bharat told me that on a certain day thousands of goats were killed, sending rivers of blood down the streets of Bamako. He said goats were brought into Bamako from all over Mali before this festival and sold to Muslims for as much as £70 per goat.

I spent the next three days (they were match-free) discovering Bamako. It certainly was a very interesting place. Incredibly dusty and dry, it had a strong Chinese influence, with electronic gadgets and textiles made in China on sale everywhere. I wondered how Mao would feel if he saw how Chinese goods infiltrated the free market economies of Africa and his countrymen were running cheap brothels in Bamako.

I also spent a day in an orphanage with David and Geraldine, who were also staying in the Hotel Maxim. They were a couple from Paris, who had come to Mali to adopt a baby. They said that they could be waiting for years in France, but that things moved much faster in Mali. They had just received their little two-month old daughter called Aïssé and they wanted to go back to the orphanage to thank the staff.

The woman in charge explained that all the children in her home had been abandoned at a very early age and were being kept in the orphanage until such time as adoptive parents could be found for them. She said that they were lucky as most children found parents before the age of three.

David and Geraldine showed me around. The children were housed in dormitories according to their ages and all dormitories were meticulously clean. We stopped in the one in which the youngest babies were kept. About ten babies lay in cots standing around the room and three helpers were feeding and soothing babies. David and Geraldine sat down with Aïssé and started to feed her. We stayed there until Aïssé had finished her bottle and then went on. The home also had a dormitory filled with disabled children and, as I stood in front of them, I thought of the life they faced in a country such as Mali, where the opportunities to succeed are already so far and in between. What chance did they have in life, I wondered?

The final was on Sunday and as Mali had already lost the third-place play off the day before, organisers had decided to allow fans free entry into the stadium for the game between Senegal and Cameroon.

It was not a brilliant game, but Cameroon was clearly the better side and in the end won on penalties to become the first country since Ghana in 1965 to successfully defend their title.

After the game I had to file several stories as well as do an interview with Schäfer and by the time we left, it was not only dark, there were also only a few people remaining in the stadium. We saw only one taxi and walked up to the driver who was leaning against the door. "Taxi," we asked?

"Oui," he answered.

"Hotel Maxim."

"No," he said and turned his head.

We had no idea why he had turned us down, but not wanting to beg, we walked to the road, hoping to see a taxi passing. Unfortunately, there was none and an hour later we were still standing on the side of the road. By now we were getting pretty desperate as all we wanted to do was get home to our hotel.

James suggested we walk back towards the stadium in the hope that we could catch a ride with one of the vehicles that was still periodically leaving the stadium. After a few minutes wait, a car stopped opposite us. In it were two passengers and we asked the driver if he could take us to the Aqua Bar, which was close to our hotel. The driver said that it would cost 6,000 CFA, but as we had no alternative, we accepted.

Once we were on our way the two passengers told us that they were Swiss journalists and that the taxi was taking them to their hotel. We looked at the driver and we suspected him to be the driver who had earlier turned us down. Some twenty minutes later, the taxi stopped at a hotel, which was very close to ours, and the two journalists got out. We then told the taxi driver to proceed to the Hotel Maxim. Surprisingly, he did not ask where it was.

It was then that we both realised that the driver was the same who had taken me home from an earlier game and had felt cheated. Unexpectedly, he had received a chance to pay me back and he had taken it. First, he had been able to turn us down, forcing an hour's delay and then he had been able to charge us what he wanted.

We could not help laughing at his change of fortune and paid him the money he wanted.

My flight back to South Africa was scheduled to leave at 5am the next morning and as I wanted to be at the airport three hours before, I decided to spend a last evening in the Chinese restaurant-cum-brothel, savouring their culinary delights before heading out straight for the airport.

Once I had arrived there, I got into the Air Cameroon queue. After about 30 minutes, I had finally made it to the check-in counter.

"Can I check my luggage through to Johannesburg, please?"

"No, you can only check in at 6am," he woman behind the counter said.

"But we are supposed to leave at 5am. When are we going to leave," I asked.

"I don't know, maybe 7am."

I now was a worried man. My connection time in Douala for my flight to South Africa was only two hours and as the next flight from Cameroon to South Africa was four days later, I saw myself stranded in the humid airport lounge in Douala. "But I have a connecting flight, what am I going to do about that?" I asked her.

She was unsympathetic and cold. "I don't know."

In desperation I turned to another Air Cameroon employee. He assured me that he would send a telex to Douala, informing them of the situation. He then told me to come back in four hours.

Anybody who has ever spent four hours sleeping on a floor in the Bamako airport - or any other airport for that matter - will believe me that the next four hours were not the best four hours I had spent during this trip. Far from it. I was exhausted, but could not really sleep on the hard floor. I tried though, but when I went back to the check-in counter at 6am, I was not a satisfied customer. The same unsympathetic woman, who had probably gone home and slept in a wonderfully soft feather bed, said she had no idea when the plane for Douala (which incidentally was again going via Abidjan and Lagos) was going to leave, or for that matter, what was going to happen to me in Douala if I missed my connecting flight, which by now seemed more than probable.

"I don't know," she said. She might as well have added: "And I don't care," for that is certainly the attitude I felt.

Luckily, the man who had promised to send a telex on my behalf was standing close by. He assured me that Douala had sent him an answer informing him that they would wait for me.

After my experiences with Air Cameroon, I am not sure to what degree I believed him, but as I had little choice, I proceeded to wait. Finally at 8am, we checked in.

That, of course, did not mean much. And it certainly did not mean that we were about to leave. In fact, there was not a single plane in sight in the airport. Two hours later, a plane arrived. I got really excited when I saw that it was an Air Cameroon flight. At 11am, we were finally air-borne and six hours later, we touched down in Douala.

Once there, I realised why the official had been so positive when he told me that the plane would wait for me in Douala. Once again, there was no other plane on the tarmac, only the one in which I had just arrived. My usual question about the departure date met with the usual response: "Maybe at nine."

Surprisingly, we left only an hour later (six hours after the scheduled departure time). This time though, there must have been enough passengers to make it worth their while to stop in Kinshasa, for in Kinshasa we stopped. It was only a short stop though and at 4am we finally arrived in Johannesburg - I had been travelling for 24 hours, been awake for 36 and would have killed for a nice bed.

Instead of a nice bed though, there was a further six-hour wait in Johannesburg and a two-hour flight back to Cape Town!

19

HAS ANYBODY GOT A WHISTLE?

ONCE THE NATIONS CUP WAS OVER, I had lost the chance to continue pursuing a footballing story of international dimension. Instead, I would have to return to parochial reporting, hoping at best for a trip to Bobo-Dialasso or Bamako in between.

Just how parochial, I realised a short while afterwards. Ajax Cape Town was playing Orlando Pirates in a top-of-the-table league clash in Cape Town. There was no score at half time and both sides were eager to get on with it. The players were doing a few exercises on the field to keep warm, the referee and his two assistants were standing on the field, and the ball was placed on the centre spot. Everything was ready for the second half to begin.

It did not. Instead, the referee started fumbling about in his pocket. He then started walking around on the field, obviously looking for something. He had lost his whistle! After searching in vain for a few minutes, he decided to approach the fourth official and ask him if he had a spare whistle. Luckily he did and the second half could begin.

The incident took me back a few years. I had accompanied the South African Olympic football team on a three-match tour to the USA. During the trip, I had spent quite a bit of time with Mich D'Avray, who at the time was coaching the team. D'Avray was a South African by birth but had spent a long time in the then English first division in a successful spell with Ipswich Town, before winding down his career in Holland. D'Avray had then returned to South Africa, where he took over a league club called Moroka Swallows. From there he had moved to Cape Town Spurs. After winning the league and cup double with Spurs, he had been given the task to coach the South African Olympic squad. D'Avray was one of the most professional men involved in South African football. He always returned calls, went out of his way to help journalists and obviously knew what he was doing.

Shortly after returning from the USA trip, his side was scheduled to play a friendly against the Australian Olympic team. As the hosts, the Australians were guaranteed a place at the Olympics, and the match would prove a good indicator of South Africa's strength. The game had been scheduled as the curtain-raiser for the World Cup qualifying match between Bafana and Zaire. It was to be played at the FNB Stadium in Johannesburg.

I visited D'Avray in the team hotel the night before the match. I asked him how preparations had gone and what his experiences were.

"I think we've got a pretty good side and I am confident that we have a good chance. Australia has an excellent development programme in place and they are always very strong at youth level. Are you coming to the match?"

"Of course," I said.

At FNB Stadium journalists with press tickets are permitted to use the players' entrance. It takes you past the change rooms to the tunnel that leads to the field. I arrived at the stadium at 12.10pm, eager not to miss too much of the game.

I need not have rushed, as when I entered the stadium, I saw the Australian and South African players sitting on the floor outside the change rooms. D'Avray was pacing up and down in front of them. I went up to him and asked him why the match had not yet started.

"You won't fucking believe it, these idiots have not organised a referee." D'Avray was a committed Christian and I had never heard him swear before. He was furious! "Somebody is running around at the moment trying to do something, I have no idea what, though."

Ten minutes later the manager of the South African side appeared and said that they had found a referee in the stands. I knew the referee. He was from Durban and officiated in the second division there. This was probably his first international match, but the game could begin.

That at least, is what everybody thought. But nothing happened. The players continued sitting on the ground, D'Avray continued pacing up and down and the referee stood in the middle of it all chatting to the manager.

"Mich, what is the problem now, you need to be finished with the game by quarter past two at the latest?"

He looked at me and just shook his head. "I don't know whether I should laugh or cry, but there is no whistle. The referee has no whistle and it seems there is nobody with a whistle in the stadium. I feel so embarrassed."

I felt bad for him. Here was an honest guy, trying to get the South African Olympic team qualified for the Olympics and his association couldn't even organise a friendly match without any hitches. I felt just as sorry for the Australians. They had flown thousands of kilometres to play two international friendlies against South Africa, and now one of them was in danger of not being played at all because the referee did not have a whistle.

"Let me see if I can help you," I told D'Avray. I rushed onto the field to see if there was anything that could be done. A few photographers were on the field already, waiting for the game to begin. I went to Gavin Barker, who was a photographer with one of the local football magazines. I told him why the game was not starting and asked him if he had any suggestion. He said that he thought that another of the photographers, whom he knew, and who was also waiting on the field, normally carried a whistle with him. He ran over to the photographer and asked him. He then turned around to me and gave me the thumbs up sign. Barker took the whistle and rushed up the tunnel to where the referee was still deep in conversation with the manager.

As soon as Barker gave him the whistle, he blew. The players got up and walked onto the field. The game could finally begin! Or so everybody thought. The next problem was one of timing. The main game between Bafana and Zaire was scheduled to start at 3pm, the South African under-23 manager could hardly go to the match officials and say, "Sorry, but we did not have a referee and a whistle for the game between the South African and the Australian Olympic teams. Would you have a problem starting a bit later?" As both sides were eager to play though, a compromise was quickly reached and the match was reduced to a friendly that would not count towards the statistics. It would be played thirty minutes each way. And then the game finally began.

Looking back at that game, I suppose both sides had very little to complain about, as the match at least took place. I have been to cover matches where that had not always been the case.

In 1998, South Africa was bidding for the World Cup and the world controlling body, FIFA, had sent an inspection group to South Africa to determine whether the country was in a position to host such a huge tournament. The visit created an enormous amount of interest worldwide and I went to take photographs at a local league match between Hellenic and Free State Stars, hoping to be able to use them to document a story I was writing about the visit. The venue was the Greenpoint Stadium in Cape Town, which was not far from where I stayed.

The home side, Hellenic, is a club with a rich tradition in South African football, but does not attract many supporters. I was thus pleasantly surprised when I arrived at the stadium and saw hundreds of cars parked outside.

I drove up to the gate and showed my league press card to the security guard standing at the gate. "Sorry sir, we can't let you in," he said.

"What do you mean you can't let me in? I always park my car inside, I have never had any problems."

"But we can't let you in today, sorry sir."

I showed him my card again. "Surely with that, I am entitled to park inside."

"That card means nothing to me. I have my orders and that is to let nobody in."

At this stage, I was furious. "What do you mean you have orders not to let anyone in? Who gave you those orders?"

"The headmaster."

"The headmaster? The headmaster of what?"

"The headmaster of Khayelitsha Secondary School."

I felt like jumping out of the car and throttling the guy. Only, he was bigger than me. So I remained calm. "The headmaster of Khayelitsha Secondary School told you not to let me in. What has he got to do with this?"

"He organised it, sir."

"He organised the game. Between Hellenic and Stars?"

"No, he organised the athletics meeting that is being held here at the moment."

"What do you mean athletics meeting? There is supposed to be a Premier Soccer League match here today."

"I don't know about that, sir. All I know is that there is an athletics meeting."

At that moment, one of the Hellenic officials was leaving the stadium. I turned to him. "What is going on? Aren't you supposed to be playing against Stars today?"

"Yes, but it seems there was a double booking and the field is being used for a school athletics meeting. Even the referees are there, but they said that even if the meeting stopped, they could not go ahead with the game, as the field is not ready, so we have all gone home."

I went home too.

Shortly afterwards, I was chatting to Eric Dalton. He was a football official who had become the manager of one of the professional clubs in Cape Town. We were talking about the league, about how many things go wrong and how much money the league is generating nowadays.

"Yes, but they could be doing much more. Just imagine how much money the league would get if they organised football pools like in Europe. I am sure they would make millions every week," I said.

"You are probably right. But can you just imagine if the league tried to introduce football pools. It would be chaos. But then, they might introduce truly South African football pools. Instead of predicting what the result will be, you just have to predict if the game is going to be played or not. That will be difficult enough."

How true!

South Africa is not the only place where games do not take place. To prepare for the finals of the 2000 African Cup of Nations, the Zambian national team embarked on a ten-day trip to Ghana and Côte d'Ivoire.

But if the officials were hoping that the matches were to prepare the national team, they were in for a rude shock. What they had forgotten is that a training match only provides training if it is actually played and for it to be played, it has to be organised. And organisational skills were something that the Zambian FA (FAZ) was obviously sadly lacking.

When the team arrived in Côte d'Ivoire, they discovered, much to their embarrassment, that they had not only forgotten to confirm arrangements, they had in some cases not even told their potential hosts that they were coming. The Ivorian national team was preparing for an international, that much was true, but it was not against Zambia. They were scheduled to play Burkina Faso. A hastily arranged friendly against the Ivorian military team, SO Armee ended in a 1-0 defeat for the unorganised visitors.

They then left for Ghana, where Zambia had hoped to play two matches against top club sides, Goldfields and Hearts of Oak. Both clubs, however, were otherwise engaged in cup-ties.

FAZ president Teddy Mulonga sheepishly admitted that there had been a major mix-up. "I have to apologise to the nation for this mess," he said.

The FAZ acting general-secretary, James Mazumba, was less apologetic. "OK, maybe we did not get any response to the messages we sent telling them about our plans to visit their countries, but we did fax and the messages went through," he insisted.

Running football in South Africa is not an easy task. The game evokes so much passion amongst the people, that it is by far the most popular sport. To ensure the smooth running of such an organisation is a huge task. As a journalist, I often have occasion to contact the various associations for information.

On one such occasion, I had been asked by a club in Austria to see to it that the South African Football Association sent its Austrian counterpart an international clearance certificate for a South African player they had just bought. The Austrian club had received my name from a journalist with whom I had worked and as I liked the player who had been transferred, I agreed to help.

I contacted the South African Football Association (SAFA) headquarters in Johannesburg and spoke to the person responsible. I explained the situation to her and she told me that she would see to it immediately.

Two days later, I got a phone call from the manager of the club. "We want to use the player on the weekend, but we have not yet received the clearance. We can't register him if we do not have the necessary documentation."

I promised to look into the matter straight away. I phoned the SAFA official and asked her whether she had had a chance to send the clearance, as she had promised.

"Yes, I sent it the same day," she said.

I phoned the club and told them that it had been sent two days ago. The manager said that he would contact the Austrian FA and find out what the problem was. He phoned me back a short while later and said that they had not received anything. I decided to go to the SAFA offices and speak to the official personally. I tried my humble-pie approach.

"Hi, sorry to disturb you. The club has asked me to ask you if you could please send it again, as the Austrian FA has misplaced it."

She was friendly. "Sure, I can do that. I will do it now. Just wait a minute."

She went to a cupboard and pulled out a file. I was impressed. It was the green international FIFA clearance. "I have never seen those," I said. "Would you mind showing it to me?" I asked, going up to her.

"Not at all," she replied as she gave it to me.

Attached to the green paper was the fax transmission report. I looked at the number. It started with 09-61-2 that was enough for me to realise that something was not right. I looked at the clearance certificate. It had been neatly typed. Player name, his previous club, the club he was going to, the country that was releasing him, and the country that he was going to. Whoops. The country that he was going to? It said Australia.

I looked at the official and showed her the form. "It says here the player is going to Australia, but he is in fact going to Austria."

"Oh, is that not the same place?" she asked innocently.

"No, it is a different country. Could we please send another one?"

"Yes, of course. Sorry about that."

This time I waited with her until the clearance certificate had been correctly filled out and sent to the Austrian FA. I then phoned the club and told them that everything should be in order now.

After that, nothing should have surprised me anymore. Not even when I contacted the league offices for some statistics. The league does not compile its own statistics and therefore there are no records of the number of games played by a player in the league. Some magazines have attempted to keep their own records, but most of these are rather sketchy.

I wanted my statistics to be as accurate as possible and asked the league to grant me access to the official match reports of the past few seasons. After a week of toing and froing, during which time I had to explain to countless officials why I had wanted the statistics, I was finally given permission to look at the league records. I was taken to a strongroom in the league offices and told that everything was there.

What was there was an absolute mess. Piles and piles of folders, papers and record books were stacked all over the floor and there seemed to be no system to it. I spent the first day sorting everything out. At the end of the day, I had managed to bring enough order into the place that I felt I could start to compile the records.

I arrived the next morning and was allowed into the strongroom. I started writing down the information I needed. After having compiled statistics for two seasons, there was a break. The match reports for the next two seasons were missing. I went to the official in charge of the matches and asked where the referee reports for those two seasons were.

"We burnt them."

"What do you mean you burnt them? Why?"

"When we moved to new offices, we burnt them because we did not have enough space."

I looked at him. He was being serious. I did not know what to say, so I said, "Oh." I decided to leave it at that and returned to the strongroom. I continued to compile the records from those referee reports that had not been burnt.

Since then, whenever I see league statistics about South African players, I am a bit weary. If a magazine or newspaper writes that so and so is playing his 200th league game, I think to myself that what they are actually saying is that, 'According to the statistics that have not been burnt and are still available, so-and-so is playing his 200th game. It could also be his 203rd game or his 204th. But it is somewhere in the region of 200.'

To be fair, in the last few years, statistics have been updated on a more regular basis and the younger generation of players has benefited from this. Their statistics are nearly up to date.

It is still frustrating though when, on a Monday morning, one looks at the South African league table and sees three different tables in three different publications. Even the respectable Reuters news agency sends out incomplete (and often incorrect) tables on a weekly basis.

Being a referee in South Africa is not an easy job. Like anywhere else in the world, they are criticised and subjected to abuse from the players, the fans and club officials.

Not surprisingly then, they don't take too kindly to their match reports being burnt. They like it even less when the meagre remuneration they receive for taking all the abuse is not paid on time.

In November 2000, referees in Cape Town decided they had had enough, or better said, they had decided that they had not had enough of the money that was due to them. They decided to down their whistles during a weekend. All matches that were scheduled to take place in the second division that weekend were not played because there were no referees. The players were at the field, the few fans that watched second division matches were at the field, there was even an occasional dog running around on the field. Not there, were the respective match officials.

Needless to say, the decision taken by the referees spurred the league into action and during the course of the following week, the referees were paid and they returned to work.

Their decision to boycott their matches must be considered quite mild, compared to an event that I covered a few months earlier. It happened during an amateur match somewhere in one of the rural provinces in South Africa. The referee officiating decided that he would no longer take the constant abuse and intimidation he had been subjected to during the match. One of the players in particular had irked the referee to such an extent that he decided that a red card would just not do. He pulled a gun out of his pocket and shot the offending player dead.

The story went through the world press. The referee was arrested and put on trial; presumably he is now officiating at prison matches.

'Referee shoots player' is not the only headline that has come out of South Africa in recent times. 'Referee is shot at', is another.

In this case a Johannesburg referee, Moses Soko, who officiated at first division matches decided that he would take the idea of being a 'whistle blower' further than intended. It is a well-known fact in South African football that there are attempts to rig professional matches. In some cases, these attempts are successful.

Soko decided that he no longer wanted any part in this and, in return for indemnity from prosecution, offered to blow the whistle on others on the take. He fingered several officials and his evidence caused much consternation in footballing circles in South Africa. The effect must have been so threatening that one of the offenders decided that he no longer wanted Soko around. An attack on his life was planned and carried out. Luckily for Soko, though, he survived the attack and after spending a lengthy time in hospital, continued to give evidence. He was later banned from refereeing for life.

Shortly after the referees had staged their strike, the sports editor of a German newspaper visited me. We went for supper and spoke about football in Africa. He knew quite a bit about our players and about the national teams in Africa. He was impressed with the standard of play of African players that played in Europe. "It's a pity that South Africa did not get the 2006 World Cup. It would have been good for the country," he said.

I agreed with him. "I am sure that it will be Africa's turn in 2010 or at the very latest 2014."

He nodded. "I think that an African country can even win the World Cup then, if not sooner."

I shook my head. "I can't see Africa winning the World Cup for quite a few years."

HAS ANYBODY GOT A WHISTLE?

He was surprised. African countries had long left behind the legacy of being 'soft points' in international competitions. Not only had Ghana and Nigeria won youth world championships, Nigeria had beaten both Argentina and Brazil on their way to an Olympic gold medal in Atlanta in 1996. Cameroon had emulated their triumph four years later in Sydney. Why then, he wondered, could I not see an African victory at the World Cup soon?

I could have told him about the juju man, or I could have spoken about the missing whistle or burnt referee's reports. I could have told him about the professional players earning £130 a month, while officials were stealing hundreds of thousands. I could have told him about officials that are incapable of organizing matches.

But I could have also told him about the children on the streets of Grahamstown laughing, as they kick a ball made of rags on the dusty township field. I could have told him about the football fans in Burkina Faso, for whom their country's success at the finals of the African Cup of Nations meant so much, and I could have told him how football in Africa means so much to millions of people all over the continent.

But I did not say any of that. Instead, I just shrugged my shoulders and looked at him.

"Well, Africa is just Africa. It's just different," I said.